CONTENTS

Part III
"THE GREATEST DAY IN THE HISTORY OF *THE WASHINGTON POST*"

Part IV
"DUDE! COOL!"

Part V
"MARCUS WAS AS GOOD AS BRADLEE AND DOWNIE"

Praise for Dave Kindred's

MORNING MIRACLE

"*Morning Miracle* may be the best semi-insider's account we'll get about a newspaper's losing season of red ink, cutbacks and institutional angst amid the current industry crisis. . . . Kindred is a connoisseur of journalists' voices. . . . [He writes with] a sportswriter's unfailing good humor and sympathy for his chorus of ink-stained wretches."
—*The New York Times Book Review*

"An intimate look at one of America's most prestigious and powerful newspapers. . . . A heartfelt—and often heartbreaking—tale of the challenges faced not only by the *Post* but by every other American newspaper. . . . *Miracle* is both a tribute to journalists and journalism and a case study of the ramifications of the corporate downsizing of newspapers. It also captures the odd yet committed nature of journalists."
—*The Columbus Dispatch*

"Addictive. . . . Like all good reporters, Kindred tells this informative and entertaining story through people—the *Post*'s stars and drudges, its curmudgeons and eccentrics—to elucidate its triumphs and failures."   —*Richmond Times-Dispatch*

"A rich portrait. . . . With a romantic's love of the reporting life, unique access to the inner chambers of the *Post* and a gift for hand-tooled writing, Kindred tells how, as the subtitle implies, a great newspaper fights for its life. The result is a book as engaging as any contemporary novel and as telling as any history about America today."   —*The Roanoke Times* (Virginia)

"Kindred epitomizes the classic sports columnist: dogged, eloquent, skeptical yet enthusiastic, dedicated more to his craft than his 'brand.' His eight-page introduction alone is worth the cost of the book. . . . For anyone interested in how newspapers work, [*Morning Miracle*] is a must-read."
—*The Courier-Journal* (Louisville, Kentucky)

"*Morning Miracle* is both a love letter to newspapers and an elegy for days long gone. . . . [Kindred] nails what's wrong with newspapers in general, and with the *Post* in particular."
—*AARP Magazine*

"Busy and exciting and fun to read. . . . Kindred has a real gift for describing his fellow Posties. . . . [And] is equally adept at describing action in the newsrooms. . . . His book successfully takes the reader inside a great newspaper as it tries to endure."
—*Columbia Journalism Review*

"There's always some guy in the newsroom who knows the real story."
—Roger Ebert

"Kindred's book is the miracle, making this old *New York Times* man wish he had spent at least one shining moment in the heartbreaking romance of the *Washington Post*."
—Robert Lipsyte

"This is a book about reporting and reporters. The best reporter involved in it is the one writing it. Through his talent, his wit, and his uncommon humanity, Kindred demonstrates a love for journalism as a job, as a craft, and, above all, as a calling. In fact, he loves it more than it probably deserves to be loved anymore."
—Charles P. Pierce

DAVE KINDRED
MORNING MIRACLE

Dave Kindred has reported and written for newspapers and magazines for forty-five years. He has been a Washington correspondent, sports columnist, and general-interest columnist. His work has won the Red Smith Award, sports journalism's highest honor, as well as a National Headliner award for general-interest columns. Kindred's stories have been anthologized in the *Chicken Soup for the Soul* series. He is the author of eight books, including, most recently, *Sound and Fury*, the dual biography of Muhammad Ali and Howard Cosell.

MORNING MIRACLE

Inside

THE WASHINGTON POST

A Great Newspaper Fights

for Its Life

DAVE KINDRED

Anchor Books
A Division of Random House, Inc.
New York

For

Dan Foster, Deborah Howell, Barry Lorge,

John Mashek, and Van McKenzie,

who loved the life

FIRST ANCHOR BOOKS EDITION, AUGUST 2011

Copyright © 2010 by Dave Kindred

Grateful acknowledgment is made to the following for permission to reprint previously published material: *The Washington Post* Writers Group: Excerpt from "Post Co.'s Graham and Wife to Separate" by Frank Ahrens (*The Washington Post*, November 10, 2007), copyright © 2007 by *The Washington Post*; excerpt from "John Updike's Lyricism Exalted the Everyday and the Unglamorous" by Henry Allen (*The Washington Post*, January 28, 2009), copyright © 2009 by *The Washington Post*; excerpt from "Why Oh Why: The Epistemology, Philosophy, History, Psychology, Anthropology, Aesthetics and General Absolute Necessity of Making Lists" by Henry Allen (*The Washington Post*, June 12, 1977), copyright © 1977 by *The Washington Post*; excerpt from "Jimmy's World" by Janet Cook (*The Washington Post*, September 28, 1980), copyright © 1980 by *The Washington Post*; excerpt from "Growing Up Rodham" by Sally Jenkins (*The Washington Post*, December 9, 2007), copyright © 2007 by *The Washington Post*; excerpt from "That Was the Desk I Chose to Die Under" by David Maraniss (*The Washington Post*, April 19, 2007), copyright © 2007 by *The Washington Post*; excerpt from "Soldiers Face Neglect, Frustration at Army's Top Medical Facility" by Dana Priest and Anne Hull (*The Washington Post*, February 18, 2007), copyright © 2007 by *The Washington Post*; excerpt from "In Flag City USA, False Obama Rumors Are Flying" by Eli Saslow (*The Washington Post*, June 30, 2008), copyright © 2008 by *The Washington Post*; excerpt from "Barack Obama for President" by *The Washington Post* Editorial Board (*The Washington Post*, October 17, 2008), copyright © 2008 by *The Washington Post*; excerpt from "Can One of the Nation's Great Musicians Cut Through the Fog of a D.C. Rush Hour? Let's Find Out" by Gene Weingarten (*The Washington Post*, April 8, 2007), copyright © 2007 by *The Washington Post*; and excerpt from "McChrystal: More Forces or 'Mission Failure'" by Bob Woodward (*The Washington Post*, September 21, 2009), copyright © 2009 by *The Washington Post*. Reprinted by permission of *The Washington Post* Writers Group.

William Morris Endeavor Entertainment: Excerpt from *The Front Page* by Ben Hecht and Charles MacArthur, copyright © 1928 by Ben Hecht and Charles MacArthur. Reprinted by permission of William Morris Endeavor Entertainment.

The Library of Congress has cataloged the Doubleday edition as follows:
Kindred, Dave.
Morning miracle: inside the Washington Post: a great newspaper fights for its life / by Dave Kindred.—1st ed.
p. cm.
1. Washington Post (Washington, D.C.: 1974). I. Title.
PN4899.W31W346 2010
071'.53—dc22
2009044885

Anchor ISBN: 978-0-7679-2814-4

Book design by Michael Collica
Author photograph by Dom Furore / Golf Digest © Condé Nast Publications

www.anchorbooks.com

Printed in the United States of America.
10 9 8 7 6 5 4 3 2 1

We ought to call this thing "The Morning Miracle."
It's a miracle we get it out every morning.

—Ben Bradlee, during his tenure as executive
editor of *The Washington Post*

ACKNOWLEDGMENTS

Len Downie made this book possible. He also made the work a pleasure. Don Graham is every newspaper person's idea of a dream owner; he also is every inquiring reporter's idea of a frustrating interview (so much there, so little said), and yet he kindly accepted my appearances at his office door. Bo Jones, Katharine Weymouth, Marcus Brauchli, and Jim Brady answered every question, even the impertinent ones. To them all, and to everyone in the *Post* and Washingtonpost.com newsrooms who made me feel welcome, thank you.

My agent, David Black, was again expert in every phase of the game. At Doubleday, editor Phyllis Grann showed a hopeless romantic that less is more; copy editor Rosalie Wieder did work invisible to the reader and priceless to the writer; and associate editor Jackeline Montalvo's grace matched her efficiency.

Extraordinary news people allowed me into their lives and work: Dana Priest, Anne Hull, Gene Weingarten, Anthony Shadid, David Maraniss, Sally Jenkins, Steve Fainaru, Walter Pincus, Omar Fekeiki, Tony Reid, Deborah Howell, Eli Saslow, Bob Kaiser, Dan Balz, Ben Bradlee, and Bob Woodward. All were generous, and I am forever grateful.

Gary Pomerantz, Jane Leavy, Tom Callahan, John Feinstein, and Verenda Smith are great friends from my newspaper days. They picked me up every time I stumbled. Working overtime, Verenda took notes on Bradlee at the Illinois Prize dinner, and she stood in the street at dawn to flag down the Pakistani who delivered her *Post*.

In the summer of 2009, I returned to Atlanta, Illinois, for the fiftieth reunion of my high school graduating class. It was also my fiftieth year as a newspaperman. Better yet, for the fiftieth consecutive summer, I went to the movies with the prettiest girl in school, Cheryl Ann Liesman. She has made my life possible.

MORNING MIRACLE

PROLOGUE

Reporters and Editors

BRADLEE, BEN

In retirement since 1991, the editor who came to fame with the *Post*'s coverage of the Watergate scandal kept an office alongside the newspaper's corporate executives. As to what he did as a vice president at large, Bradlee nodded to an open door and said, "I'm a stop on the tour."

Such a look on the man: silver-haired, chesty, the jawline square and strong. Every rough-cut line in his face suggested a rogue's mischief. He might have been a pretty-boy boxer who quit only when his nose got busted a fifth time. In my reading, I noticed the year 1933 was important to him. He was eleven years old and in the tender care of a nubile Swiss governess who practiced public nudity so spectacularly that sixty years later Bradlee wrote, "I shall always be grateful to the highest authority that hers were the first breasts I ever saw." Now, even at eighty-eight, Bradlee gave everyone reason to think newspapering could be sexy. Women blushed in his presence and men straightened up.

"So," I said, "is the *Post* in trouble?"

"I dunno," the old lion roared. "But I know, whatever happens, there'll always be a few of us, a band of brothers, or a band of sisters—a band of people, damn it—who call themselves journalists, who will write what they believe the truth to be."

BRODER, DAVID

On an election night, I would have stepped inside David Broder's office except there was no room for a second person. It was a tiny mess of a space with paper everywhere, scattered and stacked— newspapers, books, letters, documents, five large plastic U.S. Postal Service crates, and eleven cardboard filing boxes filled to bulging. It seemed to have been arranged by an explosion. There remained one open space near the door. By turning sideways, Broder folded himself into a chair at his computer. Surrounded by the residue of a pundit's research, Broder resembled a slight, wizened Yoda figure. He was seventy-eight years old, a Pulitzer winner, a Washington monument. His hands and head trembled. He wore orthopedic shoes.

"The office," he allowed, "is a little out of hand now."

Broder knows newspapers. A piece of his 1973 Pulitzer speech ought to be on every newspaper's front page, up there in the ear where every wingnut can read it. He said:

Instead of promising All the News That's Fit to Print,
I would like to see us say—over and over, until the point has
been made—that the newspaper that drops on your doorstep
is a partial, hasty, incomplete, inevitably somewhat flawed
and inaccurate rendering of some of the things we have
heard about in the past twenty-four hours—distorted,
despite our best efforts to eliminate gross bias, by the very
process of compression that makes it possible for you to lift it
from the doorstep and read it in about an hour. If we labeled
the product accurately, then we could immediately add: But
it's the best we could do under the circumstances, and we
will be back tomorrow with a corrected and updated version.

CILLIZZA, CHRIS

A thirty-year-old political junkie working in print and online, Cillizza represented the future of journalism—if the future wore blue jeans and vowed not to shave its beard until the presidential campaigns had chosen their candidates. Along with the pollsters and other pundits, Cillizza had foreseen a victory for Barack Obama in the New Hampshire primary. When Hillary Clinton won, Cillizza popped out of his chair to declare, "I know nothing about politics! NOTHING!"

At night's end, the poor misguided political junkie asked if I wanted to go with him.

"Where to?"

"Doing *Larry King Live* from midnight to one."

At that hour, apparently, a guest who knows nothing—NOTH-ING!—becomes an oracle.

I chose TiVo.

DOWNIE, LEN

Big-time executive editors of sustained excellence—the legends—were not always stars beyond reach. Len Downie was a high school sportswriter whose column appeared in the *John Marshall Interpreter* under the headline "Downie's Drivel." At Ohio State, he was the *Lantern*'s sports editor. This sports journalism helps explain one thing.

In 1977 there was a maniacal fan courtside at a Washington Bullets basketball game. When upset with a referee's call, this man executed several dance steps at hyperkinetic speeds. He raised one leg Rockette-style. Balanced there, he rotated his arms with a velocity that might have achieved flight had he not simultaneously brought the raised leg down against the floor with a crash. These movements were accompanied by loud shoutings of a disagreeable kind.

I asked the *Post*'s basketball man, "Who is that?"

"Our Metro editor," Paul Attner said. "Len Downie."

Thirty years later, I said, "Len, at Bullets' games—what was that about?"

Laughing: "When I wasn't a sportswriter anymore and could root, I just lost it."

GRAHAM, DON

Now chairman of the board and chief executive officer of the Washington Post Company, Graham started at the newspaper as a general assignment reporter and became sports editor before moving to the business side. When I told him this book would show reporters and editors at work, his response was curious. He said, "Making the sausage—isn't that boring? Like that movie, all that newsroom stuff, wasn't that boring?" He meant *All the President's Men*, which many newspaper hacks consider the greatest movie ever made.

He also said, "If your book was up to me, I'd say no ... It takes just one person saying something stupid to hurt you."

Then Graham deferred to Len Downie and publisher Bo Jones. "But I spend almost no time in the newsroom anymore. It's Len and Bo's paper. If they say okay, it's okay."

"They're okay with it," I said.

"Good luck, then," Graham said.

Leaving his office, I passed through a bright, airy vestibule. There hung three regal oil paintings of his grandfather and parents. On the left was Eugene Meyer, the patriarch who bought the *Post* at a bankruptcy auction in 1933. In the center was Phil Graham, the star-crossed figure whose ambition and tragedy changed the newspaper forever. On the right was Meyer's daughter and Phil's wife, Katharine Graham, who led the *Post* in its finest hours.

HOHMANN, JAMES

James Hohmann was a kid. I had shoelaces older than James Hohmann. A tall, lean midwesterner, blond and blue-eyed, firm of handshake and resolute of purpose, he could pass for the correspondent from Lake Wobegon.

As a 2008 summer intern at the *Post*, Hohmann worked in the suburban Prince George's County bureau. He had long been a veteran of the business. As his first journalistic effort, he reported, wrote, edited, designed, published, and sold his own newspaper. He called it the *Hohmann Times*. It specialized in reporting on family members, immediate and extended.

He sold it to them for one dollar a copy.

He was five years old.

HULL, ANNE

As proof that God has a sense of humor, Anne Hull, who did long-form narrative, first worked at a desk in the National pod alongside the hard-news geezers Walter Pincus, Dan Morgan, and George Lardner. "I represented the end of journalism as they knew it," she said.

With a nod from a judge here or there, she might have been the all-time champ of Pulitzer Prizes. On our first meeting, she had been a finalist in features and national reporting six times.

"Neglect, abandonment, injustice, and personal awakening." Those were her consistent themes. "I tend to write about the marginalized, the forgotten, or the shunted aside. Individuals swimming upstream who have more quiet courage than bravado. As a journalist, it's important to shine the light where people aren't looking and compel them to look. But it's more than social justice that keeps me reporting in this realm; it's sheer awe and respect for the tenacity to survive."

JENKINS, SALLY

Whatever story a newspaper needed, Sally Jenkins could do it. The week after 9/11, she wrote a New York firehouse piece that should be required reading for anyone who can read. The week after Katrina, she drove through Mississippi and found a piano in a treetop. The first week of the Olympics in Beijing, she arranged a clandestine meeting with a Chinese dissident, the sort of edgy reporting that prompted her father, the novelist Dan Jenkins, to send her this e-mail:

> If a Chinese government agency is reading this, I just want to say that my daughter, Sally Jenkins, hasn't been feeling well lately. Her mind has been affected by being so far away from home. As a family, we have always loved China, and feel badly for the unfair press it has received regarding the Olympics. Some of our best friends are Chinese, and we love Chinese cuisine, even the little things we can't identify that we know are exquisite. Congratulations on a wonderful Olympics. Go, China!

PINCUS, WALTER

On a windswept winter day, I stood outside the Madison Hotel facing the *Post*. Here came Walter Pincus across Fifteenth Street.

Short and broad-shouldered, he wore a trench coat, open with the belt dangling loose, the wind stirring his white hair. He walked with a limp (bad knee). His thick, wild, graying eyebrows went every which way, suggesting that he had more important obligations than clearing his line of vision. He spoke in a low rumble of mumbles that once caused Ben Bradlee to say, "Damned if half the time I know what he's saying, but I believe him." His fine suit of an understated copper color was matched by a silk tie. This was not the disheveled look familiar in newsrooms but the wardrobe of a Yale graduate who taught at Stanford University's Washington program.

If you were an ink-stained soul who fell for newspapers when newspapers mattered, Walter Pincus was your man. The paper's elder, seventy-six years old, he was so familiar to Washington sources that Anne Hull one day heard him say into the phone, "It's me, he in?" He worked national security and intelligence. When I asked why he was a reporter, he answered clearly, quickly, and with a large helping of why-else: "To change the world."

The Pincus signature was the hard-news story advanced daily. He had never done long-form narrative. "Crap," he called it. He was a dinosaur so happy to be walking the earth that he intended to do it most of forever. His friend Herb Block, the *Post* editorial cartoonist, died at ninety-one, six weeks after drawing his last cartoon. Pincus said, "I'm going for Herblock's record."

PRIEST, DANA

Early on, her mother noticed that Dana had an unusual reaction anytime she saw a door marked DO NOT ENTER. "She immediately went in," Shirley Meyer said. "She was always adventurous, inquisitive, and unusual."

An inquisitive person will not sleep, or let you sleep, or let anyone else sleep, until she gets an answer to whatever mystery last made her inquisitive. Add in the adventurous and the unusual and you have a starter kit for building a reporter who will, one day, cover the Pentagon, walk in Kosovo with soldiers in full battle-rattle, and go jogging at dawn in the war-zone mountains of Afghanistan while Marines sleep in, the wimps.

Dana Priest's stories usually were built by talking to People

Who Can Not, Must Not, and Will Not Be Named or Else. At her desk, there was a cartoon—two guys in a prison cell, and one says, "I got caught up in the secret domestic wiretapping and financial-monitoring program. What are you in for?" The other replies, "Reporting on it."

I loved Dana Priest.

REID, TONY

Tony Reid, first a reporter and for twenty-one years a *Post* copy editor, explained why people work as reporters and editors when newspaper pay is famously low. "It's so much fun," he said. "They get us cheap because they know our dirty little secret—we'd do this for free."

SHADID, ANTHONY

Hands or legs?

Which would you rather lose?

Anthony Shadid chose hands, Steve Fainaru legs.

The foreign correspondents debated the question during idle moments in their coverage of the war in Iraq.

"Anthony had this obsession about his legs," Fainaru said. "He didn't want to be in a wheelchair."

Fainaru wanted to keep his hands to play catch with his son.

Each man won a Pulitzer.

"Shadid is the soul of the *Post*," Sally Jenkins said.

WEINGARTEN, GENE

The humor columnist Gene Weingarten insisted, "The only humor columnist in America is Dave Barry." As an editor at the *Miami Herald*, he had hired Barry out of nowhere, and years later Barry thanked him by writing a foreword to one of Gene's books. "Gene Weingarten," his friend wrote, "is a weird kind of person."

Weingarten once made a graduation speech to journalism majors in which he said, "Our field is changing rapidly. Technology is overtaking us at an unheard-of pace. The journalists of tomorrow may not look anything like the journalists of today. I mean, literally. For all we know, they might have gills and three buttocks. That's how fast things are changing. But rest assured that, however dizzying the rate of change, when what's at stake is the sacred art of truth-telling, there is always one constant. One thing will always stay the same: Your editor is going to be an idiot."

WEYMOUTH, KATHARINE

The *Post*'s mystery woman was Katharine Weymouth.

Everyone knew the name. They knew she was Don Graham's niece. They knew that she had worked for the *Post* on the legal and business sides. They knew she might be the newspaper's next publisher, the ultimate boss making all the most important decisions. She was forty-one, a divorced mother of three children under ten. They may have known that, but there were unanswered questions: Did she want the big job? Did she know anything about journalism? Anyway, who was she?

A partial answer to the last question came from a man who said, "I was at a party where she jumped into the pool. That's not something Don would do, but he would enjoy seeing it done." Also: "She's brilliant, forthright, fun, salty—and hot."

She was the tall, strong, blond, ballerina-graceful, could-play-Joan-of-Arc type. About every six weeks, she joined girlfriends for poker night, which caused me to ask, "Any cigar smoking?" "No cigars, sadly," she said, "but in the good old days, cigarettes." As for the pool, yes: "Hey, it's midnight, it's fun, in we go, three girlfriends, with all our clothes!"

WOODWARD, BOB

His Watergate reporting, eleven number one bestselling books, and continuing association with the *Post* have made him perhaps the most influential reporter of his generation. Almost certainly, he is the only reporter who ever actually asked to work for free. But various laws insisted that the *Post* pay him something, so he settled for $193.46 a week. At age sixty-five, he had started work on an Obama book.

"I love the news, newspapering, and book writing," he said. "What better life? I don't know of one."

INTRODUCTION

Because I am a hopeless romantic about newspapers, it was good and right that I should meet another such madman early in the work on this book. His name was Gene Weingarten. Had he satisfied his parents' wishes and become a doctor, we never would have met—because he, for one, would be dead. "A doctor! With access to all those drugs!" he explained. Instead, we shared coffee and newspaper war stories.

We sat in a shop near the Capitol, both of us wearing the sneakers, blue jeans, and T-shirts of men without jobs. At fiftysomething, he was an endearing eccentric who did humor columns and long-form narratives for the *Post*. He also conducted a weekly online chat, subtitled "Tuesdays with Moron," in which he might do a mathematical proof that there is no God, followed the next week by pungent ruminations on potty-training gone bad. Like so many journalistic dreamers of the early 1970s, Weingarten had been set on fire by the Watergate reporting of Woodward and Bernstein. He escaped college to write a feature on New York street gangs. Next thing he knew, he materialized in an autopsy room.

"Think about this for excitement," he said. "A Schenectady woman's body was dragged out of the Mohawk River bound in chains. I walked into the autopsy like I belonged there. That's the way it works. Pretty soon you actually believe you belong there. I could see that the woman's head had been staved in. The cops had said the husband was not a suspect, but here it is, 6 a.m, and for the heck of it, I call him. 'Mr. Smith?' I say. 'Yeah,' he says. And I say, 'What's your reaction to the discovery of your wife's body?' He actually sucked in his breath! That enabled me to write that the husband 'reacted with shock and hung up the phone.' "

Weingarten was then a kid reporter for a paper in Albany, New York. No flashing neon light on his forehead identified him as a newspaperman. For a moment, at least, he passed as a mature person, perhaps a city official with reason to be in the autopsy room. He made notes on the condition of the poor woman up from the cold waters where her killer believed she would stay. Then he woke the husband before dawn with the news that the chains hadn't worked all that well.

"Imagine the thrill of notifying a killer!" he said. "You gotta be a reporter to do that! You get in the middle of life!"

About here, he interrupted himself to ask, "So, what's your book about?"

It was early. I had no real idea. I knew only that it would be a reporter's book. "Probably," I said, "a valentine to journalism."

I had gathered rose petals to spread along the way. I knew that Matthew Arnold had called journalism "literature in a hurry." Whitelaw Reid did literature for the *Cincinnati Gazette* from Gettysburg: "The Rebel line was five miles long and a Nation's very existence trembled before its clangor—the great, desperate, final charge was about to come." I made notes when smart people said good stuff, such as the Bogart character in *Deadline USA* telling an eager kid that reporting isn't the oldest profession but it's the best. Dan Jenkins caused a novel's heroine to say, "Journalism is a seductive profession, and it is irresistibly so, I think, when there's big stuff to write about. No other writing compares with it." Jimmy Cannon had been to a war and written it and he'd been to games and written them, and he said, "I sat, most of my life, at glad events, as a sportswriter, amid friendly multitudes, gathered for the purpose of pleasure." Newspapers sent me to the Kremlin, Kathmandu, Yankee Stadium, and Monkeys Eyebrow, Kentucky. In Bloomington, Illinois, I had stood so long at the chases in the *Daily Pantagraph*'s

composing room—looking at type upside down and backwards—
that I learned to read a subject's mail from my side of the desk. I
love the smell of newsprint in the morning, and my favorite time
of day is thirty minutes to deadline. I believe in going to the losers'
locker room, I believe in a god of journalism who answers our
prayers if we make one more phone call, and I believe Ben Bradlee
had it right when he said, "Nothing's better than a big story, not
even sex."

For seven years, I was a sports columnist at the *Post*, one of those
overcaffeinated social misfits on the fifth floor at 1150 Fifteenth
Street, five minutes from the White House. The newsroom was
alive with idealists and skeptics, literati and hacks, all on fire to
know, before the world knew, what the hell had happened and
why. A state editor bragged about "my Harvard key," to which a
curmudgeonly copy editor (the only kind) replied, "Big deal. On
my garage, I got a Yale lock." We ran a dead pool on the formerly
famous, five dollars to enter, the pot paid to the scribbler who
came nearest predicting the expiration date of, say, Joe DiMaggio.
A newpaper's nature was forever fixed for me by a friend who
had been a vagabond, not sure where she belonged in life until
she first spent a day in a shabby, disgusting, derelict newsroom.
"I finally felt at home," she said. "I had found my chimpanzee
family."

The degenerate chimps had a story to tell, a newsroom story on
the adrenaline buzz, on how the newspaper was reborn every day.
The consultant Mark Potts wrote in an unpublished memoir of his
time at the *Post*, "Unlike any other product, newspapers are con-
ceived, designed, and produced virtually from scratch every single
day. We used to take executives and research-and-development
people from computer companies through the *Post*'s eighteen-
hour daily production cycle, from initial story meetings to throwing papers off of trucks. They were invariably flabbergasted. And
multiple editions blew their minds."

The movies showed twine-tied bundles of papers thumping
down on sidewalks with headlines advancing the plot. Reporters
were wisecracking men in fedoras, press cards in their hat bands,
happy miscreants shouting into saloon pay phones, "Get me rewrite,

sweetheart!" In 1940 the nineteen-year-old Ben Bradlee saw *Foreign Correspondent* four times. The hero uncovered kidnappings, assassinations, and international conspiracies. But editors wouldn't print his stories out of fear they'd ignite a world war. The hero said, "I came four thousand miles to get a story. I get shot at like a duck in a shooting gallery, I get pushed off buildings, I get the story, and then I've got to shut up!" Romance! Glamor! Danger! Young Bradlee wanted it all.

In the 1920s, Ben Hecht and Charles MacArthur lived in Chicago newsrooms. Here was newspapering as sent up in their *Front Page* dialogue:

> Listen to who's talking. Journalists! Peeking through keyholes! Running after fire engines like a lot of coach dogs! Waking people up in the middle of the night to ask them what they think of Mussolini. Stealing pictures off old ladies of their daughters that get raped in Oak Park. A lot of lousy, daffy, buttinskis, swelling around with holes in their pants, borrowing nickels from office boys! And for what? So a million hired girls and motormen's wives'll know what's going on . . .
>
> I don't need anybody to tell me about newspapers. I've been a newspaperman fifteen years. A cross between a bootlegger and a whore. And if you want to know something, you'll all end up on the copy desk—gray-headed, humpbacked slobs, dodging garnishees when you're ninety.

John Boyle O'Reilly, a nineteenth-century Irish novelist and reporter, saw a newspaper as more respectable: "It is the biography of a day. It is a photograph, of twenty four hours' length, of the mysterious river of time that is sweeping past us forever . . . tales of sorrow and suffering, and joy and success, and ambition and defeat, and villainy and virtue . . . and a heart feels the touch of the wonderful human sympathy that makes us brethren of the men of all climes and all ages."

When I was eleven and twelve years old, my grandmother sent me on my bicycle to the train station every Sunday morning to pick up the Chicago newspapers, the *Tribune*, the *Daily News*, and the *American*. With the funny papers and baseball box scores, a kid was set for hours and ultimately for years.

So, yes, a hopeless romantic would make the book a valentine. This mild assertion caused Weingarten's mustache to twitch.

"No," he said. "I'll tell you what your book's about."

Not hearts and flowers, not with newspapers in crisis, not when millions of Americans believe newspapers tell them lies, not when Weingarten himself had written an in-house critique of the *Post* that began, "How can we still wonder why our profession is swirling counterclockwise down the toilet in a maelstrom of irrelevancy, a relentless vortex fed by the fetid stench of our shocking ineptitude . . ." Bob Woodward, the *Post*'s legend, also voted against the valentine. "You have to be tough," he said. When I asked Marilyn Thompson, once a foreign desk editor, what to look for at the paper, she arched an eyebrow and said, "You mean, besides the death throes?"

And one day I walked into the *Post*'s lobby. For almost thirty years, a wall there had been covered with a collage of larger-than-life photographs depicting *Post* history. But now the pictures were gone.

Bob Woodward and Carl Bernstein as boy reporters—gone.

Ben Bradlee and Katharine Graham, gloriously vital—gone.

The distinguished founder of the modern *Post*, Eugene Meyer—gone.

These mythic figures had been disappeared in favor of a flat-screen slide-show monitor.

At that moment, my valentine was dead. I had hoped to shade the misery into the background. But, no. I could read the headlines in publications covering the trade:

WASHINGTON POST LOSING ADS, CIRCULATION,
INCOME, EVERYTHING

ARE JOURNALISTS THE 21ST CENTURY'S BUGGY
WHIP MAKERS?

THE NEWSPAPER INDUSTRY KNEW IT WAS DOOMED
30 YEARS AGO

The Internet had started the greatest revolution in communication since Johannes Gutenberg created his printing press six hundred years earlier. In the meanest of ironies, newspaper websites drew millions of users and made no real money. Charging for access drove users to free sites, and advertisers, with thousands of sites available, could buy space cheaply. As a result, newspapers' online revenue was one-tenth that of print. Then came a recession, the economy slowed to a walk, and newspapers suddenly became an endangered industry.

More than 100,000 newspaper jobs went away in four years. Papers applied tourniquets in the forms of four-day workweeks, mandatory furloughs, and pay cuts. By the fall of 2009, ten chains holding hundreds of newspapers declared bankruptcy. Desperate for cash, the *New York Times* accepted a $250 million loan at 14 percent interest from a Mexican billionaire once described on its editorial pages as a robber baron. The celebration of Sam Zell's rescue of the Tribune Company's papers lasted only until the leveraged deal led to bankruptcy. Knight Ridder's dailies were sold to the McClatchy Corporation, which unloaded a dozen to pay down debt. Detroit cut free home delivery to three days a week. The *Christian Science Monitor* went online-only. Papers died in Ann Arbor, Seattle, and Denver. When the *San Francisco Chronicle* aimed to be a world-class newspaper, it hired managing editor Robert Rosenthal; when losses reached $1 million a week, it forced Rosenthal out. He told his staff, "We all are caught in the greatest upheaval our industry and the institution of journalism has ever faced."

Warren Buffett had seen trouble coming. He owned more than a million shares of Washington Post Company stock, was a confidant of Katharine Graham, and mentor to her son and successor, Don. Buffett's 1991 Berkshire Hathaway annual report warned shareholders that media businesses "will prove considerably less marvelous" than expected. From his 2006 report: "For most of the 20th century, newspapers were the primary source of information for the American public. Whether the subject was sports, finance, or politics, newspapers reigned supreme. Just as important, their ads were the easiest way to find job opportunities or to learn the price of groceries at your town's supermarkets . . . No paper in a one-paper city, however bad the product or however inept the management, could avoid gushing profits." As the Internet rose, newspaper executives "were either blind or indifferent to what was going on under their noses." And now the truth was unavoidable. "Almost all newspaper owners realize that they are constantly losing ground in the battle for eyeballs. Simply put, if cable and satellite broadcasting, as well as the Internet, had come along first, newspapers as we know them probably would never have existed."

Then came the national recession of 2007 and 2008. What might have happened to the *Post* over the next decade instead happened in a single year. In 2007 the company's newspaper division, primarily the *Post*, achieved only a 2 percent profit—the lowest in its thirty-six years as a publicly traded company. In the next twenty-one months, the division lost $359 million. Those kinds of losses had caused Buffett to warn that unless the newspaper industry found a profitable online/print combination, it faced "an economic doomsday."

It was here that Weingarten reached across the table and brained me with a skillet. That, or he said ten words in a simple declarative sentence. Either way, my head hurt.

"Your book," he said, "is about a great newspaper dying with dignity."

My great friend Jane Leavy, the writer, believed this book's title was wrong. She said, "It should be 'Morning Miracle, R.I.P.'"

I heard her and I heard Weingarten, but, no, I would not prepare the body for viewing. I would not stand by the casket to whisper with strangers. The book is not about dying, however much dignity is involved.

In the fall of 2009, *Vanity Fair* decided the *Post* had "devolved from heralded heights to mere ordinariness, if not haplessness." *The New Republic* followed with a piece headlined "Post Apocalypse." They, too, were wrong.

The newspaper still won Pulitzers. It still mattered in any national political debate. Even with a shrunken newsroom, the *Post* still had two hundred more people than in the Watergate years. Washingtonpost.com usually stood among the top three or four most-visited national news websites. More important, though it lost money, the news organization was part of a well managed, financially robust, multibillion-dollar company with a global reach whose CEO, Donald Edward Graham, first walked into his grandfather's newsroom at age ten and never really left. Graham's commitment was evident in his 2008 letter telling shareholders that no one knew if any newspaper ever again could be consistently profitable. "But the *Post*," he said, "will get every chance."

And *that* is what this book is about. It's about a great newspaper doing its damnedest to get out of this mess alive.

Part I

"IT MAKES THE PAPER
SAFE FOR DONNIE"

1.

BALLS AND GHOSTS

Eugene Meyer's first steps into newspaper history came on the staircase of his baronial country estate in Mount Kisco, in Westchester County, just north of New York City. Meyer was a titan of American business, wealthy beyond an ordinary man's dreams, and newly resigned from President Roosevelt's Federal Reserve Board. At age fifty-seven, he had become worn and weary; his wife, Agnes, saw him at "death's door." He had decided to retire and make way for the next generation, an idea that made sense in the abstract. In practice, however, it was hell. For a man accustomed to the frenzied swirl of political and financial action, a retiree's regret set in quickly. Two weeks of sleep, rest, and nothing to do had made Meyer bright-eyed, alert, and restless. As he descended the curving staircase, running his fingers along the bannister, he felt dust.

He murmured to his wife, "This house is not properly run."

She answered, "Eugene, it's time you bought the *Post.*"

The famous British publisher Alfred Charles Northcliffe had said, "Of all the American newspapers I would prefer to own *The Washington Post,* because it reaches the breakfast tables of the members of Congress." Agnes Meyer's order to her husband was born of prior knowledge, for Meyer had tried to buy papers in Washington and was still eager to own the *Post.* "If he succeeds," Mrs. Meyer wrote in her diary, "it will be a sensation and we shall have a reputation for Machiavellian behavior"—they had told friends they were done with Washington. As for the inevitable expense, she wrote, "what after all is money for if not to be used . . . It is a great opportunity for E. to be a dominant influence in this formative period of the new America . . . a great chance to be creative."

On this day in May 1933, *The Washington Post* was not the powerful, proud journal of Lord Northcliffe's memory. It had fallen so far from grace that its very survival was in question.

The newspaper's owner was Edward Beale (Ned) McLean. He had inherited great wealth and married a woman even richer than himself. The fool's one original idea in a lifetime of profligacy seemed to have been the jury-rigging of a handkerchief sling to steady his drinking arm. His wife, Evalyn, the daughter of a prospector who found gold in the Rocky Mountains, spoke of Ned as "a queer, queer fellow" whose problems were "the natural consequences of unearned wealth in undisciplined hands." As a measure of her own self-indulgence, she lived with the adulterous sot for twenty years.

They shared a mansion on I Street where Ned McLean kept a llama and a long-tailed monkey named Babe. "A mad place, truly," Evalyn wrote, "with a monkey in my bathroom, a llama on the lawn, and our corridors shrill with the curses of our parrot (learned from a diplomat)." The monkey once "snatched from a table on the porch a tall glass of lemonade or something, and scampered up the side of the house by clutching vines and projections; and then everybody had forgotten about the little beast until it dribbled the contents of the glass down on the striped flannels of President Harding."

No one knew if his life of dissipation had ruined Ned McLean's mind, or if his ruined mind led to the life of dissipation. He once swore under oath, in a lawsuit, that he did not urinate onto the leg of the Belgian ambassador, though undenied was the report of a second stream directed into a White House fireplace. Inevitably, his newspaper's best use was as a covering for the bottom of his parrot's cage. The *Post* ran fifth in a five-paper town and some days printed no more than twelve pages of its thin gruel. It did not send a reporter to cover the Lindbergh baby kidnapping/murder drama. It had no one in Chicago for the Democratic convention that nominated FDR. Its star White House man, Ed Folliard, covered Herbert Hoover's renomination and then was fired to save money. The *Post* paid small notice to FDR's promise of a "new deal" and even less to Hitler's rise.

McLean's grandfather and father had built an empire on newspapers. Washington McLean was a Cincinnati boilermaker who got into politics in 1852 by making the *Cincinnati Enquirer* the loudest Democratic party voice west of the Alleghenies. His son, John, got rich a dozen ways before gaining control of the *Post* in 1905 and inviting Ned in. The family connections gained Ned favor with the Ohio politician Warren G. Harding, whose troubles only began with Babe the monkey.

Ned and Evalyn Walsh met as children in a dance class in Washington. Her father, Thomas Walsh, after discovering gold, left a wooden shack in the Colorado outback to build a palace on Massachusetts Avenue. It cost $835,000 and had sixty rooms, a four-story reception hall, an elevator, and a Louis XIV ballroom. A biographer called Evalyn "a wild, gay child with an early developed taste for alcohol . . . Her small face with large houri eyes framed by dark hair . . . was wistfully pretty . . . Although undisciplined, uneducated, semi-literate, her mind—unlike Ned's—was sharp and alert, a quick if malformed intelligence."

When Evalyn and Ned married, they treated themselves to a European honeymoon on their fathers' wedding gift of $200,000. At Cartier's in Paris, Evalyn bought the Star of the East diamond for $120,000. On a later trip to Cartier's, with McLean co-signing a note, she committed $154,000 to buy the Hope Diamond, the blue stone of malevolent reputation that may or may not have belonged to Marie Antoinette, who in either case lost her head.

Shortly, McLean's cozy relationship with Harding ripened into scandal. He had been the president's poker buddy, golf partner, and traveling companion. One Christmas, when Harding had received death threats, Evalyn insisted that the president stay at her I Street house. There he chewed tobacco and played poker until two in the morning. Amused by the fuss, Harding said, "I am very grateful to my assassins for a very pleasant Christmas Day."

After Harding's sudden death in 1923, investigators discovered that officials in his administration had allowed private oil companies to tap into public reserves at the Teapot Dome field in Wyoming. The scandal snared Ned McLean. He had agreed to fake a loan for a friend under investigation who needed to explain $100,000 in his bank account. Then McLean lied about the deal. Finally, to avoid perjury charges, he told the truth to Congress. Two lines of eight-column type on the *Post*'s front page read:

E.B. MCLEAN ANSWERS CLEARLY AND FRANKLY ALL
QUESTIONS OF SENATE OIL INVESTIGATORS

Years later *Post* historian Chalmers Roberts called the headline "the most humiliating ever printed in a publisher's own paper." That year, 1924, the newspaper began its slide into insolvency, which led to the public auction held June 1, 1933, on the steps of the *Post*'s building at E Street and Pennsylvania Avenue. By that day, and for the rest of his days, Ned McLean was locked away in a private psychiatric hospital in suburban Washington.

Though there were only three bidders at the auction, the *Post* reported that "important personages of the worlds of finance and journalism mingled with the merely curious." Evalyn McLean, there to bid, wore the Hope Diamond. William Randolph Hearst, owner of the *Herald*, sent his executive editor. A lawyer, George E. Hamilton Jr., represented a secret bidder—Eugene Meyer, who stayed in New York lest his presence drive up the bidding.

Twice before, Meyer had offered to buy Washington newspapers, first the *Herald* in 1925 and four years later the *Post*. But Hearst would not sell, and McLean turned down Meyer's offer of $5 million. Now, at the auction, Evalyn McLean dropped out at $600,000. Hearst's editor fell silent when Hamilton jumped every bid by as much as $50,000. The auction's climax was reported by the *Herald*:

A pleading note in his businesslike voice, the auctioneer exhorted: "Eight hundred thousand dollars bid. Do I hear 825? I have $800,000. Will you offer 25?"

From Hamilton, wedged in the center of the throng, near the auctioneer, came an offer of $825,000.

Bidding ended at this point, but not until [the lawyer Nelson T. Hartson] had again run back to see Mrs. McLean. Impatient at this further delay, Hamilton threatened to withdraw his bid unless the sale was promptly closed.

Three short words marked the passing of The Post into new hands: "Going, going, sold."

For less than 20 percent of what he had offered four years earlier, Eugene Meyer was back to work—this time as owner of *The Washington Post*.

Born in 1875, the first son of a French immigrant merchant who settled in Los Angeles, Meyer made himself a Wall Street financier and multimillionaire. Six presidents invited him into their administrations. He did sixteen years of public service work, from World War I into the Depression. One admiring journalist called Meyer "a remarkable combination of amiability, pugnacity, reliable judgment, and special audacity." All those elements were present one night at the National Press Club when Fleming Newbold, a vice president of the *Post*'s afternoon rival, the *Washington Star*, complained of insomnia.

"I think I can help you," Meyer said.

"How?"

Meyer said, "Don't read your paper until you go to bed."

Across the next decade he spent millions raising the levels of the *Post*'s talent and resources. Though far from the breakfast-table necessity of Lord Northcliffe's imagining, the paper did turn a profit in 1943. Soon, Meyer thought in terms of legacy. His daughter, Katharine, had worked briefly as a reporter. Her husband, Phil Graham, a lawyer who had imagined himself in the U.S. Senate, became the *Post*'s publisher in 1946. Meyer and Phil Graham decided that to achieve and sustain dominance for generations, they had to end Washington's morning-newspaper war. Graham advocated buying the *Times-Herald*. On March 17, 1954, the deal was done at a cost of $8.5 million.

Meyer was seventy-eight years old and thinking even a generation past Phil and Katharine to their child, his grandson, Donald Edward Graham, then eight years old.

"The real significance of this event," the patriarch said, "is that it makes the paper safe for Donnie."

Katharine Meyer's life with Phil Graham began in the fall of 1939 when she hit him in the head with a window screen. She had been to dinner and a party with friends. Back at her house on S Street near Connecticut Avenue, she was calling good night from a second-floor window when she caused the screen to fall onto the people below, striking Graham. Their eyes first met when he "looked up to see me staring down with my mouth agape."

She was twenty-one, he was twenty-three. She was a child of the manor, pampered and privileged. He was raised on a houseboat in the Everglades, brilliant and ambitious; only years later could anyone imagine him as the haunted man of Edward Arlington Robinson's poem "Richard Cory," a character who "fluttered pulses when he said, 'Good-morning'" and "one calm summer night, Went home and put a bullet in his head."

Katharine and Phil were born to exceptional families. Katharine's parents were the Meyers—Eugene, the self-made money man, and Agnes, a harpy when drinking and an intellectual who suffered no fools and inflicted upon her daughter harsh memories that she carried forever. Ernest, Phil's father, was a rough-cut engineer up from nothing in South Dakota to a race for the Florida governor's job; his mother, Florence, was a schoolteacher who owned her son's heart and died of cancer when he was nineteen.

From Harvard Law School, where Phil had been elected president of the *Law Review*, he went to Washington to clerk first for Supreme Court Justice Stanley Reed, then for Justice Felix Frankfurter. On his third date with Katharine, he proposed and soon presented his plan for their life together. They would live in Florida, but she had to understand one thing: she would have only two dresses because he "would never take anything from my father or be involved with him and we would live on what he made." That determination changed after World War II. On discharge, U.S. Army Major Philip Graham went to work for his father-in-law.

Don Graham was born April 22, 1945. Fixing the future for the boy might have been the grandfather's ambition from the time he first saw him in the crib. Meyer wrote Phil a letter in which he said he had decided to call Donnie "Judge" because he was

> calm and quiet, and seems to be balanced in a sort of judicial manner. I don't think anybody is going to get him excited if he can help it, and I think he thinks he can. If you think he is going to be a torchbearer for any of the "isms" that you want to hand him or try to instill in him, I feel it my duty to tell you I think you are going to be disappointed. On the other hand, if you have anything to say to him on a factual basis, with good evidence and perhaps a witness or two, I believe you may interest him in your presentation.

The "judge" was three years old when Katharine discovered him reading a primer that belonged to his sister, Lally, then five. At twelve he was a gambler making horse-race bets with a teacher, the stakes a candy bar. In golf games with his father, the bets were nickels, dimes, and quarters. Neighborhood boys came to the Grahams' R Street mansion to play, sometimes with the father. "All my friends just loved him, he was so damn funny," Don said years later. "He played these wildly competitive, funny, joking, teasing tennis games. He talked all the time, too, needling you, urging himself on, making jokes about himself nonstop."

Friends noticed, though, that there sometimes was an edge to Phil's chatter, especially when it was directed to Donnie. At bridge games, the boy seemed less his son to be praised than a rival to be beaten badly. Nicholas Friendly, a friend of Don's, would say, "I don't think he made enormous efforts to build Don's confidence. And Phil was such a brilliant, brilliant man. Having to live up to that kind of brilliance was a pressure I wouldn't have wanted to have."

Donnie was precocious and lonely. As a high school athlete, he chose sports pursued alone: wrestling and tennis. He didn't drink, smoke, or show interest in girls. His idea of partying was a trip on Saturday night to the Howard Theater, two dollars for the midnight show, to hear the jazz of Miles Davis, Herbie Mann, and John Coltrane, the iconic music of James Brown, Otis Redding, and

Aretha Franklin, and the comic riffs of Moms Mabley and Redd Foxx. Every season he also attended a couple dozen Senators baseball games.

He worked on the school newspaper, the *St. Albans News*. At home he met Washington's most prominent people, among them historian Arthur Schlesinger, columnists Joseph Alsop and Walter Lippmann, and the *New York Times*'s James Reston. It was clear that Donnie was headed for the *Post*, as his grandfather had announced after the purchase of the other morning paper. Back then, though, all Donnie knew was how exciting it had been when his father came home by taxi in midafternoon to show him the *Times-Herald* comic strips that now belonged to the *Post*.

He was thirteen when Phil took him on a visit to the Senate majority leader, Lyndon Johnson. "My dad took me down with him one night to see Johnson and explained in advance what he was doing and why," Don said. "He wanted to get Johnson to show off for me about being Senate majority leader. Then he wanted to get Johnson to leak him a document for the *Post* for a story about some Texans in the oil and gas industry. They had thrown a fundraising dinner for Joe Martin, the Republican leader in the House, after the House had voted down an oil and gas regulation bill. It happened just as my dad wanted. Johnson was organizing a new Senate committee on space in the aftermath of *Sputnik*. He put young Senator Scoop Jackson on speaker phone so I could listen to Jackson's arguments about why he ought to be on this committee and hear Johnson masterfully answer the arguments. Then he explained he wouldn't put him on the space committee, but he was going to do him lots of other favors. I was a little political junkie at the time, and I was quite fascinated. In the end, Johnson gave my dad whatever document it was he wanted. And they wrote about it the next morning."

In the late 1950s, Phil's work came in frenzied spurts, always passionate but not always rational. After injecting himself into the political machinations surrounding the Little Rock school desegregation efforts, he was spent. Katharine saw him as "a rocket fizzling out—still giving off sparks and even occasional bursts of flame, but steadily burning down." She reported in her autobiography that on October 28, 1957, "in the middle of the night, he broke. There is no other way to express it. All of the latent physical and psychological symptoms came to such a sudden crisis that I didn't even connect them in my mind. He was racked with pain and in despair, in a total and overwhelming depression. He wept and wept and couldn't stop. He said that he felt trapped, no longer able to go on, that everything was black."

The trial lawyer Edward Bennett Williams, Phil Graham's friend, once told Katharine he felt Phil was troubled by self-doubt— "whether he could have been as successful as he was if he hadn't married you. In other words, whether or not he would have hit the heights that he did professionally if he hadn't been Kay Graham's husband, Eugene Meyer's son-in-law, and hadn't had the *Post* stock given to him. Whether he would have made it as just Phil Graham . . . I used to say to him, 'How in the hell can you have doubt when you were Felix Frankfurter's clerk?' . . . It was inevitable that he was going to be a top-flight success, but that doubt drove him absolutely bananas."

Katharine later wrote of vile treatment by her husband and of his repeated demands for divorce during a public affair with a *Newsweek* stringer, Robin Webb. In her autobiography, she re-created ugly scenes born of his manic depression, an illness now known as bipolar disorder. She also wrote of a night in December 1962:

> We were at home, and he had had a lot to drink and was saying some wild things, most of which were not very rational. I finally got him to go to bed, but not until around two in the morning. When I came out of our room to turn off the lights throughout the house, I saw Don, looking spectral and drawn, sitting at my desk in the room right next door to the bedroom. He was seventeen years old, a freshman at Harvard, home for the holidays. "How long has this been going on?" he asked, referring to Phil's drinking and the row. I confessed that it had been for some time. "Why have you never told me?" he asked.

Early in 1963, Katharine reached "the bottom moment for me." Phil wanted a divorce in order to marry Webb and he intended to make the *Post* theirs, shoving aside Katharine. "Phil knew that he controlled the *Post* because my father had given him the majority of A shares," she wrote. "He felt he owned it because he had worked for seventeen years to make it a success, so from his point of view the paper was his . . . I saw his plan as a logical aspect of his illness, and I knew he was really ill, but by now the effect was real and I was frightened." She also knew her father's money had bought the paper and sustained it in lean years; also, the Grahams had lived on her money, allowing Phil to use his income from the paper to buy stock. "So my bitterness about his plans was extreme, and my intention to dig in was total. I was not about to give up the paper without a fight." Mrs. Graham resolved not to agree to a divorce unless her husband gave up enough controlling stock to leave her with the majority interest.

Twice that year, Phil Graham was admitted to a private mental hospital in the Washington suburbs. On August 3, he persuaded doctors at Chestnut Lodge to allow him a break at the family's country estate, Glen Welby. There he and Katharine had lunch on the back porch. They listened to classical music and then went upstairs for a nap. "After a short while," Katharine wrote, "Phil got up, saying he wanted to lie down in a separate bedroom he sometimes used. Only a few minutes later, there was the ear-splitting noise of a gun going off indoors."

She found him in a downstairs bathroom tub. When Don arrived at Glen Welby, he walked with his mother along a country road, away from the pain and grief. The next morning's *Post* reported: "Shortly after 1 p.m., while Mrs. Graham was in her room upstairs, Mr. Graham killed himself with a .28 gauge sportsman's shotgun. He was alone in a first-floor room. The only other persons in the house were the servants." Phil Graham was forty-eight years old.

Freud called a father's death "the most important event, the most poignant loss, of a man's life." Long after that day at Glen Welby, one of Don's colleagues at the newspaper, the columnist Bob Levey, said, "Don is a rare and puzzling combination—a guy with big balls but also a guy with huge ghosts weighing on him. His father's death crushed him, and I think it still crushes him." A longtime *Post* editor said, "Don was eighteen. There can be no more critical time in a young man's life to lose his father. And to lose him by suicide prompted by what is now known to be a genetically based psychiatric disorder—for the next thirty years, I would be worried."

After graduating from Harvard, Don Graham made two unusual decisions. First, he enlisted in the army and was sent to Vietnam in 1966. As a short-timer with fewer than thirty days left in his tour, Graham, a public information officer, choppered into Khe Sanh, "the fire base, a terrible battle going on, just to do a story for some army rag," a friend said. Second, when he came home, he joined the District of Columbia police force. In D.C.'s Ninth Precinct, he patrolled a bleak part of a murderous city. "Goes into domestics with his gun in its holster, thinks he can talk to them, going to get himself killed," the police chief said.

Years later, Graham discounted the melodrama. "In Vietnam, I went where they sent me," he said. "Our division was sent to Khe Sanh in April as the relief expedition and we were very frightened going in. But there were four hundred helicopters and quite a few thousand American soldiers and when the North Vietnamese saw us coming, they just said, 'Well, the hell with that,' and they got out."

His mother had wanted him to work at the *Post*. "As throughout her life," Don said, "she was quite concerned about herself and worried that she wasn't doing the job. She was, in effect, asking for help. And Vietnam had made it clear the importance of getting difficult stories right, made clear the importance of work reporters do. Then, two months before I came home, there had been the riots in Washington following Martin Luther King's assassination. After that, I felt that I would do a better job on the *Post* if I learned about the city from some other point of view.

"I thought briefly about teaching," Don said, "but I couldn't teach because I didn't have the degree required. I thought about the poverty programs starting up. At the same time, the police were desperate for people. A sergeant in recruiting actually called me—they were calling discharged veterans—and asked what I thought about going on the department. I said if I joined, I would only stay about eighteen months. He said, 'That would be above average.'"

As a D.C. police officer, Graham worked in a low-income, high-crime area notorious for burglaries growing from heroin addicts needing money for their buys. "A time or two, it seemed danger-ous," he said. "But Vietnam was much more dangerous. The dan-ger to police is random. In the time I was a police officer, there were two officers killed. One was an undercover officer making an arrest and a uniformed cop came up on him, not realizing he was an undercover man, and killed him because he had a gun out. The second officer killed was in suburban Maryland answering a call for a loud radio. Someone in an apartment building had com-plained. It turned out the guy playing the loud radio was wanted for a felony and assumed that's why the cop was knocking at the door. And shot him."

Graham acted on the honorable principle that a Harvard degree should not exempt a man from a war while his country drafted poor high school kids. He also believed a man who would run a newspaper in the nation's capital ought to know more about the city than how to find a parking space in Georgetown. Those were good reasons for the way he shaped his life; they may even have been the real reasons. Still, here was a gifted young man with a brilliant future who, in the immediate years after his father killed himself, put himself at risk. Perhaps the simplest explana-tion makes the most sense. Don Graham needed to know that he had the balls to confront a ghost.

Then, and only then, did he begin work at the paper that his grandfather had preserved for him. In 1971, Don Graham joined the news staff as a general assignment reporter in Metro. There he met Leonard Downie Jr.

2.

"I'M AN INVESTIGATIVE REPORTER!"

Because the boys of Metro in 1971 were ambitious, rambunctious, and undisciplined, Ben Bradlee sent over a hard-assed newsman named Harry Rosenfeld to shape them up. The first thing Rosenfeld did was ask deputy Andy Barnes to take Len Downie to the cafeteria. There they changed Downie's life.

"You're the new day city editor," Barnes said.

"But I've never been an editor," Downie said.

"Doesn't matter."

"But I've loved being an investigative reporter."

"Doesn't matter," Barnes said. "You don't have a choice, you'll do this."

Downie had been a reporter seven years and had never thought of doing anything else. But when an order came from Bradlee through hard-ass Harry, no one argued past two sentences. To Downie's surprise, he quickly came to like the new work. He cared about words saying precisely what they were meant to say; in fact, other reporters often had brought their copy to him for a first reading. Now, instead of the isolation that was a reporter's normal milieu, Downie was responsible for news coverage decisions that extended beyond himself. As he put it years later, "I was bossing people around! And I liked it."

He first met Don Graham when the publisher's son was doing the usual daily run of Metro stories. On May Day in 1971, Graham covered a protest march with another young Metro reporter, Carl Bernstein. Later, he did a series on alcoholism. The young editor Downie's take on the young reporter Graham: good with the facts, pretty good writer, overall very workmanlike.

Downie graduated from Ohio State University in 1964 and came to the *Post* as an intern. He found himself among Ivy Leaguers, each more sophisticated than the last. A city editor pitted him against a Yale man, Robert G. Kaiser, promising that the kid with the most bylines that summer would get a job. This was the Midwest kid in polyester against the elegantly dressed son of the U.S. ambassador to Senegal, a wunderkind so confident of others' admiration that he once propelled himself on the seat of his pants across a row of metal desktops, past Downie, sliding to a stop in front of assistant city editor Leroy Aarons.

"Hi, Roy, I'm back," Kaiser announced.

Oh, shit, Downie thought, *this is what I'm up against.*

By summer's end, the city editor declared the contest a draw and both Downie and Kaiser began *Post* careers that took them, as a team, to the top jobs in the newsroom. Into the winter of 1965, twenty-three years old and working at $105 a week, Downie had done the usual run of neophyte fodder: "Disaster Loans Dry Up SBA Aid to Negroes." "Winter Rainfall Here Held Vital in Drought." That changed when he was sent to the city's Court of General Sessions, a legal Bedlam. Downie's job was to find out what was wrong.

He hung around the corridors listening to judges, lawyers, cops, bail bondsmen, defendants, and jurors. Downie dug for news, often by hand. Before the days of computer data banks, he learned about the thousands of cases that moved through General Sessions by reading and tabulating the records himself. Along the way, he noticed that money changed hands in the corridors and whiskey bottles appeared from brown bags. One day, a veteran judge, Thomas C. Scalley, spoke to him from the bench. For weeks he had seen Downie scribbling in notebooks. The judge asked his name.

"Leonard Downie, from the *Post*."

"I know what you're doing here," the judge said, "and it doesn't bother me a bit."

He had heard that Scalley went easy on defendants who pled guilty and saved time for the court. One lawyer told a client that if he insisted on a jury trial—he had pled innocent—he did so at the risk of Scalley's wrath.

In court, the client hesitated when asked his plea, and the lawyer said, "He wants to plead guilty, Your Honor."

The client was confused into silence, and Judge Scalley's voice boomed down from the bench, "C'mon, we can't take all day for you."

The lawyer turned his client away from the judge. His exasperated stage whisper carried to Downie's ears. "Do you want probation or don't you?" Then the lawyer said, "He's going to plead guilty, Your Honor."

The clerk of the court asked the defendant, "Is that what you want to do?"

"I guess so," he said.

A week later, the defendant appeared for sentencing. Scalley noted that the defendant had previous arrests and gave him not probation but sixty days in jail. Later, when Downie asked if Scalley would comment on the way he handled cases, the judge said, "I wouldn't tell you guys anything. You just go ahead and write what you want to write."

And Leonard Downie Jr. wrote it all down. He did a seven-part series called "People's Tribunal." The first story began:

Confusion rules the criminal court building on a typical day as several hundred citizens charged with everything from illegal parking to murder are paraded past half a dozen judges.

Noisy groups of lawyers, policemen and defendants mill constantly around the judge's bench in each courtroom, bargaining back and forth as they hurry through the day's long calendar of cases.

Money can be seen changing hands in halls throughout the building as defense lawyers demand cash on the spot before advising newly assigned clients. Bail bondsmen solicit fees from relatives and lawyers of defendants who want to get out of jail on bond.

Whisky, carried in coat pockets and lawyers' briefcases, also is consumed publicly in the court building and empty bottles can be found in hallways and rest rooms by the end of the day.

This is a picture of justice as it is done daily a few blocks from Capitol Hill in 1966 in Washington's overcrowded and long-neglected Court of General Sessions.

The series made Downie a finalist for a Pulitzer Prize. Ramsey Clark, the U.S. deputy attorney general, came to lunch to say the government's own investigation of the court agreed with Downie's. Then he asked, "Who would you recommend as the new chief judge of the court? From your stories, it looks like it should be Harold Green. Do you agree?" Downie stammered a non-reply because a journalist had no business making a recommendation. As it happened, Green had been one of his sources. Thirty years later, Judge Green officiated at Downie's third marriage.

President Lyndon Johnson's administration overhauled the city's court system, at least partly in response to the *Post* series. The work also changed the reporter. Downie realized he liked the archaeological dig of reporting, he liked standing up for people who had no voice, and he especially liked the idea that he could ask governmental officials to account for the way they did the public's work. "It made me an investigative reporter," Downie said.

Leonard Downie Sr. was born in 1918 to English immigrants and came of age in the Depression. He delivered milk by day, tended bar at night. He met Pearl Evenheimer during productions of high school plays; she was the makeup girl, he was the gregarious, singing star. She raised four sons and in sixty-seven years of marriage kept a closed fist around every dollar her husband made. Because Leonard Jr. was, by three and a half years, the oldest boy, he was often the man of the house in his father's absence. He brought home money, too, the first of it from newspaper work: he delivered the *Cleveland Press*.

His father wrote essays, songs, and poetry, some intended for publication in the local papers. "Had it not been for the Depression," Len said, "he might have gone into the newspaper business." Because Leonard Sr. admired the *Cleveland Press*'s crusading editor, Louis Seltzer, he took his son, then in the sixth grade, to hear the newspaperman speak. "I fell in love with the business," Len said. That same year, he won an elementary school essay contest by explaining the St. Lawrence Seaway's impact on the city.

While his choice of topics suggested precocious maturity, Downie knew better. "At eighteen," he said, "I was a mess. There was part of my life I wouldn't show." His father fixed up an old Plymouth for him, only to have Len get in an accident that ripped off the passenger-side door. Worse was the day his mother took the car to the grocery store and discovered a case of beer in the trunk. Then came the senior prom, after which Len reported that his girlfriend was pregnant.

"My father was furious," Downie said. It wasn't only the teenage sex. "Dad was embarrassed because he had always gotten along well with my girlfriend's father. Now, this." The girl had wanted to attend Ohio Wesleyan with plans to become a lawyer; instead, she married Downie and went to Ohio State with a husband whose interest in family life ran second to journalism. A second child arrived three and a half years later. In graduate school, Downie went on staff at Ohio State's monthly magazine and did freelance work for an insurance company's in-house magazine.

On graduation, then, Len Downie, the son of honorable, hardworking parents, was a hungry, eager competitor ready to take on the fancy-pants Ivy Leaguer who slid past him that day in the *Post* newsroom.

A veteran by the winter of 1967, Downie holed up in a squat, ugly warehouse that stored files created by the District of Columbia Recorder of Deeds. He wanted to know who stood to get rich quick from the federal government's spending on urban renewal. Who owned the houses and apartment buildings in the city's poor Shaw neighborhood? The only way to find out was to nail his butt to a chair in that filing room and read hundreds, even thousands of deeds.

Doing a search, a reporter was usually alone in a room where fluorescent bulbs hummed overhead. It was slow going because he did it by hand, and though haste made mistakes, the human impulse when faced with tedium is to hurry, get done, get a beer. And in a three-newspaper town—the *Post*, the *Star*, the *Daily News*—a reporter's pulse quickened at the thought of the competition.

Downie grew anxious when he saw a tall, hulking guy making notes. Maybe he was not alone in searching for the Shaw information. As the man worked, Downie noticed that he went to lunch every day at the same hour. He left his notebook on a filing cabinet. Downie soon learned the big man's identity by doing what comes naturally to the best reporters.

"I started reading his notebook."

Without qualms?

"No! He left it there uncovered! I'm an investigative reporter! I read stuff upside down on people's desks. That was fair. If I left my notebooks behind and somebody read them, I would expect that, too. I didn't go into his locker, into his office or his home. He left the notebook on top of a file cabinet in a public building."

The man turned out to be a reporter from the *Star*.

"From his notebook, I calculated how many weeks ahead of him I was," Downie said.

"He was still there taking down records while I was writing."

What Downie wrote for the *Post* was that thing every reporter wants—a five-part series already in type while his competitors slept.

"The series started on a Sunday," Downie said, "and I heard from friends in the newsroom, 'There's a crisis at the *Star*.'" It had two reporters working Shaw, one the records guy, the other talking to residents. "The street guy woke up that Sunday morning, picked up the paper from his front porch, went in to his editors, and said, 'I want to kill myself.'"

Under the headline "Slum Landlords Buy Up Shaw Houses," Downie reported that twelve Washington slumlords owned nearly seven hundred Shaw properties valued at $10 million. The story began, "The city's slum landlords have been quietly buying up the Shaw neighborhood, even as Shaw has been deteriorating into the city's worst slum, The Washington Post has found from a study of city land records . . . Some of these landlords reaped profits of from 25 to 100 percent by selling property to the Government in a nearby urban-renewal project, Northwest, in recent years."

The numbers in that paragraph were not produced by computer in two-tenths of a second. They were produced by ballpoint pen on a reporter's notebook in weeks—which explains Len Downie's raucous exclamation seven years later when he saw Jack Nicholson as private detective Jake Gittes in the movie *Chinatown*.

Like Downie, Gittes did a records search. Like Downie, Gittes found the records he wanted. Unlike Downie, Gittes did not have time to make notes of those records.

So Nicholson as Gittes says to the filing room clerk, "Can I check one of these volumes out?"

"Sir, this is not a lending library, it's the Hall of Records."

Nicholson smiles tightly. "How about a ruler?"

"A ruler?"

Nicholson says, "Yeah. The print's real fine. I left my glasses home. I'd like to be able to read across."

The clerk hands him a ruler, which Nicholson places vertically on a page of the records book. Then, while coughing to cover the sound . . .

"He just rips the page out!" Downie said. "How many times did I want to just rip the page out and take it with me back to the office! I cheered, 'Yeah! Go! Do it!' People in the theater must've thought I was crazy."

Donald Edward Graham and Leonard Downie Jr. came from different worlds. Graham was a son of privilege, Downie a son of a milkman. Graham's future was assured, Downie's was to be earned. What they had in common was more important. They were smart, earnest, and competitive. They were contented loners, happier at work than at a party, driven to prove they belonged. Graham needed to prove it to himself, Downie to everyone else.

From that first meeting on the Metro staff in 1971 to a last embrace in the newsroom in 2008, Graham and Downie were integral parts of a newspaper so good, so rich, so powerful that many people made the mistake of thinking it would never be anything less.

After all, they worked with a force of nature named Benjamin Crowninshield Bradlee, who one day in 1965 said, yes, absolutely, he'd love to have lunch with Katharine Graham.

3.

HOLLYWOOD ON THE POTOMAC

By buying and closing the *Times-Herald*, Eugene Meyer and Phil Graham may have made the paper "safe for Donnie." Yet for a decade and more, the *Post*'s reputation mirrored the city's as an underling to New York. The sophisticates of Gotham considered Washington a steaming southern colonial outpost, a brackish backwater bereft of everything that made life worth living. In 1955 Washington had three newspapers of middling quality while New York's seven included the *Times* and the wonderful *Herald Tribune*. The nation's capital had only a handful of decent restaurants and no quality theater. Of its art galleries, the *Post*'s critic, Paul Richard, said, "Thirty thousand years of paintings, from cave walls on, and I am older than the National Gallery." The Washington Redskins played within walking distance of the Supreme Court that made segregation illegal, but their roster included no black players; the irony was often pointed out by the *Post*'s sports columnist, Shirley Povich, who once noted that Jim Brown "integrated the Redskins' goal line with more than deliberate speed." Povich was so persistent in his crusade that team owner George Preston Marshall came to say, "When they circumcised Povich, they threw away the wrong part."

Even with morning delivery to itself in the 1960s, the *Post* ran second-best in town to the *Washington Star*. In those desultory days, the ambitious kid reporter Ben Bradlee worked for *Newsweek*, the magazine owned by the *Post*. He made his bones with Phil Graham as the weekly's Washington bureau chief—all the while lusting for the power of the *Post*. "I was in awe of the paper's immediacy, its incredible impact on the community, and the shadow it cast on the government," Bradlee wrote in his autobiography. "A crook could be exposed, wrongs could be righted overnight. A victim could be extricated before a news magazine could make up its mind. And the urge to right wrong was the urge that made us journalists in the first place."

Bradlee was many things. Bashful was not one of them. He demonstrated as much in March of 1965 at that lunch with Mrs. Graham. With Bradlee's enthusiastic assistance, the lunch . . .

Produced one of journalism's all-time great quotes.

Changed the character of the *Post*'s newsroom.

Suggested action that would move Mrs. Graham into the ranks of America's most powerful women.

And set in motion, within a decade, a series of journalistic and political events so unusual that they would be recorded in American history books forever.

Mrs. Graham had invited Bradlee to the F Street Club. The ostensible purpose was to talk about his future at *Newsweek*. But she also asked the question he had hoped to hear. Might he ever want to return to the newspaper? Twenty years earlier he had been a cityside reporter before satisfying his teenage ambition to experience the glamorous work of a foreign correspondent. He had done that as *Newsweek*'s man in Europe. Now, at lunch with his patron's widow, he made the heroic effort necessary to keep from leaping across the table and embracing her for having asked if he'd thought of returning to the paper.

Thought of it?

Had he *thought* of it?

"If Al Friendly's job ever opened up," he said, "I'd give my left one for it."

Post historian Chalmers Roberts characterized Friendly as "a man of erudition and sophistication with a facile and witty pen . . . without doubt [he] presided over a transition from an essentially provincial and local paper with a fine editorial page to a *Post* poised on the brink of greatness." By 1965 he had been in the job ten years. Mrs. Graham came to lunch feeling that the paper had lost zest. Bradlee's testicular message tingled with zest. Three months later Mrs. Graham created a deputy managing editor's job for him, and four months after that she made room at the top by shunting Friendly into a writing role.

And from there, all else flowed.

Bradlee made the newsroom his stage. He managed by walking around, and no one in any newsroom ever did it better. "Whatcha workin' on?" he asked at every stop. Occasionally he wanted a specific answer, as when he saw a scoop in another paper and marked it in red ink, asking his people, "What's this?" He moved with the confidence of a man who knew that people liked what they saw when they saw him moving their way, smiling and cocky. By the mid-seventies he decorated himself in finely made, fancily colored, imported Turnbull & Asser shirts, a hundred bucks a copy, stretched tight against a thick chest. Ben Bradlee loved being Ben Bradlee. Henry Mitchell, the kindly gardening columnist, called him "The Beast." He saw charm in Bradlee's face—and a coyote. Cataloged in his youth as "a personality boy," earthy, profane, a man's man, Bradlee had held his life in his hands, a survivor of childhood polio, an officer on the bridge of a destroyer in a tin-can navy that swept the Pacific. And with all that came more. There was something—vibes, unspoken signals, pheromones, something—and for three frightening one-hundredths of a second, you saw on his face the moving shadow of the beast. So when Bradlee chose to smile on you—thank you, God!—you fell in love.

At Bradlee's start, the *Post*'s newsroom was a small space. An editor or two still wore green eyeshades against the glare of incandescent bulbs. "We had some weird characters," Paul Richard said. "If somebody walked in off the street and told Bradlee they spoke Chinese, he figured, 'Why not?'" Make Bradlee laugh and the chances were you'd be hired.

An ex-Marine named Henry Allen became a copy editor in Bradlee's new features section, Style. He arrived with long hair, a mustache, and an attitude. It was four years after his tour of duty in Vietnam. He had taken eight months off to backpack to India by way of Iran, Pakistan, and Afghanistan. "Afghanistan!" he said. "Those are some warlike motherfuckers! And they've all got guns!

On the streets of Kabul, they're all carrying British Enfield rifles. I knew the Russians were in for it when they went in there." He came to Washington four months removed from a wanderer's life in a tent on the high desert of New Mexico. "Yes, the whole '60s show!" He stopped in the nation's capital to get his car repaired. "I had $800 on me, all the money I had, and getting the car fixed cost a lot." He figured he'd see if the *Post* could use a guy who had newsroom experience at the *New Haven Register* and *New York Daily News*. From his first day, November 8, 1970, Allen wanted it to last forever. "I knew I was home. The people in there were hip, witty, sophisticated, aggressive—and they didn't give a fuck what anybody thought."

Across twenty years, Bradlee built a staff that at its peak reached seven hundred. His lieutenants came mostly from the ranks of men who considered charm the least necessary of their attributes. He once told Metro editor Tom Wilkinson why he rejected one prospect: "When he walks, he doesn't clank." One old hand said of Bradlee's crew, "Some were born bullies, others were made." They were also effective in producing stories that Henry Mitchell thought of as Bradlee's signatures: "We do two kinds of stories. One is 'Oh, the horror of it all,' and the other is 'Oh, the wonder of it all.' "

Then, in 1971 the *Post* became a big-time player by printing stories based on the Pentagon Papers, the government's secret account of the conduct of the Vietnam War. The *New York Times* had published its stories five days earlier. The *Post* matched it despite an aroused administration's attempts to quash publication. When a court ruled for the *Post*, Bradlee and Mrs. Graham danced out of the federal building, laughing like lovers who had invented Journalism with a capital *J*—and maybe they had.

Already their newsroom hummed with the energy of the young and ambitious, among them Bob Woodward and Carl Bernstein. Woodward was a buttoned-down Yale graduate and ex–navy officer who had decided reporting was more fun than lawyering. Bernstein was a college dropout with a counterculture look, disheveled and long-haired, a full-time reporter since he was nineteen, and at the *Post* since 1966.

A Woodward story about the D.C. police department—published

May 11, 1972—brought the former city patrolman Don Graham to his desk. The story reported that police officers had barricaded two of the three lanes of "busy New York Avenue between 5th and 6th Streets NW and are using the space as a parking lot for their private cars." Graham was then the paper's sports editor. But he so often came through his old haunt in Metro that reporters called him "the prowler." He told Woodward he'd heard complaints that the story wasn't fair. "He was not happy about it, the story, and what I'd done," Woodward said years later. He thought it "a little heavy-handed" that the publisher's son would squeeze a new reporter that way. Woodward was only in his eighth month on the job. His reaction to the pressure was "a little bit of, 'Okay, that's interesting. The reporting shows you're wrong.' And a little bit of 'Fuck you.'"

One month and seven days later, on June 18, Woodward and Bernstein were among eight reporters listed as having contributed to a story under the byline of veteran police reporter Al Lewis. The story ran at the top left of the *Post*'s Sunday editions with the headline:

5 HELD IN PLOT TO BUG
DEMOCRATS' OFFICE HERE

The next day, Woodward and Bernstein shared a byline under the headline:

GOP SECURITY AIDE
AMONG 5 ARRESTED
IN BUGGING AFFAIR

That was the first Woodward-Bernstein story on a botched break-in at the Watergate apartment-office complex on the Potomac River.

They were six months into the story when Katharine Graham asked them to lunch. Bernstein was at a funeral and couldn't attend. Woodward walked alone through double glass doors onto thick white carpet that led to the corporate suite on the eighth floor. As he entered Mrs. Graham's office, he saw managing editor

Howard Simons with a drink in hand. Simons had said, "The boss wants to talk to the reporters." Woodward felt intimidated and thought, *Is this the interview before we get fired?* They sat in a corner, away from her desk, and Mrs. Graham seemed serene.

Richard Nixon's men had been emboldened by the president's reelection in a landslide achieved despite the *Post*'s reporting of corruption. Secretary of State Henry Kissinger persistently complained to Mrs. Graham. Attorney General John Mitchell told Bernstein, "Katie Graham's gonna get her tit caught in a big fat wringer." Others suggested the Post Company could lose its television licenses. Post stock fell precipitously. At that dark moment in January of 1973, Woodward, making $156 a week, arrived for a command performance. Mrs. Graham's questions included a quote from the *Chicago Tribune* and she quickly demonstrated a mastery of Watergate detail that surprised Woodward. By the time she asked the identity of sources, Woodward believed the owner only wanted to learn, as gracefully as possible, whether the young reporters had put her newspaper in peril legally or ethically. He told her the names and positions of sources: a district attorney's investigator, several Justice Department attorneys, an FBI agent, a White House aide, the former treasurer of the Republican National Committee. As for "Deep Throat," Woodward said he had told that source's name to no one.

"Tell me," Mrs. Graham said.

Woodward froze, thinking, *God, I don't*...

He said he would give her the name if she wanted it, but before he could say anything more, Mrs. Graham laughed and touched his arm. No, no. She didn't want to carry that burden. The relieved, grateful Woodward took a bite of his eggs Benedict, by then cold.

Instead, she asked the killer question.

"When is the truth going to come out about Watergate?"

Woodward said, "Carl and I believe, and have written, that it was a criminal conspiracy, that they frightened and scared people, that they compartmentalized information. So the answer, Mrs. Graham, is never. The whole truth is never going to be known."

Here, Mrs. Graham fell silent. She seemed hurt. And then she said, "Never? Don't tell me never."

Thirty-five years later, no longer wondering if he could be fired,

Woodward remembered Mrs. Graham saying those words softly. He had come to consider the words not a threat but a challenge: Use the resources of the newspaper to get to the bottom of this.

Mrs. Graham's court fight to print the Pentagon Papers was a signal to her newsroom that no ambition was too great. That triumph led directly to the resolve that sustained the paper's Watergate coverage. It also produced a newsroom moment that helped define the young Metro editor, Len Downie.

Richard Harwood, the feared and respected National editor, had decided his people should take the Watergate story.

"It's time for the grown-ups," he said.

Downie said, "It's Metro's story, it's staying in Metro."

As sure as Harwood was of his journalistic cojones—Ben's men clanked—Downie stood his ground. He could do that, and do it loudly, because he knew his own boss, Harry Rosenfeld, would keelhaul him if he didn't.

The story stayed with Woodward and Bernstein, in Metro, under Rosenfeld's direction with Downie at his right hand. And on August 8, 1974, Woodward sat in a chair at his newsroom desk. Bernstein was on the floor, Downie behind them. They watched television, along with dozens of other reporters and editors. They heard President Nixon say, "Good evening. This is the thirty-seventh time I have spoken to you from this office . . ."

There was silence at Woodward's desk.

Nixon continued. "I have never been a quitter. To leave office before my term is completed is abhorrent to every instinct in my body. But as president, I must put the interest of America first. Therefore, I shall resign the Presidency effective at noon tomorrow."

Until that night, Downie said, he never thought it would happen.

The Watergate reporting produced a Pulitzer, two Woodward-Bernstein books, and a movie in 1976 with Robert Redford and Dustin Hoffman as the boy reporters, and the powerful actor Jason

Robards as Bradlee shouting from his office doorway, "Woodstein!" From the Pentagon Papers to Watergate to Bradlee's penchant for the holy-shit story and his creation of the sassy, take-no-prisoners Style section, this was Hollywood on the Potomac. "We were gods striding the Earth," said Henry Allen, by then a star feature writer in Style. "Bumper stickers around town said, 'Thank God for The Washington Post.' And we thought, 'Damn right.'"

On July 12, 1979, eleven days before her twenty-fifth birthday, Janet Cooke, a reporter on the *Toledo Blade*, wrote a letter to the top god. "Dear Mr. Bradlee," she said. "I have been a full time reporter for The Blade for slightly more than two years, and I believe I am now ready to tackle the challenge of working for a larger newspaper in a major city."

Her résumé said she was a 1976 Phi Beta Kappa graduate of Vassar who had studied at the Sorbonne. She was also beautiful, stylish, African American—and she could write. Nine months after being hired by the *Post*, she wrote about an inner-city child named Jimmy.

The story began: "Jimmy is 8 years old and a third-generation heroin addict, a precocious little boy with sandy hair, velvety brown eyes and needle marks freckling the baby-smooth skin of his thin brown arms."

Jimmy became an addict at age five, Cooke wrote, and the junk had shaped his life for a future as a drug dealer. The "cherubic faced" boy's favorite subject in school, on the few days he attended, was math. "I want to have me a bad car and dress good and also have me a good place to live," he said. "So, I pretty much pay attention to math because I know I got to keep up when I finally get something to sell."

Jimmy's house was a "comfortably furnished home in Southeast Washington" where every day "junkies casually buy heroin" in the dining room "'cook' it in the kitchen and 'fire up' in the bedrooms." The boy's mother had been raped by her mother's boyfriend; Jimmy was the result of one such encounter. Later becoming a prostitute to support her heroin addiction, the mother had a live-in lover, Ron, who started Jimmy on the drug. From Ron: "He'd be buggin' me all the time about what the shots were and what people was doing and one day he said, 'When can I get off?' I said, 'Well, shit, you can have some now.' I let him snort a little and, damn, the little dude really did get off." Six months later, Cooke said, Jimmy was hooked. He said the heroin "be real different from herb (marijuana). That's baby shit." Every day someone plunged a needle into Jimmy's arm, "sending the fourth grader into a hypnotic nod."

The 2,256-word story ended with Ron shooting up Jimmy.

He grabs Jimmy's left arm just above the elbow, his massive hand tightly encircling the child's small limb. The needle slides into the boy's soft skin like a straw pushed into the center of a freshly baked cake. Liquid ebbs out of the syringe, replaced by bright red blood. The blood is then reinjected into the child.

Jimmy has closed his eyes during the whole procedure, but now he opens them, looking quickly around the room. He climbs into a rocking chair and sits, his head dipping and snapping upright again, in what addicts called "the nod."

"Pretty soon, man," Ron says, "you got to learn how to do this for yourself."

The powerful story putting the boy's face on a twentieth-century plague ran on the *Post*'s front page of September 28, 1980, with the headline "Jimmy's World." Bob Woodward, by then the Metro editor, submitted it for journalism's highest prize, the Pulitzer. The day "Jimmy's World" won for feature writing, April 13, 1981, was the day Janet Cooke's lies surfaced.

People at the *Toledo Blade* noticed discrepancies in an Associated Press report of her background. After hours of questioning by *Post* editors, she finally confessed to her colleague David Maraniss that she had made it all up, the story, her résumé, everything.

The Pulitzer was returned, Cooke resigned, and critics saw the affair as evidence of the corruption inherent in the *Post*'s celebrity culture. Cooke did a national television appearance the next winter in which she said she created the lies in answer to pressure from editors for sensational stories. Within three days of Cooke's resignation, the newspaper's ombudsman published a fourteen-thousand-word report of the affair. Its most damning indictment of *Post* editors was that they knew of Cooke's history of reporting errors, careless writing, and naked ambition—yet they allowed publication of the inflammatory, unsourced story.

Don Graham stood with Bradlee, literally.

Graham, as publisher, first refused the editor's offer to resign. He then attended a national editors' convention in Washington at which photographers "must have taken hundreds of pictures of me," Bradlee later wrote, "but damn few—if any—without Don Graham's arm around my shoulder. I'll never forget it, and all these years later, his presence and his show of confidence still makes my neck tingle."

Four years later, in 1985, when a Social Security form letter reminded Bradlee that he was sixty-three and eligible for benefits, he asked Graham if it was time to retire. Again, Graham said no— but with a difference. This time he had a successor in mind. Bradlee's managing editor, Howard Simons, had left the paper. The leading candidates for the newsroom's number two job were Len Downie, then the National editor, Jim Hoagland of Foreign, and Shelby Coffey from Style. Coffey, a Bradlee protégé, was the editor's favorite. But Graham preferred grit over glamor, substance over style. When he chose Downie, one erstwhile rival told a gaggle of ambitious young men that they all had lost out in the chase for Bradlee's job.

"Graham has now told us," he said, "that there's a chemistry between him and Len that the rest of us don't have. He's gonna pick Downie. Get used to it."

The choice of Downie was more than a matter of chemistry. It was also a corrective. Bradlee's newspaper—too often self-indulgent, overreaching, sensation-seeking—had done itself harm before and after Janet Cooke.

A smirky feature written by Sally Quinn, later Bradlee's wife, reported in 1979 that Jimmy Carter's national security adviser, Zbigniew Brzezinski, had unzipped his fly in front of a female reporter. When that reporter denied it, Brzezinski threatened to sue, and the paper published a retraction. In her second week on the job in 1981, gossip columnist Diana McLellan reported that Rosalynn Carter had told "pals" that, by bugging the Blair House residence of visiting dignitaries, the White House had eavesdropped on the incoming Reagans. The *Post* printed another retraction, and Don Graham wrote a personal letter of apology. More seriously, the *Post* lost a libel suit growing from a story done by investigative reporter Patrick Tyler. In 1982 Mobil Oil president William Tavoulareas won a judgment of $2.05 million. On appeal, the verdict was reversed. One morning in 1988 at their regular Tuesday breakfast, Graham said to Bradlee, "How about working until you hit seventy?" This time they agreed. A few months later at the paper's annual off-site meeting of top editors, Graham almost casually made the announcement of Bradlee's successor. By then it was no surprise that the next executive editor would be perhaps the only man in the newsroom who never imagined himself in a Turnbull & Asser shirt.

For starters, Leonard Downie Jr. could ill afford such finery; at the time he had four children by two wives. His Midwest roots also bent him toward a J.C. Penney's wardrobe. More important, Downie's highly developed political instincts had told him years before that glitz would be counterproductive. Better to be the not-Bradlee than Bradlee-lite because next time it would not be Mrs. Graham going for zest. It would be Don choosing competence.

On Bradlee's retirement in 1991, the job was Downie's.

Soon after, Henry Allen told a colleague, "It's going to be different around here."

"That's right," said a voice behind him, loudly.

It was Downie passing by.

Allen's comment was truer than he could have known. He had thought of differences in personalities and management skills. But the real difference would come in the business itself. While Bradlee's *Post* had enjoyed an uninterrupted rocket ride to prosperity, Downie's tenure began with a distant warning signal that change was coming.

Downie's old Ivy League rival, Bob Kaiser, was now his managing editor. Kaiser had been to Japan for an international conference on multimedia communication. There he saw high-tech astonishments that had nothing to do with newspapers as he had known them. He was at once thrilled and frightened, for either he had seen the future of the *Post* or he had seen the instruments of its death.

4.

BOILING FROGS

Like most newsroom executives in 1992, Bob Kaiser had only a passing acquaintance with computers. Typewriters had been his tools, his favorite a black Royal of sweet feel and sound. On it he wrote a book about Russia and another about Middle America. In Saigon, his typed copy went to the Reuters wire service, which transmitted it home. In Moscow, once he finished a story, he had to retype it into a machine that punched holes in a tape which then was flown to Washington by a genie wearing green curly-toed shoes (for all Kaiser knew).

He had first worked on computers as part of the *Post*'s newsroom editing systems in 1979. His first laptop was the rock star of the early eighties, the Radio Shack TRS-80, famous for its six-lines-of-copy screen and known as the "Trash-80." Now, as managing editor, he had two terminals at his desk, one for the newsroom system, another for a Macintosh with a dial-up connection that made him the first *Post* editor to do e-mail from the office.

In those dark ages, Kaiser qualified as a newspaper visionary. So the entrepreneurial geniuses at Apple Computer invited him to Japan for a multimedia conference at the Hakone Resort. After doing some technology reporting from Silicon Valley, Kaiser considered the Japan trip another piece of his education. Instead, it became an epiphany. He was convinced that newspapers would never be the same. The character of the changes and their significance, he did not know. But the future had announced itself dramatically. Flying home first class on All Nippon Airways, Kaiser took out his laptop and wrote a seven-page memo to his bosses. Read even at a remove of almost twenty years, the memo fairly vibrated with exuberance.

At the *Post*, however, the excitement seemed pretty much his alone. He set up a study committee and hired an expert to teach computer-assisted reporting. But nothing much else happened—until Mark Potts came to him with yet another problem.

Potts often voiced the kind of complaint made by newsroom whiners grumbling about management's failure to recognize their brilliance. This is not to say that Potts whined. But years later he wrote an essay in which he allowed that certain events had identified him, at age thirty-five, as "something of a problem child." He also characterized Kaiser as a stuffed-shirt Ivy Leaguer given to pinstripes, bow ties, and pomposity. Small surprise, then, that whatever was bothering Potts this time, Kaiser didn't care. But he did have a use for Potts.

He knew that Potts, reporting in the business section, had dabbled in technology coverage and was one of the newsroom's few computer geeks. He gave Potts a copy of his Japan memo.

"By the time I got back to my desk," Potts said, "I was in shock. Here was the managing editor of *The Washington Post* spouting the kind of futuristic vision that I was used to hearing from techies. In short, he got it!"

On a gorgeous weekend in August of 1992, Potts saw none of the sunshine. With Kaiser's memo in hand, he descended into his basement. When he came up three days later, the problem child may have saved the empire.

Kaiser's memo to his bosses described wonders he had never imagined. The personal computer would become a virtual supercomputer capable of transmitting and storing large quantities of text, video, photographs, and graphics. The machines would be more user-friendly than the day's PCs, able to take voice instructions, and read handwritten commands. "None of this is science fiction," Kaiser wrote, "it's just around the corner."

Dated August 6, 1992—four years before the Internet became a widely used public tool—Kaiser's memo reflected his newfound belief that newspapers must join the electronics revolution immediately. The memo went to Don Graham, Len Downie, company president Alan Spoon, and every vice president on the roster. Despite the memo's excitement and urgency, a reasonable interpretation of the response from *Post* executives was: What, us worry?

The *Post* was lord of all it surveyed, unassailable behind walls of myth and money, the flagship of a mighty, diversified company. As much as anyone, Bob Kaiser believed in the *Post*'s mission of journalism. He believed the *Post* of 1992, as created by Eugene Meyer and the Grahams, would be the *Post* forever.

But that was before he went to Japan and heard the pioneering computer genius Alan Kay talk about a boiling frog.

Kay explained that an electronics revolution was under way and the world's entertainment and news media better get on board. He said it's like the boiling frog. You can put a frog in a pot of water and slowly raise the flame under the pot until the water boils, but the frog will never jump. Its nervous system cannot detect slight changes in temperatures. Next thing the frog knows, it's dinner.

Kaiser wrote, "The Post is not in a pot of water, and we're smarter than the average frog. But we do find ourselves swimming in an electronic sea where we could eventually be devoured—or ignored as an unnecessary anachronism."

That revolution promised amazements. "A fiber network [Kaiser wrote] could carry two to three thousand times the stream of data that can be sent over the air in all the existing radio frequencies!" This would make possible "packages of text, photos and film that could be used to create customized news products at many different levels of sophistication. At the top end, such a product might contain the text (or spoken text) of a Post story on the big news of the day, accompanied by CNN's live footage and/or Post photographers' pictures."

A new reality was being created, a telecommunications/infotech/entertaintech universe. What that universe would finally look like, no one could know. It would come from "a collision of technologies," one conference participant said. Kaiser wrote, "If we're riding dodge 'em cars, drawing conclusions is risky. I'll offer a few tentative ones."

He called for action. "No one in our business has yet launched a really impressive or successful electronic product, but someone surely will. I'd bet it will happen rather soon. The Post ought to be in the forefront of this—not for the adventure, but for important defensive purposes. We'll only defeat electronic competitors by playing their game better than they can play it. And we can."

He made two proposals.

(1) Take the *Post* online by designing the world's first electronic newspaper: "Our electronic Post should be thought of not as a newspaper on a screen, but (perhaps) as a computer game converted to a serious purpose. In other words, it should be a computer product."

(2) Do online classified advertising: "Figure out how to capture and organize the digital computer information that we already create for each day's classifieds into a user-friendly data bank . . . Would someone looking for a reliable car for a kid going to college prefer our current listings, or a list of all small cars with less than 60,000 miles selling for $5–7,000? I suspect the latter would be the choice."

Kaiser was bullish. "We could sell an entire electronic Post for several times the newsstand price without using an ounce of ink or a roll of newsprint—all gravy at the bottom line . . . The use of computers to transmit information of all kinds is growing at a frantic pace . . . There's a big and important role for The Washington Post in this new world."

Potts worked around the clock on his Macintosh LC. On Monday morning, he downloaded his work onto a new Mac PowerBook laptop. By coincidence, he had scheduled a get-my-act-together lunch with assistant managing editor Steve Luxenberg. Over pastrami and corned-beef sandwiches outside Loeb's delicatessen, Potts waxed lyrical about Kaiser's memo and offered to show Luxenberg what he had put together. "I think Steve agreed to look as much to humor me as anything else," Potts said years later.

Back at the office, Bill Casey, just hired to teach computer-assisted reporting, told Potts, "You really ought to be at the committee meeting this afternoon." Potts replied, "What meeting?" Kaiser's committee—charged with studying the possibility of an electronic version of the *Post*—was a product of his Japan trip and nagging by Larry Meyer, editor of the paper's National Weekly Edition and a Macintosh devotee. Casey wangled an invitation for Potts, who then was told to sit down and speak only when spoken to. "So I took a seat in the corner with my PowerBook in my lap," he said.

Imagine a schoolboy who knows all the answers. Imagine the teacher telling him to sit still, be quiet. This fidgety boy, Mark Potts, heard the committee talk in the most theoretical ways about the stuff he had spent the weekend actually doing. "I was having a lot of trouble containing myself," Potts said, "and Casey and Luxenberg weren't much better." Because Jen Belton, the newsroom's head of research, noticed the three men's agitation, she said, "Why don't we just see what Mark has done?"

He had created an embryonic electronic newspaper. He first called it ElectroPost, then PostCard—puns on the newspaper's name and HyperCard programming language.

In his unpublished memoir, Potts later wrote,

I created a front page based on that Saturday's front page of
The Post and added stories from all over the paper, typing
many of them in word by word. I didn't have access to
digitized photographs, so I adapted crude clip art files to
create graphics. I put together a rough version of The Post's
logo. I dug into my collection of fonts to find typefaces that
replicated The Post's Bodoni headlines . . .

But this couldn't be just a newspaper pasted on a computer
screen, as Kaiser had pointed out. To take advantage of the
computer's power to do things differently than the printed
page, I added sounds and animation. Hurricane Andrew's

destruction of Florida was the big news that weekend, so I
held the Mac's microphone up against the television speaker,
recorded quotes about the storm from President Bush and
the governor of Florida and attached them to the stories
about the hurricane. I put together a crude animated map
that showed the hurricane sweeping across the Florida
peninsula. Clicking to go to the Weather page brought the
sound of thunder (that was the forecast) taken off of a
record I had. Also recorded off the stereo: a snatch of Bruce
Springsteen's "Hungry Heart" that played along with the
printed review of his concert in Washington that weekend.

Larry Meyer's committee members crowded around Potts and
his little Powerbook. He said, "I clicked a button and George Bush
held forth on the hurricane. I touched another area on the screen
and Hurricane Andrew stormed across Florida."

That was enough for Meyer, who hurried to a phone and told
Kaiser, "You've got to see what Potts has done."

An hour later, Kaiser shouted, "This is it! This is exactly what I
was talking about in my memo."

Then it was up to Don Graham. With his memo and with Potts's
electronic model, Kaiser had outlined action that he deemed essential and that likely would call for tens of millions of dollars in
investment without promise of return.

"Don being the world's most conservative manager, he was
extremely reluctant to go into anything like that," Kaiser said. "His
slogan became: 'Forty million dollars.' That's what Knight Ridder
had lost in an online project. Don thought it was a sinkhole."

Two days before Christmas in 1992, an enthusiastic Potts met a
discouraging Graham.

"Basically, Don said he'd be happy with an electronic crossword
puzzle," Potts said. "My reaction was, 'Oh, Christ. Is Knight Ridder
hiring?'" But Kaiser told him, "Don't worry. The key thing was, he
didn't oppose it. We'll show him the way."

As time was measured in the newspaper business world—by

years—Graham moved quickly into electronics. But by the ever-accelerating clocks of the electronics universe, his movements were those of a nineteenth-century mogul. He might not have moved at all except for one piece of disturbing information.

In 1994 the *Post*'s circulation figures fell for the first time in decades. Downie and Kaiser were stunned. Since their days as interns in 1964, the *Post*'s daily circulation had more than doubled to 900,000. Sunday's paper, stuffed with advertising, went to over 1.2 million customers.

"The decline was only a few hundred, but it made a deep impression on us," Kaiser said.

"I told Len, 'You and I do not want to be remembered as the editors who presided over the decline . . . We have to be the ones who say, 'This is unacceptable!' Len agreed, and we tried to do something, but none of the vice presidents wanted to take it on. It was like they had all agreed to minimize it, not overreact to it. We made a stink, but basically were told that we were a 'mature' business whose greatest growth was behind us and that the challenge now was to preserve what we had."

Only years later did Kaiser admit why he and Downie were upset. They hoped to fix the blame on corporate lethargy, on fat-cat smugness, on misguided business strategy—they searched for a reason other than what they feared to be the truth. He said, "We didn't want to acknowledge that the glory days were ending."

The transition from print to electronics had started, and smart people knew it was time to move.

Alan Spoon, then the company president, was a techie who had been online as a student at Massachusetts Institute of Technology in the 1970s. He led the *Post*'s journey into the uncharted territory that separated print from electronics. "I had a headache all through the nineties," he said. "By October of 1995, the headache had become a migraine." The *Post*'s online efforts were weak. "We charged maybe twenty dollars a month and had twenty-nine thousand subscribers. Some people thought that was a great number. I said, 'Yeah, we just won the county track meet. Trouble is, we want to compete in the Olympics.'"

The step up began in a taxi. In October 1995, Spoon shared a ride with Graham from O'Hare International Airport to down-town Chicago. Change, already dizzying, had picked up speed. "I told Don, 'We gotta go to the Web.'"

This was three years after Kaiser's memo, which had said nothing about the World Wide Web or the Internet—for the good reason that the Web was in its infancy, and the Internet worked mostly with academia and government agencies. But now, with the CEO captive in a taxi, Spoon said it was necessary to give up the money gained by subscriptions. He advocated a free website where audience would grow exponentially and advertising revenue would follow.

And so, on June 17, 1996—three years, ten months, and eleven days after Kaiser's boiling frog memo—the *Post* took a major step into the electronics revolution. It relaunched Washingtonpost.com, this time on the Web.

It was a big-money gamble.

"It took a hundred million dollars to get Post.com to profitability," Spoon said.

Potts said, "Every time Don sees me, he says, with mock bitterness, 'You cost me two hundred million dollars.'"

Len Downie's newsroom thought in terms of fully realized news stories. Editors and reporters balked at satisfying the website's demands for immediacy. The newsroom's argument was that it couldn't give the website the story until it was ready for publication. The webbies answered: In a 24/7 world of news, we must not wait, we cannot wait.

The newsroom's mindset began to change when the website's editor, Doug Feaver, told reporters it would be helpful if they filed something quickly for the dot-com. Not a full story, a few paragraphs. Dress it up later.

"Is that all you want?" David Broder said. "That's easy enough."

Broder was the most respected newsman in the room. After that, young reporters covering big stories were eager to file for the website. Rajiv Chandrasekaran covered the Microsoft antitrust trial, Frank Ahrens the shenanigans at Enron, and Peter Baker did the Monica Lewinsky soap opera in ways he had never worked before. "It was a real sea change in thinking to put up original content on the website in the middle of the day," Baker said.

We had never done it before, and I'm not sure any other newspaper had done it. But obviously there was such enormous public appetite for this story in particular that we realized waiting for the next morning was no longer good enough. For me, it was challenging learning how to turn something around that fast. I don't think a lot of newspaper reporters ever fully appreciated just how tough it is for wire service reporters to crank out smart, fair, accurate, and lively copy almost instantaneously. None of us quite realized at the time, I don't think, just how much this was the beginning of something almost revolutionary about our journalism and how we present it to our readers.

The idea of revolution became undeniable on September 11, 2001. On that day, news five minutes old was useless. That day, newspapers were revealed as anachronisms, made obsolete by events moving so quickly that even an "extra" rushed onto the streets had the feel of a relic. That day, Don Graham came into the *Post* newsroom, and people heard what they had never before heard. They heard Graham cursing. "God damn it," he said, "we gotta get this stuff up on the Web as soon as we get it!"

No one knew if the *Post* had come to the electronic revolution too late, but the feeling was that it had not embraced it. Website users thought of the Internet as the Wild West, as a life in which you made up new rules. That was too much for the high-church journalists of the Graham-Downie generation, and in 2004 Washington post.com still came off as your grandpa's newspaper taped to the monitor screen.

One day, Jim Brady, the executive editor of Washingtonpost.com, told me something that sounded like this:

"The bots feed RSS geo coding to internal client tools that Flash morph through HTML until it aggregates in the IM search engines, if you can believe that Twitter."

I said, "Really?"

Then he started up again and seemed to say, "Otherwise, the

broadband wiki widgets spike Technorati uniques into a time spent in the blogosphere metric."

"Oh," I said.

Before becoming fluent in the language of revolution, Brady had been a sportswriter and news editor at the *Post*. He did four years at America Online, then returned to the website. In 2004 he wrote an eighteen-page memo that helped earn him the website's top editorial job. Much of the memo (written in English) defined what the website was and what he wanted it to be:

"We are not attracting the younger users that will make up the next generation of Web users.

"People are increasingly using non-traditional web media sources—Drudge, blogs, wikis, etc.—to get news and information.

"Most Web media experts agree that audio and video will be playing larger roles as the broadband revolution continues, and text will have to start sharing the playing field. We are not necessarily built to handle this change.

"Wireless is coming, and coming fast, and nothing is less friendly to a small wireless screen than newspaper articles."

Brady wanted the website Bob Kaiser had imagined, a real computer product. But he knew that the bosses first needed to understand what a website really was.

"We do have to look at the Web as a different medium than the newspaper, one with different users, different usage patterns, and a very different future. For the first 10 years of TV, it was nothing more than people doing radio in front of a camera. Up until now, I think, media companies have used the Web as a mirror that reflects their core mission." But in ten years, he wrote, the Web, like TV, would have become its own thing. Meanwhile, a strong brand and strong content made Washingtonpost.com a first-class website. "But it can't end there. We have to web-ify the brand in ways we have not done to this point."

To web-ify was to do a story as it could be done only on the Web with features and tone impossible to reproduce in print.

For instance, he asked me, "Have you seen the ambush video?"

Ambush video?

"Nelson Hernandez got caught in an ambush, outside Baghdad, and did video of it."

It was a news story set to gunfire.

Nelson Hernandez Jr. was the *Post*'s man on a convoy of water trucks. He stepped out of an armored truck that had carried him four hundred miles from the Persian Gulf across Iraq's southern desert. All his life he had been a word guy, a schoolboy debater, a writer, and recently an escapee from a Yale University master's program. So how did a scholar/reporter come to ride with British mercenaries delivering a water truck to Baghdad?

The immediate answer was that he simply asked if he could go along. The full answer began in his childhood. Then he saw his father—the son of an immigrant from the Dominican Republic— serve as an Army paratrooper. While a student at St. John's College in Annapolis, Maryland, Hernandez worked as an intern at the *Post*. Five years later—after his brief flirtation with Yale, where he rebelled against a historian's idea that "all truth is subjective"— Hernandez worked on the *Post*'s foreign desk. He was young, single, and hungry, an ideal candidate for a posting to the most dangerous job in journalism. "I thought Iraq would go down as the news story of my lifetime," he said. "So I wrote an absurdly macho memo asking for it, something about 'I was born for this job.'"

He joined the Brits at the Iraqi port of Um Qasr. He rode in a rear seat as the convoy moved north on a two-lane paved road across the desert moonscape. He had seen no bad guys, but only sensed . . . something. "There was a war lurking in the shadows," he said later, "and it felt like it would snatch at you, and you're gone."

On the convoy's arrival at the Baghdad Water Directorate, they parked inside a walled compound to unload. Watching the water truck back off its carrier, he heard the explosive *crump!* of a rocket-propelled grenade. Next came gunfire from somewhere above the compound's walls. One of the British guards shouted at Hernandez, "Get in the truck."

Wearing a flak jacket but no helmet, he leaped into the truck's rear seat. He fell onto the day's lunch of ham and cheese sandwiches and reached across the seat to shut the door. A machine gun mounted in the truck bed began clattering out return fire. He saw one convoy guard take aim at a shooter. He saw another guard sprint to open a compound gate so the trucks could get out of there.

Even as the gunfight raged around him, Hernandez thought to pull out his video camera. The website's video man, Chet Rhodes, had trained him in the use of a camera about the size of a pack of cigarettes. Hernandez recorded the British guard firing a rifle from in front of the truck. He captured the sounds of the gunfight. The camera bouncing askew as the truck roared away, he showed the compound gate coming open.

He said he never thought about being shot. "I was carried through on a wave of pure adrenaline. If I had actually seen one of the insurgents aiming at us, I might have had a different reaction. But I do remember thinking that the people outside the truck, shooting back, were doing something incredibly dangerous." On the raw video not used online, Hernandez could be heard saying, "Jesus Christ."

His written account of the convoy's trip and ambush appeared on the newspaper's front page. That same morning, users of Washingtonpost.com could see a three-minute video scripted and narrated by the reporter himself.

John Walsh, an ESPN vice president and once editor of a sports magazine published by the *Post*, bumped into Don Graham at a dinner in the summer of 2007. As always when journalists met, talk turned to the crisis. Walsh said, "Newspapers have just been too slow catching on to the Web."

Graham demurred. "You wouldn't say that if you saw our business reports of the last few years. Through the mid-nineties, we lost thirty or forty million dollars on the website."

So confusing were the times that to have spent tens of millions without return was seen as a good thing, an investment rather than a loss. "Then you're ahead of the curve," Walsh said.

Graham replied, "We now make more money online than the *Wall Street Journal* does. It's a hundred-million-dollar business for us."

Then, almost as an aside, the chairman added, "Online—it's everything to us now."

Nelson Hernandez Jr.'s video ambush was the news web-ified, as Jim Brady wanted it. In 2005, Brady made Washingtonpost.com the first major American news site to carry a staff-written blog— done by feature writer Joel Achenbach. "That was a big cultural step," Brady said, "especially since most of the print newsroom was against launching blogs, mostly because they thought blogs were done by ill-informed people ranting about stuff they didn't under-stand." The site was also the first to link to bloggers and first to print users' comments on the site's articles. "The idea was to make readers feel like we were letting them into the conversation. We were successful in that—as one blogger wrote, we made the *Post* feel like it wasn't just 'on the Web' but 'of the Web.' "

By the spring of 2007, Brady estimated that 40 percent of con-tent was web-ified by his staff of sixty-five people. There were eighty hours of chats in which *Post* reporters including Dana Priest, David Broder, Michael Wilbon, Gene Weingarten, Carolyn Hax, and Warren Brown took questions from users. Maybe thirty reporters chipped in with blogs, among them Achenbach, Marc Fisher, Howard Kurtz, Dan Froomkin, and Dan Steinberg. "And there are maybe fifty reporters carrying video cameras," Brady said.

Washingtonpost.com was the future in which Don Graham had made a huge investment. Still, it had not yet produced anything near the revenue necessary to sustain a large news operation. The investment could more accurately be portrayed as a high-stakes gamble.

The chairman was betting that this new thing would work.

If it didn't, the game was over.

Part II

"HOW COULD ANYONE NOT WANT TO BE A REPORTER?"

5.

EXISTENTIAL CRISIS

Breakfast with Walter Pincus, the curmudgeon in full growl . . .

"So do you want two, three Pulitzers?" he said over muffins, burnt.

"Sounds good," I said.

"Or a hundred and thirty thousand more readers?"

"Well . . ."

The number was not plucked from the sweet air at the Madison Hotel. A man who does a big-league newspaper's most arcane beat—national security and intelligence—does not imagine facts. He finds them. In 1954 Pincus began his search for answers to riddles inside enigmas. Out of Yale, he became a copy boy at the *New York Times*. There he met Hanson Baldwin, the *Times* military correspondent. Pincus said people "read him to find out what the hell was going on."

What the hell's going on? Pincus had asked that as a newspaper reporter, television producer, and in the sixties as an investigator for J. William Fulbright's Senate Foreign Relations Committee. (In the Dominican Republic, he used a microfilm camera to photograph documents showing a dictator's attempt to influence U.S. sugar policies. Pincus as James Bond.)

Early in 2007, what the hell was going on was that newspapers were going to hell. Readers abandoned them, advertisers followed. The news was everywhere on the Internet, delivered instantly, at no cost, with none of that pesky newsprint piling up in the house. The industry was still a multibillion-dollar money machine, but sputtering. Even the *Post*, once thought impervious to financial distress, was proven vulnerable. In 2006 it bought out 193 staffers, its second round of buyouts in three years. As Pincus said, daily circulation in the last ten years had fallen by 136,000; Sunday's figure was down almost 200,000. Don Graham's annual report to shareholders said: "Our company owns four large businesses, and it was a terrific year for three of them. It was a poor year, however, for the business we are named for, The Washington Post. Circulation continued to fall and a sharp drop in classified advertising raised questions about the future of the business. I don't have all the answers for these questions."

Nor did anyone else have answers, and there was some concern that answers needed to be found soon. Some concern, but not all that much. After all, the Dow was over 10,000 on its way to a record 14,000. Smart folks said the only way the newspaper industry would fall dead was if the nation's economy went into the tank, and there was no way that would happen.

What the hell's going on? Pincus had his theories about newspapers.

"The Internet is not the problem," he said.

"But Walter . . ."

"There's no audience for it."

"Walter, those millions of visitors to websites . . ."

"The only time anybody's on is between ten and four when they're at work. It's a headline service, not news. People think it's the tail that wags the dog. No, it's nothing but the tail. And nobody's on it on the weekend." Anyway, he said, so what if the *Post* had to cut staff? "We could be a great newspaper with half the people we have now."

Pincus believed newspapers, among them the *Post*, had become self-indulgent. They wrote for themselves rather than readers. They published blockbuster projects designed to win prizes rather than satisfy the reader. For instance: "We're inundated every day now with political campaign coverage. The campaign hasn't started— except in newspapers writing for each other."

He believed newspapers had lost their way, beginning with the pretense that they were what they could never be: neutral. "The idea of 'objectivity'—that a person shouldn't have an opinion—is ridiculous. Everyone knows that is a lie." Newspapers should find a story, tell it, tell it again, tell the truth from the lies, tell it until the powers that be do the right thing. "What's wrong with crusading? That's why newspapers exist."

He blamed *Post* management for a change of attitude that damaged reporters' morale and diminished the daily product. He said the paper was driven from the top down by editors deciding what reporters should do. "From my discussions with AMEs," he said of assistant managing editors, the top level of newsroom management, "it's frightening how contemptuous they are of reporters." He saw that as a sea change from the days when the *Post* gave proud, passionate reporters the freedom to find stories that leapt off the page and caught Ben Bradlee's full attention.

"Ben is the last man standing and he was the greatest journalist of all time. He'd take chances. He was always in the newsroom wanting to know what you were working on. That doesn't happen now."

He worried about the *Post*'s future.

"The first American newspapers were aligned with political parties. Businessmen and politicians owned them for the influence they could have. There were papers coming from every persuasion, so people could read them all and decide. Then, when people saw there was money to be made, papers were corporatized as businesses more than journals of opinion. Along came the chains, putting papers together to make even more money, the Gannett crap. The question today is 'Will the *Post* be the last family-owned paper?' Don Graham is a great businessman who hasn't made the mistakes the young Arthur Sulzberger has made at the *Times*."

Both the *Times* and the *Post* had two levels of stock ownership that gave the families control of their newspapers. But families can turn dysfunctional when confronted by sweet-talking billionaires raising their offers. Family control was never guaranteed, as proven when the Binghams sold out in Louisville, when the Chandlers sold the *Los Angeles Times*, and the Bancrofts sold the *Wall Street Journal*.

So I asked Pincus what he thought would happen at the *Post* when Don Graham, then sixty-three years old, retired. His answer came quickly.

"Katharine's great," he said. "She's smart and she has surrounded herself with bright young people."

He just dropped the name into the conversation. No last name, just "Katharine." The allusion was to Katharine Weymouth, the daughter of Don's sister, Lally, and Katharine Graham's namesake. Ten years earlier she had come to the newspaper as legal counsel. She moved to Washingtonpost.com in advertising and then returned to the *Post* as vice president of advertising. More important, she and Don were the only members of the Graham family working for the newspaper.

So casually did Pincus mention her name, I took it as a given that a plan of succession had been made. The only question seemed to be: When would she take the obvious next step and become publisher?

Soon after, I brought up Weymouth's name in conversation with Tony Reid, who in twenty-one years at the *Post* had been the copy desk chief in sports, foreign, and business.

Reid always looked mischievous, his pleasant face rearranging itself every few seconds as if a startling insight were about to be announced at full volume. He was at once the newsroom's oldest imp and its youngest curmudgeon. He had built a reputation as a wordsmith and conversationalist. When not untangling reporters' syntax, he talked and then he talked some more before talking again. Because he started in the business as a reporter in sports and features, he spoke the star reporters' language and was brash enough to chat with them. That way Reid learned stuff. In the *Post* sports department, he was, pound for pound, the all-time watercooler champ. He also ran the foreign copy desk before moving to business. At age fifty, he knew the room and he would dish.

He said to me, "You started in Louisville."

"Sure."

"And you know what happened there."

"Don't remind me."

The *Louisville Courier-Journal* had been among America's best newspapers. The owner, Barry Bingham Sr., was content with a 2 percent profit margin. Then a daughter started a family financial feud that ran through the 1970s and ended only when the patriarch sold the paper to the Gannett chain. I can still see that daughter on a *60 Minutes* television segment. Asked if she was sorry the squabbling had led to the sale of an institution that had served Kentucky for a hundred years, she half smiled and said, "Oh, yes, sorry," or some such piffwaddle.

"So," I said to Reid, "what's your point?"

"People in the newsroom here are worried about what happens after Don. He's sixty-three and he won't be here forever. When he goes, what's next?"

I said, "I thought worrying was for people at other papers."

"Only as long as Don is here," Reid said. "People see him as the protector of the newspaper. They know he understands the paper economically and culturally. He wouldn't change much for economic reasons alone—maybe reduce the foreign staff. And he lets the culture function and thrive. The big thing is, Don has a profound feeling for the *Post* as a family business. But once he leaves, who knows? Other members of his family might not feel that way. The thing could descend into a Louisville-type situation ending in the sale of the paper."

I asked, "What about Katharine Weymouth?"

"Almost nobody in the newsroom knows Katharine Weymouth from Catherine the Great," Reid said. "They don't even know what she looks like, let alone what she stands for. There's this great uncertainty in the room, this apprehension about anybody who isn't Don."

Now, after two rounds of buyouts had sent nearly 250 newsroom people into retirement, Reid heard grousing about a hiring freeze and a third buyout.

"Those people upset that we're not hiring anybody don't understand that we're trying to survive," he said. "On the buyouts, the first one, in 2003, just felt like a bunch of people retiring. Most of them were of the age where that might happen anyway, and their leaving didn't seem to make much of a dent in the paper's mission. And many of those didn't really leave; they got contracts to keep working, so it seemed kind of fraudulent, like nothing was really going to change. But the second one, last year, was entirely different. One great reporter who'd been here for thirty years said, 'This one has an end-of-empire feel to it.'

"That was when they told reporters to stop taking cabs and use the Metro instead. They talked about combining the weekly sections; people who left weren't replaced; someone was leaving for the *New York Times* every week and we weren't trying to keep them. The average age in the room dropped noticeably. They talked about closing bureaus overseas, including Paris, and everyone began waiting for the other shoe to drop."

He said the other shoe would be a third buyout.

Or it might be Downie's retirement.

Or both.

"Just call us unsettled," Reid said.

Corporate greed through the 1980s that prompted cost-cutting when none was truly needed had left American newspapers shells of their robust, feisty selves. The inimitable Molly Ivins wrote that she didn't so much mind newspapers dying, she just hated to see them kill themselves with the suicide of a thousand cuts. Now, at *The Washington Post*, in the wake of two buyouts with a third rumored, the Metro columnist Marc Fisher said, "You won't want to do that."

I had wanted to be with him on an election night to watch him work at a campaign headquarters so I could show how a news guy with an elegant writer's touch did the hard work of producing literature in a hurry.

"I won't be going out," he said.

"What?"

"I'm going to do radio," he said, "and I'll be doing a chat."

Instead of doing the Murray Kempton/Mike Royko/Jimmy Breslin column that reported the news even as it took the reader into the color and passion of an event, Fisher would stay at home

with his telephone for the radio reports and his laptop for the online chat with Washingtonpost.com users.

"Now you have to live in fear of being the only guy who didn't
catch the next wave," Fisher said. So he was no longer just the best
Metro columnist the *Post* ever had. In addition to two or three
columns a week, his work would include a daily blog and chats on
a regular basis. By hurrying to catch the next wave—whatever it
might be, wherever it might take him—Fisher no longer had time
to go to a campaign headquarters where, perhaps, a senator would
be elected who might, four years later, be president of the United
States.

I understood it.

"This is an existential crisis we're in," he said.

And I hated it.

Through it all, Fisher said, the *Post* had been able to do meaningful journalism because Len Downie had been the newspaper's
leader. The *New York Times*, to name another paper, had chosen as
its executive editor Howell Raines, who brought to the Gray
Lady's pages what Fisher called "flash and buzz." There was none
of that in Downie's work. "Len just kept plowing ahead, the ultimate news guy doing the news, doing accountability reporting. It's
not an accident that the *Post* didn't make all the mistakes the
Times did under Raines."

Downie had presided over the growth of the *Post*'s newsroom to
over seven hundred people with a budget of $100 million. Now the
paper was no longer the one he had built. "The fact is, we can't
cover everything the way we did. And Len has to be weeping
inside. Inside, he's in pain. But what a spine he has. There's not a
whisper of complaint from him."

What if he were to retire?

Who'd be the next editor?

"There's no one in the newsroom today who I can even imagine
being Len Downie's successor."

If delivering the goods online was every newspaper's future, as
Marc Fisher knew it was, creating those goods was every reporter's

future. Most likely, that work would be done the way it always had been done. An old newspaperman named Ray Ring knew how that went. He even did a riff on it in his novel *Arizona Kiss*. He caused his alter ego, photojournalist Russell Macky, to say:

> I can tell you what it's like to work for a newspaper.
> Imagine a combine, one of those huge threshing machines
> that eat up a row of wheat like nothing, bearing right down
> on you. You're running in front of it, all day long, day in,
> day out, just inches in front of the maw, where steel blades
> are whirring and clacking and waiting for you to get tired
> or make one slip. The only way to keep the combine off you
> is to throw it something else to rip apart and digest.
> What you feed it is stories. Words and photos. Ten inches
> on this, fifteen inches on that, a vertical shot here and a
> horizontal there, scraps of news and film that go in the
> maw where they are processed and dumped out on some
> page to fill the spaces around the ads. Each story buys
> you a little time, barely enough to slap together the
> next story, and the next, and the next. You never get far
> ahead, you never take a breather, all you do is live on
> the hustle. Always in a rush, always on deadline, you
> keep scrambling to feed the combine. That's what
> it's like.

Macky's tone was world weary, as if he knew all that running would, in the end, lead to nothing. Okay, he could play the jaded, burnt-out character. But the reader knew the greater truth about Russell Macky. He loved it. He loved running in front of that ass-eating combine. Only by getting out there did he have a chance to nail the bastards. "That's the real purpose of journalism, why it rates up there in the constitution and the courts, because it's the only tool with which certain people can be nailed," Macky says. "Every journalist has a high-sounding rap, and that's mine."

In the real world at the *Post*, as surely as in a novelist's world, the good ones all love the running. Here, see how they run . . .

Dana Priest and Anne Hull on an investigation that changes lives.

Gene Weingarten doing a virtuoso's work about a virtuoso.

A newsroom at full throttle on a national tragedy.

From Iraq, by Anthony Shadid, the most beautiful, harrowing stuff you're ever likely to see in a newspaper.

Here, see how a great newspaper nails the truth . . .

6.

DANA PRIEST AND ANNE HULL

Don Graham had said no to an interview.

An hour later he saw me with Dana Priest.

"Went right to the top, eh?" he said.

The Madison Hotel's lunchroom was all gold and silver, shimmering in a soft light. In such a milieu, and in the company of a Pulitzer Prize winner, some people might be thrown off their game. I, however, spilled my coffee onto the silk tablecloth only twice. With a grace that surprised onlookers, I used a fork, left-handed, to stab pieces of Caesar salad that had fallen into my lap. With my right hand, I took notes on a conversation with Priest.

Articulate and telegenic, a moonlighting correspondent on television network news shows, Priest was the *Post*'s spymaster. She worked national intelligence and security. In 2005 she did stories revealing the Central Intelligence Agency's clandestine transportation of detainees to prisons in Eastern European countries where interrogation under torture was legal.

For that, the Bush administration threatened her with jail time, which in turn presented me with the possibility of a Brenda-Starr-in-distress narrative with the smart, pretty, twinkly-eyed girl reporter telling the president of the United States to get off her case.

"So, Dana, are you going to jail?" I said.

"Doesn't look like it," she said.

"Darn," I said.

She had stayed out of the paper most of that summer. "The administration went on the warpath for people poking around in those sort of things," she said, the things being national security matters, the people being mostly her. "So I took the long-term view. 'Okay, I can sit this out for some months, let things cool off.'"

Then came a phone call.

"The unusual part is that the person actually did have the beginnings of a story—and that never happens," Priest said. "This was someone who followed my work for a long time, an acquaintance of an acquaintance. She said it had to do with Walter Reed, how they're not treating soldiers right, that the soldiers and their families were frustrated in dealing with the military bureaucracy."

Hundreds of soldiers wounded in Iraq and Afghanistan—an inordinate number amputees, the result of roadside bombs—were treated at the Walter Reed Army Medical Center. It was a state-of-the-art facility a twenty-minute drive from the White House. If soldiers were treated poorly there, it was unconscionable. Priest wanted to find out.

Two weeks in, she decided to ask for a reporting partner. "I usually am totally off on my own, and I thought I needed a change of pace," she said. "I also thought working with somebody would be fun."

That's when she walked across the newsroom to Anne Hull.

Priest went to Hull because she saw Walter Reed as more than a story about bureaucratic incompetence, which was her thing. She saw it as a story about people—Hull's thing.

Anne Hull called herself a lone wolf. She was small and thin and unadorned, an ascetic who said her mother was forever after her to brush her hair. Her brown eyes, once locked on a target, let go only when there was nothing more to see. She asked her subjects if she could be in their lives momentarily. Then she did the most important trick in journalism. She listened. She slipped into the silences and heard real people talk about real things. She was fluent in journalism-seminar language: "Immersion, the anthropological, sociological stuff—that's what I really really like." Which meant she liked to get on a bus filled with pigs and chickens and get off four days later, stinking, and feel in her trembling body the lives of twenty-two young Mexican women. "It opens your heart," she said, "to what you're writing about."

She moved in society's margins, with the forsaken and the uncertain, and more often than not she transformed their troubles into a redemptive poetry. Of a young Mississippian who might enlist in the army: "He lives in a mobile home with his mother and younger brother on Old Highway 80 on a piece of land that never quite dries." Of a woman who had waded through flooded New Orleans with her six-year-old grandson in a red Spider-Man T-shirt: "Near the collar, his grandmother had written in ballpoint pen, 'Eddie Picou, DOB 10/9/98.' 'I put that on so they could at least identify who he was,' Picou said, and she began to weep."

Six times in ten years, Hull was a finalist for a Pulitzer Prize, but the judges settled for someone else each time. The winners' stories provided closure to events rendered melodramatically. In contrast, Hull's stories examined complex social issues that defied ready resolution. "The Pulitzers deal in black and white," she said. "The things I write are always dwelling in the gray."

"Why is that?" I asked.

"Because it's life. That's where life happens."

She looked away.

"I don't put happy endings on my stories."

Now Dana Priest stood by her desk, elegant and cool, as if it were her habit to drop by when in fact they had met only at a lunch for Pulitzer finalists a year earlier. Armed with the knowledge that Hull's work included a feature on amputees at Walter Reed, Priest asked, "What's the hospital campus like?"

Hull answered, even as she wondered, *What's this about?*

Priest: "Do you know anyone there?"

Now I know what she's doing, thought Hull.

"How hard is it to get in there?"

She's laying bread crumbs.

"I've got a tip on a story."

Suckering me in.

Hull was happy to oblige. At day's end, she sent Priest an e-mail: "That sounds great. If you want some help on the story, I'd love to do it."

The cold call to Priest came from a woman fed up with the army. "There's a right way and a military way, and because the military way always wins," she said, "the soldiers pay with their pain and frustration." She had complained up the line and gotten nowhere. Back from Iraq, back from Afghanistan, soldiers had come home in pieces, wounded in ways seen and unseen. She knew the people at Walter Reed did heroic work under heavy workloads. Still, hundreds of soldiers were lost in the military bureaucracy, misplaced, warehoused, even forgotten. She told everybody the story. One day she told it to her hair stylist.

"You should call a reporter," the stylist said.

"I would," she said, "but I don't know any."

That's when the stylist dropped Dana Priest's name.

In other circumstances, Priest would have passed the Walter Reed caller to another reporter. She usually dealt with ghosts, sources developed over years who could never be named. She could not remember the last time she had done a story that began with a cold call. But this time, she listened. She had come to admire and respect the military. The year after 9/11, she had traveled with soldiers, Marines, special operations forces, and four-star generals for a book, *The Mission*, which described the military's work around the world. This time, instead of talking to ghosts, Priest would do shoe-leather reporting. Go there, ask questions, listen, watch, ask more questions. Not many papers would give you months to do it, but the *Post* did. When you know the story, you write.

There was a world out there and Dana Priest wanted at it. Eight years old, she walked on top of a fence to peer into neighborhood backyards and write up her discoveries in a two-page xeroxed newspaper. "A snoop, even then," she said. When first she decided to quit school and learn about the world on her own, she was in the eighth grade. Her political instincts had been awakened in social studies class. "I was soaking it all up," she said. She understood César Chávez's motives in organizing migrant workers. She knew why Angela Davis called for social revolution. The Black Panthers were afoot, Vietnam was ablaze, and there was poor Dana Priest, fourteen years old, stuck in a Los Angeles suburb, Canoga Park, left behind by the day's great events. How would a girl ever catch up?

She ran home from high school to watch the Watergate hearings, when North Carolina senator Sam Ervin took off after all the president's men. "I was glued to it. I hated Nixon, and my parents didn't. Mom was conservative, Dad was libertarian. Dad and I could not even talk about the subject. Neither one of us would back down. The whole idea—I mean, that you could be dishonest at the level of the Vietnam War!" In college, to do a photographic essay, she took a bus to Seattle intending to ride the rails back with hoboes (until a yard man described hobo bodies frozen in the Cascades).

As a junior at the University of California, Santa Cruz, she wrote for the school paper, such as it was. "No faculty adviser, no journalism school. It was the blind leading the blind. We could investigate whatever we wanted to, and because we had no one overseeing us, I'm sure our stories were laden with our own opinions." When Americans were taken hostage in Iran, Priest called Iran. "We called students in the Iranian embassy who had taken the Americans hostage. The coolest thing in the world! I wanted to know what, exactly, our government had done with the government of Iran? I was a contrarian even then."

It was the maddest fun an inquisitive kid could dream up. "It gave me a taste of the power that you have as a journalist and the unlimited adventure that you can have, which is really unbelievable." Laughing like she was twenty years old again, she said, "There is nothing like it. You get to go places you're not supposed to!"

A year's internship on the foreign desk at the *Post*—"I thought I'd died and gone to heaven"—preceded a year covering county government for the *St. Petersburg Times*. Back at the *Post*, she did government in the suburbs before returning to foreign. As military action was about to begin in the first Gulf War, she traveled to Baghdad to report on Saddam Hussein's release of 950 hostages who had been held in Kuwait. She was five months pregnant at the time, but did not consider refusing the assignment to Baghdad.

"This," she said then, "is what I'm living for."

Anne Hull goes to this nowhere place in the central highlands of Mexico. Comes back to North Carolina with twenty-two young women, seasonal laborers, hired by a crab house to do the primitive, prehistoric work of picking meat out of crabs. From their mountain town they ride a pigs-and-chickens bus, the first of many buses because North Carolina is four days away. No one can sleep doing that, no one has bathed, everyone is shaky. They arrive at midnight and a woman takes them to a little trailer where they will live for the season. "Good night, ladies," she says in English to women with no English. "See you in four hours."

Four hours later, a car horn honks at the door. At the crab house, blue crabs are piled onto a steel table. The young women have no idea what to do. The manager holds up a knife and a crab and says, "Knife. Crab." The crab's edges are as sharp as the knife's. For the next eight hours, they squeeze meat from the crab and pick it away with the knife. They stand on concrete, their backs and legs aching.

Or Hull goes to De Queen, Arkansas. The locals are complaining that migrant laborers are taking over the town. Are they really? At the property appraiser's office, Hull drags out those big old leather-bound deed books from the last ten years. She sits in that office looking at property transfers. She does it for six hours. And she sees the story, sees the Hispanic surnames. And now she needs a human being, she needs to feel the life of a De Queen local even as he feels his life changing. She stands outside the factory gates of a chicken plant, men leaving work, greasy, feathers falling from their boots. She asks one, Danny, if they can talk. She sits at his dining room table and drinks coffee with him until midnight and it turns out that he is not resentful; he is in awe of the migrants' ability to outwork him. Then she comes back at 5 in the morning when his alarm sends him back to the plant to pulverize chicken bones at seven dollars an hour.

Or Anne Hull risks her life by going to Newark to hang with

black gay teenagers. She lives with them at Burger King, goes to church, to basketball games. Rides city buses. Walks with them to school, a violent and poor school of the type with metal detectors at the entrance. She hangs with seventeen-year-old Felicia Holt, whose friend Sakia Gunn had been stabbed to death at a bus depot after telling a man who hit on her, "No thanks, I'm gay." And one night she goes with Felicia and her friends to a nightclub where Missy Elliott's music thunders from the bar. They throw down their puffy jackets and she sees someone asking Felicia about the white woman, "Who's that?" And Felicia says, "That's nobody. That's Anne."

Well, by damn, yes! After years of trying, Anne Hull had achieved her ideal reporter's state of being—invisibility.

The first thing Priest and Hull did together was go to a strip club. They had heard that the club put exorbitant charges on credit cards used by Walter Reed patients. They wanted to see for them-selves. Because a national intelligence reporter's work seldom took her to strip clubs, Priest asked a newsroom friend about the place. "Oh, don't worry," the friend said. "It's not really a strip club, you'll be fine."

Still, just in case, Priest's husband joined them. He came straight from a black-tie social event and may have been the first customer ever seated at the club's stage wearing a tuxedo. Thirty seconds in, three women came out dancing. It is true, as Priest's friend had said, there was no stripping involved. The dancers came onstage already nude.

Between sets, Priest and Hull sought out the dancers in a bath-room that served as a dressing room. The strippers told the reporters that, sure, Walter Reed soldiers were regular customers but they had seen none that night. Around 11 o'clock, Priest and Hull left the club to men who did not wear tuxes and women who wore nothing.

But this was one Washington story that did not have its origins in a strip club. Nor did it start with Priest in full command. She had been told she would have no problem getting on the Walter Reed grounds. It seemed improbable to her, a civilian driving alone onto a military base. But she was assured that gate guards were not crisply efficient military police.

Priest passed the guards only to get lost on the grounds. Three times she stopped to ask directions to the hospital. Some reporters beginning an investigation on a military base might have been wary of asking for help from army officers. Not Priest. She was not afraid to question authority. Three times that day, she asked uniformed officers, "Where's the hospital?"

Turned out they didn't know, either.

Like some Washington stories, this one started with that cold call to Dana Priest and a promise by an anonymous source. (Priest never told me the source's name. When I found her on my own, she said, "I told Dana, 'I'll be your Shallow Throat.' ") When they met some time later, the source guided the reporter into the darkness of Walter Reed.

"First thing you've got to see is Building 18," she said. "They put some of the soldiers there. And it's really bad."

Priest's reporter radar went *ping*. She thought, *Building 18? No name? They store wounded soldiers in a building with no name.*

In the building, they passed a lobby guard half asleep. Then they told a soldier they were just visiting and would like to look around. True enough. Priest and Hull had agreed on basic rules of conduct for their work at Walter Reed. They would avoid personnel who might ask their names and purpose. But if confronted as reporters, they would tell the truth.

Priest looked around Building 18's lobby and saw a flat-screen TV and three computer consoles, a normal hotel-like space with five or six people sitting around. Down a corridor, the soldier escorted them to one of the building's rooms, again a setting typical of a hotel rather than the open spaces of an army barracks. She saw nothing untoward and told the soldier that the room looked nice.

"That's the VIP room," he said. "That's the room they show the senators."

PingPingPing.

The idea of a showroom for politicians in a nameless building moved Priest's companion to ask, "What do people do in this building?"

From the soldier, silence.

Priest knew soldiers. On that night, at that moment, she believed the Building 18 soldier was about to cry. Finally he said, "There's a lot of depression here."

I gotta get back here, thought Priest. *There's more to this story.*

Priest and Hull made themselves inconspicuous. They wore grays and beiges, sweats, softball gear. They never took notes in public places. They melted in with families of soldiers they had befriended. They planned their cover stories if questioned— "Visiting a friend"—but did not need them. They were never asked who they were or what they were doing there. It was easy returning to Building 18.

To reach the building with no name, which stood just outside the campus gates, soldiers suffering from brain injuries, schizophrenia, paranoia, and posttraumatic stress disorder crossed a street where drug dealers worked the corners nightly.

At one of the required 7 a.m. formations, a commander bellowed, "Building 18! There is a rodent infestation issue! It doesn't help when you live like a rodent! I can't believe people live like that! I was appalled by some of your rooms!"

As if a soldier suffering from paranoid delusions should chase down vermin.

As if schizophrenics should master the use of roach bombs.

One soldier said he had been okay with mortar blasts in Iraq but stayed in his Building 18 room all day rather than face the dangers of city streets.

"I hate it," he said of the place. "There are cockroaches. The elevator doesn't work. Sometimes there's no heat, no water . . . I told my platoon sergeant I want to leave. I told the town hall meeting. I talked to the doctors and medical staff. They just said you kind of got to get used to the outside world . . . My platoon sergeant said, 'Suck it up!' "

Relatives visiting patients were allowed to get a fifteen-day advance on their $64 per diem, except they weren't really allowed to. A staff sergeant explained. The relative could take the money in cash or by electronic transfer. "I highly recommend that you take the cash," he said. "There's no guarantee the transfer will get to your bank." Only it wasn't really $64 because relatives could get only 80 percent of the advance, or $51.20. Only it wasn't really $51.20. "The cashier has no change, so we drop to $50. We give you the rest"—the $1.20 a day—"when you leave." And relatives needed to figure out how long their patients would be in the hospital because if they signed up for an advance on the $150 daily lodging allowance and the patient was discharged early, "you owe the government the advance back of $150 a day."

As if loved ones in distress came with accountants.

As if this drip-drip-drip of the bizarre was everyday life.

Priest and Hull became constant presences at Walter Reed. They worked without the permission of hospital officials but with the full knowledge of soldiers who opened their lives to them. They watched and listened. They saw soldiers who "had been blown up, shot, crushed." They saw "the maimed and newly legless." Ears had been "melted off" and faces "tattooed purple by shrapnel patterns." Eyes were gone and skulls were pieced together with implants. Soldiers described the smell of gas entering their lungs just before their bodies exploded. They ticked off their drugs: Paxil, methadone, Seroquel. The reporters heard an infantryman scream at his mother for getting high on her son's painkillers: "Quit taking all the soldier medicine!"

These were not new patients arriving from a war zone. They were outpatients waiting for further treatment, some on the campus for months, some lost in a bureaucratic miasma that obscured hope.

A mother told Priest and Hull she had spent fifteen months living on the post trying to help her son. "It just absolutely took forever to get anything done. They do the paperwork, they lose the paperwork. Then they have to redo the paperwork. You are talking about guys and girls whose lives are disrupted for the rest of their lives, and they don't put any priority on it."

It was *Catch-22*, only real. Wounded soldiers managed other wounded. Soldiers with psychological disorders were responsible for soldiers at risk of suicide.

Priest and Hull talked to John Daniel Shannon, a staff sergeant. He had been a sniper in Iraq when his eye and skull were shattered by an AK-47 round. His two years at Walter Reed began when he was given a map of the grounds and told to go find his room. He had been a reconnaissance and land navigation expert in Iraq. Now, diagnosed with PTSD, he was so disoriented he couldn't find north on the map. He stumbled through the hospital, sliding against walls to stay upright, until rescued. He needed to prove to a supply clerk that he had been in Iraq in order to get a new uniform to replace the one bloodied when he took a bullet in his skull. Shannon showed the clerk his Purple Heart.

Everywhere Priest looked, she saw damage. She saw men with metal halos holding their necks in place, men encased from shoulder to waist in metal frames. Everywhere, men once whole were held together by metal.

One day Anne Hull asked a favor of a South Carolina couple, Dell McLeod and his wife, Annette.

"Feel free to say no," Hull said. "But I want to be able to tell this story through the eyes of the family, too. I really need to experience it with you."

"No problem," Annette said.

Dell McLeod had been admitted in August of 2005, a month after a head injury. A year later, the McLeods lived in the center's Mologne House, a step up from conditions at Building 18 but no more an answer to a soldier's troubles. Annette had never held a *Washington Post* in her hand. She had read it online but then only for news of wounded veterans. But, sure, if Anne Hull from *The Washington Post* wanted to spend a night with these nobodies from South Carolina, come on.

Hull was there in room 323 when the alarm went off at 5 a.m. Dell didn't move in bed. Annette fixed a bowl of instant oatmeal before going to her husband. "Dell," she said, tapping him from behind on advice from a counselor that men back from war can wake up swinging. "Dell, get in the shower."

Then, "Dell!"

"Okay, baby," he said.

It was after 9 o'clock one night when Annette pushed Dell to practice his speech.

"My name is Wendell," he said. "Wendell Woodward McLeod Jr."

"Spell 'dog,' " she said.

"Spell 'dog,' " he said.

"Listen to me."

He repeated that, too. "Listen to me."

Dell's eyes drifted toward the TV. On the screen, muted, was an Ultimate Fighting show.

"You are not working hard enough, Dell. Wake up."

He said, "Wake up."

"Dell, come on now!"

Anne Hull wrote it all down.

Hull wrote letters to Santa. Not letters, interview requests. She wrote every year with different questions, but it always began, "Dear Santa, please answer these ten questions . . ." She grew up a country girl, running barefoot in her father's orange groves in central Florida. One day she would write for *The New Yorker* about her town's Strawberry Festival: "I must have been seven or eight when I got to ride in the parade, holding a tinfoil wand and wearing tap shoes from Jackie's School of Dance."

Out of high school, she got a job in the newsroom at the *St. Petersburg Times*. She fetched coffee, ran copy, did whatever anyone wanted done. A year and a half of college was enough for her. "From the minute I walked into the St. Pete Times newsroom," she said, "I felt at home." She wangled her way into the features department the old-fashioned way, which is to say she wrote about a trip to New York and offered it at the going rate for unsolicited freelance work by unpublished reporters—zero dollars. The *St. Petersburg Times* bought it. When the music critic was not available for a Madonna concert, Hull filled in. Then, not only improbably but for a full year, the barefoot girl from the orange groves covered fashion for the *Times*.

It was four years, maybe five, before she did a three-part series called "Metal to Bone," an account of an incident in which a fifteen-year-old boy put a gun to a police officer's head and pulled the trigger, only to have the gun misfire. "I covered the criminal trial," Hull said. "But that was really an excuse to live in a public housing project in Tampa, a really rough project." Doing that series moved Hull to a decision: "That's the kind of work I was meant to do."

It was work that some people would resent. "It's your life," she said, "and you have to give up everything and follow the story. I've missed more birthdays and Christmases and special occasions because I was in a housing project or hanging out with immigrant children in Atlanta." For her, there were no regrets. "No, no." Laughing now. "You feel fully alive when you're reporting. I just feel like you're in a moment of history. It's an addiction in some ways." And then she said, almost musically, "How could anyone not want to be a reporter?"

Every morning when Hull's stuff appeared in the *Times*, her mother, Victoria, called to wake her. She had outlined the story. She had underlined good sentences. "She would read back to me everything she liked and we'd have these long conversations about every story. In a way, I was always writing for my mother."

Victoria Desmond Hull was a middle school principal in Pinellas County. "She was always given the toughest schools with the toughest kids," Hull said. "She was a turnaround artist and loved most working at schools populated with low-income kids who'd been written off by others." Once, during a lunch break at John Hopkins Middle School, Hull drove into a parking lot behind the cafeteria. "I saw my mom's head sticking out of the Dumpster, her gold earrings sparkling."

Say what?

The charming, charismatic Victoria Desmond Hull in a Dumpster?

"She was going through the garbage trying to find a kid's watch. The kid had accidentally thrown out his watch when he put it on his lunch tray. He was from an abusive home and my mom knew he'd probably meet more abuse if he came home without the watch. So she brought her walkie-talkie out back behind the cafeteria and went Dumpster diving."

And?

"In all the milk cartons and food, she found the watch."

Victoria Hull was just out of college, the new mother of a baby named Anne, when she wrote a short-short story. Six or seven years later, on October 24, 1969, from 508 East Reynolds Street, Plant City, Florida, she mailed the story to *Redbook* magazine's fiction editor with a note saying, "The theme is a small town middle class

Negro woman's humiliation in a doctor's office. She expected things to be different today, but learned that while facilities were equal, not much else had changed."

In the story, the woman brought her infant son to the office early, ahead of everybody else, her son "who came from one body and two passions," the baby boy with a cold, who "listened as his mother told him without ever saying a word of many things. Of how handsome he was and what did he want for lunch and how lucky he was to be born in these times. The communication was there with fingers, eyes, and little noises which no one in the room understood but them."

And they waited and they waited and when the boy began to cry,

the mother nervously put a neatly folded diaper on her shoulder and hoisted the soft ball of a body into an erect position while rhythmically tapping a tune between his soft shoulder blades. Her unintended rocking caused the diaper to fall behind her on the floor in a narrow patient-lined row. It fell on the shiny shoes of a woman of unchangeable attitudes, who, feeling its weight, thrust it forward with the heel of her shoe. The eyes of the people in the crowded row remained fixed on blank pages and blank walls, as the humiliated mother contorted herself to pick up the cloth which no one had seen fall in a room where the only thing they had to concentrate on was each other.

Still the clock moved. The faces were replaced by more non-faces. The miserable boy in blue wanted to be home in his crib and the mother ached. She looked into the sepia eyes of her fine son and whisperingly declared in a sick effort of consolation, "Why it hurts so bad now is that I know things should be different. Before we were content with anything we got. Now we expect more." She beseeched of the infant an answer, "Can we call this progress?"

His lashes swept closed in sleep as he lay against her bewildered breast waiting for his name to be called.

There Victoria Hull's story ended, a story done in the grays of life, the mother's work now seen in the daughter's.

———

One sunny day, Priest and Hull decided it was time to find out what they had. They had seen the absurd and bizarre. But what was it, really? Was it a black comedy of army snafus? Had Walter Reed itself suffered a PTSD meltdown? The reporters had the human stories, good, true, and poignant. But they believed they had more. They believed they could report a systemic failure at the army's most famous hospital.

They went to Capitol Hill to meet with staffers who the year before had worked on a Walter Reed inquiry for a congressman, the Virginia Republican Tom Davis. The reporters played the meeting as an early step in what might be, or might not be, a story. Priest said, "We didn't mention we'd been up there. We just asked, 'What do you hear about Walter Reed? Is it broken?' They went, 'Broken? Oh, my God, you can't believe it.' "

The response was telling because it came from Republican staffers who might be expected to protect an administration proud of its war in Iraq. In the next few minutes, Priest said, the staffers confirmed what she and Hull believed. As they left the Rayburn House Office Building, the reporters stopped on Independence Avenue, below the shining Capitol dome.

There, in the warming sun, Dana Priest shouted, "We got it!"

Priest's source at Walter Reed had spoken to the reporter only occasionally since that first phone call. But every morning, she checked the *Post* for the story. She found nothing. For weeks, nothing. "I'd go through it, page by page. I thought I'd find it on page 18, a little thing at the bottom." For months, nothing.

Then, on Sunday morning, February 18, 2007, her husband came in from the front yard with the paper. He said, "Well, the lid's off."

"What do you mean?"

"Look at the front page."

The page was dominated by a haunting photograph of the sniper John Daniel Shannon. Taken by the *Post*'s Michel DuCille, the photograph was a shadowy portrait that ran above the fold and used almost half the space there. It showed the sergeant's good eye. It showed a graying hollow where the other eye had been. In the middle of his forehead, an indentation extended from his hairline to his brow, marking the place where pieces of his skull had been put back together.

The story's headline ran above Shannon's picture, just under the newspaper's masthead, in two lines of sixty-point type set five columns wide. It screamed for a reader's full attention:

SOLDIERS FACE NEGLECT, FRUSTRATION AT ARMY'S TOP MEDICAL FACILITY

The story began:

Behind the door of Army Spec. Jeremy Duncan's room, part of the wall is torn and hangs in the air, weighted down with black mold. When the wounded combat engineer stands in his shower and looks up, he can see the bathtub on the floor above through a rotted hole. The entire building, constructed between the world wars, often smells like greasy carry-out. Signs of neglect are everywhere: mouse droppings, belly-up cockroaches, stained carpets, cheap mattresses.

This is the world of Building 18, not the kind of place where Duncan expected to recover when he was evacuated to Walter Reed Army Medical Center from Iraq last February with a broken neck and a shredded left ear, nearly dead from blood loss. But the old lodge, just outside the gates of the hospital and five miles up the road from the White House, has housed hundreds of maimed soldiers recuperating from injuries suffered in the wars in Iraq and Afghanistan.

The common perception of Walter Reed is of a surgical hospital that shines as the crown jewel of military medicine. But 5½ years of sustained combat have transformed the venerable 113-acre institution into something else entirely— a holding ground for physically and psychologically damaged outpatients. Almost 700 of them—the majority soldiers, with some Marines—have been released from hospital beds but still need treatment or are awaiting bureaucratic decisions before being discharged or returned to active duty.

They suffer from brain injuries, severed arms and legs, organ and back damage, and various degrees of post-traumatic stress. Their legions have grown so exponentially—they outnumber hospital patients at Walter Reed 17 to 1—that they take up every available bed on post and spill into dozens of nearby hotels and apartments leased by the Army. The average stay is 10 months but some have been stuck there for as long as two years.

At her home, Priest's source looked at the page.
I asked what she thought.
"I thought, 'Holy shit!' "

7.

GENE WEINGARTEN

For a year, Gene Weingarten wanted few things more than an escape from the sun, sand, and pastel glories of Miami.

This was 1990. It was a golden time in the newspaper business. If the grown-ups in the big offices irritated you, you threw a typewriter through a window and followed it up by asking a better paper for a higher-paying job. Back then, newspapers hired good people with the idea of improving the product.

Weingarten worked at the *Miami Herald* when it was so rich its presses might have been printing thousand-dollar bills. One afternoon, a boat capsized in the Atlantic and left its occupants stranded on an island. A junior editor decided the *Herald* should go interview and photograph those people. Ten grand for a helicopter? Fine, get that bird in the air. "That," Weingarten would come to say, "doesn't happen in today's newspaper world."

It was April 26, 1990, when Weingarten, the irreparably irritated editor of the *Herald*'s *Tropic* magazine, sent a letter to Mary Hadar in the *Post*'s Style section. Weingarten recounted having turned down the *Post* three years earlier, remembered Ben Bradlee "growling that 'Miami is an asshole town,'" and explained why he must leave the *Herald*. "On Monday," Weingarten wrote, "my publisher informed me that, regrettably, as a cost-cutting measure, it had become necessary to downgrade Tropic's paper stock to, er, ahem . . . newsprint."

The publisher might have demanded a Maori tattoo on Weingarten's face and generated less resistance. Then the boss said *Tropic*'s pages would henceforth be folded, not stapled together. To Weingarten, the demotion to newsprint and the removal of staples were personal affronts. He had created a magazine that won two Pulitzers. He had hired Dave Barry. This was his thanks?

In his letter to Hadar he advertised himself as "a workaholic, a real obsessive maniac" who valued humor, the offbeat, and "the nakedly provocative." He also admitted his greatest weakness: "I need an excellent secretary or my rather stunning inefficiency in the timely movement of paper will cause whatever newspaper I work for to tremble, sway, and implode in a smoking pile of rubble."

"If we don't have a slot for you," Hadar told him, "I'll jump out a window and make one."

Within two weeks, he was at the *Post*.

He became its wizard of odd.

The beauty of Weingarten was that once he got an assignment, he improved on it. For a winter vacation travel piece, he did not study the Caribbean—he studied Alaska. Alaska was okay but he wanted to get out of Anchorage to someplace really wintry, such as Nome, the last outpost of exiles, cutthroats, and the hollow-eyed, Nome, the end of the Earth. "Only it isn't the end of the Earth," Weingarten wrote. "You can see that, right on the map." A small plane could take a winter vacationer 130 miles to an island closer to Russia than Alaska. "To the people of Siberia, this island is the middle of nowhere. On it, according to the map, is a village named Savoonga. Savoonga. Va-voom. Bunga bunga. Funny, no?"

Ideas came to Weingarten from everywhere, even from a subway station where he saw a ragged man playing a keyboard. When no one stopped to listen, Weingarten thought, *I bet Yo-Yo Ma himself couldn't get through to these deadheads.*

That's how he came to sit with Joshua Bell, one of the world's great violinists, then in Washington to perform at the Library of Congress. Over coffee on Capitol Hill, Weingarten asked one of those questions that a person would never ask if he weren't lucky enough to be paid for the impertinence of asking inconvenient questions. He asked if Bell would wear street clothes and perform at a Metro station during rush hour, just another down-on-his-luck busker with a fiddle.

"Uh," Bell said, "a stunt?"

Would he think it . . . unseemly?

Bell sipped his coffee.

"Sounds like fun," he said. "What the hell."

Weingarten was the author of a funny book about hypochondria. In its acknowledgments, he thanked several doctors who were exposed to him and lived through it. "Finally," he said, "I thank my friend Dave Barry, who gave me no assistance whatsoever except in the sense of providing me, through his work, a flawless template for timing, setup, structure, syntax, voice, emphasis, cadence, and word selection, not to mention providing a specific prototype for virtually every joke contained in these pages. I hereby forgive Dave for shamelessly imitating my style all these many years."

Along with forgiveness, Weingarten had offered Barry an escape from the sun, sand, and pastel glories of Miami. He had rescued Barry when he hired him for *Tropic* and ended his career as a corporate writing coach. But he couldn't get him to Washington. "I would have preferred editing Dave here," he said. "And I never would have tried to compete with him. But once it was clear he was staying down there . . ."

Only then did Weingarten become a humor columnist. He still did long-form pieces. He uncovered the family-secret backstory on the life and death of Bill Clinton's father. He gently removed the mask from a birthday-party clown, the Great Zucchini, whose rapport with children was inexplicable until Weingarten explained it. Garry Trudeau talked to him—and Garry Trudeau talked to practically nobody.

More often, Weingarten thought funny. One day he said, "Let me think if I want to tell you this story." He assumed a thinker's pose, an elbow propped up on the table, his forehead resting in his hand. Perhaps he considered if any of the people involved could still fire him. Soon he popped up with his mustache twitching. "It's about the Style Invitational," he said.

The Style Invitational was a puzzle contest. Under Weingarten's direction, it was irreverent, subversive, and nakedly provocative. "Potty jokes, jokes about religion, jokes about politics, all the stuff you couldn't get in the paper any other way," he said. It often was a source of despair among management types, chiefly the managing editor Bob Kaiser. "Bob thought it was 'beneath the dignity' of *The Washington Post*. Which was, of course, the idea."

Finally, Kaiser said he had decided what he would do about the Invitational—he just wouldn't read it. Weingarten called that "the second-greatest editorial decision ever made."

On Week 99, the Invitational ran an illustration under the question, "What's Wrong with These Pictures?" The joke was, everything was wrong. A man had one eye. A leg popped out of a woman's breast. A Christmas tree ornament hung from a palm tree. One reader mailed in the illustration with a circle around one tiny drawing. The reader's note said, "This is wrong."

Weingarten studied the drawing inside the circle.

"I thought, 'Pretty good. She drew in a dick and balls! Funny woman! Yep, that would be wrong.'"

Wait.

He took a second look.

Then he thought, *Hey, Gene, she did draw those in herself, didn't she? They couldn't have been in the original, could they? Couldn't be, naw.*

To be certain, Weingarten studied the drawing on the clipping sent in by the woman.

Then he looked at the original piece of art. Then he looked at each again, back and forth. *Oh, God. She didn't draw 'em in. It is a dick. And those are balls.*

It was a drawing so small that most readers missed it. But size, as we know, doesn't matter in these matters. It reminded Weingarten of a famous newspaperman's horror story. In June 1966, twenty-one-year-old *New York Times* reporter Clyde Haberman had the onerous task of typing up hundreds of awards given to City College of New York students. To relieve the boredom, he typed,

"THE BRETT AWARD to the student who has worked hardest under a great handicap—Jake Barnes." In Hemingway's *The Sun Also Rises*, Jake Barnes is sexually impotent by way of war wounds and in love with the femme fatale Brett Ashley. Haberman was fired and did eleven years of journalistic penance before the *Times* rehired him. Weingarten knew the lesson: You do not fuck with the *New York Times*.

Well, do you fuck with *The Washington Post*? With Katharine Graham's newspaper? Under the stern gaze of a bow-tied managing editor?

Weingarten leaped to the phone and fired the illustrator. He then marched in to the very same Mary Hadar who once had promised to leap from a window to give him a job. As best he could remember his mea culpa, it went:

"Mary, mumblemurmurDICK!mutterBALLS!" And, "Mumble mutterINTHEWASHINGTONFRICKINGPOST!"

Then, "MutterTHETIMESmurmurFIREDHIM!mumbleNOW FIREME!"

Hadar said, "Huh?"

Weingarten told me, "Mary looked at it for hours, though it may have been seconds. Then she made the single greatest editing decision ever. She said, 'No, no. That's not a dick and balls. That's a gun!'"

It didn't look like any gun Weingarten had ever seen, but if Mary Hadar said it was a gun, great. No one other than the one woman ever complained, not even Kaiser, and Weingarten promptly rehired the illustrator.

And he lived to invite Joshua Bell to play at a Metro stop.

Bell hailed a taxi for a three-block ride to the station.

Not for himself.

So his violin wouldn't have to go out in the weather.

It was 7:51 a.m. when Bell took up a position against a wall, beside a trash basket. As Weingarten watched from a distance, Bell removed the violin from its case and placed the case at his feet. He seeded it with a few dollars and pocket change. The violin was a 1713 Stradivarius, valued at $3.5 million. In the next forty-three minutes, 1,097 people passed by the guy wearing blue jeans, a long-sleeved T-shirt, and a Washington Nationals baseball cap. The idea was Weingarten's. He wrote in the *Post*'s Sunday magazine that it would be "an experiment in context, perception and priorities—as well as an unblinking assessment of public taste: In a banal setting at an inconvenient time, would beauty transcend?"

Weingarten on Bell: "Tall and handsome, he's got a Donny Osmond-like dose of the cutes, and, onstage, cute elides into hott. When he performs, he is usually the only man under the lights who is not in white tie and tails—he walks out to a standing O, looking like Zorro, in black pants and untucked black dress shirt, shirttail dangling. That cute Beatles-style mop top is also a strategic asset: Because his technique is full of body—athletic and passionate—he's almost dancing with the instrument, and his hair flies."

Bell "got his first music lessons when he was a four-year-old in Bloomington, Ind. His parents, both psychologists, decided formal training might be a good idea after they saw their son had strung rubber bands across his dresser drawers and was replicating classical tunes by ear, moving drawers in and out to vary the pitch."

He began the experiment with the Chaconne from Johann Sebastian Bach's Partita no. 2 in D Minor. Weingarten paid attention to Bell's playing, but all he knew was that that wasn't Lynyrd Skynyrd. The *Post*'s classical music critic, Tim Page, whispered play-by-play so Weingarten could write, "Bach's 'Chaconne' is also considered one of the most difficult violin pieces to master. Many try; few succeed. It's exhaustingly long—fourteen minutes—and consists entirely of a single, succinct musical progression repeated in dozens of variations to create a dauntingly complex architecture of sound. Composed around 1720, on the eve of the European Enlightenment, it is said to be a celebration of the breadth of human possibility." The violin became a human voice: it "sobbed and laughed and sang—ecstatic, sorrowful, importuning, adoring, flirtatious, castigating, playful, romancing, merry, triumphal, sumptuous."

Of the 1,097 people who passed within hearing distance of Joshua Bell's magic, what do you think happened?

Nothing, for the first sixty-three people.

Then a middle-aged man altered his gait for a split second, turning his head to notice that there seemed to be some guy playing music. It was almost ten minutes in before someone stopped to listen. Things never got much better. In three-quarters of an hour, seven people stopped. Twenty-seven gave money, $32 and change. This for a man who can command a thousand dollars a minute in concert halls.

"It was a strange feeling," Bell said at breakfast afterwards, "that people were actually, ah . . ."

A laugh here, at himself.

". . . ignoring me."

Of the seven passersby who stopped, only one did so because she recognized Bell. Stacy Furukawa, a demographer at the Commerce Department, had seen his performance at the Library of Congress. Now, in a Metro station, she stood dead still in front of him, ten feet away, people flowing around her. She didn't move, nor did she stop smiling, until Bell drew his bow across the strings for the last time. She said, "It was the most astonishing thing I've ever seen in Washington. Joshua Bell was standing there playing at rush hour, and people were not stopping, and not even looking, and some were flipping quarters at him! Quarters! I wouldn't do that to anybody. I was thinking, Ohmigosh, what kind of a city do I live in that this could happen?"

She stopped because she knew the violinist. Of the others who paused, just one did so because he knew the music. His name was John Picarello. He was a smallish, balding man.

The way Weingarten did this, a hidden camera videotaped the full forty-three minutes. His helpers at the station that morning got phone numbers from people of interest, telling them the *Post* might call about a story on commuters.

Of the more than forty people who were asked if they'd seen anything unusual on their commute that day, only Picarello immediately said, "There was a violinist playing at the top of the escalator at L'Enfant Plaza."

Weingarten: "Haven't you seen musicians there before?"

"Not like this one."

W: "What do you mean?"

"This was a superb violinist. I've never heard anyone of that caliber. He was technically proficient, with very good phrasing. He had a good fiddle, too, with a big, lush sound. I walked a distance away, to hear him. I didn't want to be intrusive on his space."

W: "Really?"

"Really. It was that kind of experience. It was a treat, just a brilliant, incredible way to start the day."

Picarello knew classical music. He was a fan of Joshua Bell, but didn't recognize him from across the station space. Grew up in New York. Used to play the violin. Used to dream about the violin, hoping to become a concert performer. "But he gave it up at eighteen," Weingarten wrote, "when he decided he'd never be good enough to make it pay. Life does that to you sometimes. Sometimes, you have to do the prudent thing. So he went into another line of work. He's a supervisor at the U.S. Postal Service. Doesn't play the violin much anymore.

"When he left the station, Picarello says, 'I humbly threw in five dollars.' It was humble. You can actually see that on the video. Picarello walks up, barely looking at Bell, and tosses in the money. Then, as if embarrassed, he quickly walks away from the man he once wanted to be."

W: "Any regrets about how things turned out?"

"No, if you love something but choose not to do it professionally, it's not a waste. Because, you know, you still have it. You have it forever."

"Pearls Before Breakfast" was published in the *Post*'s Sunday magazine and posted on Washingtonpost.com with video and audio embedded in the text. It brought Weingarten more than three thousand e-mails, one from a woman in Iowa who said she had been put on to it by a daughter in Bishkek, Kyrgyzstan. Washington post.com users clicked on it almost two million times. Eighteen months after publication, the video had been viewed on YouTube a million times.

The piece was so creative, evocative, imaginative, and even magical, that I said to Weingarten, "That thing can win a Pulitzer."

W: "No way. The feature Pulitzer always fits a formula. It's about a baby born without feet. The travails of dying elephants. A tornado hits and in twelve seconds lives are changed. Nothing controversial, a safe passage through adversity. This has no chance."

Me: "Still . . ."

W: "It's a stunt. They don't give Pulitzers for stunts."

Me: "They'll like what it did on the Web. They'll want to show that the Web really matters. Besides, it's beautiful."

W: "Meh."

8.

VIRGINIA TECH

R. B. Brenner, the Metro editor, was still in his workout clothes, gym shorts and a T-shirt. He hadn't shaved and hadn't turned on a radio or television. Shortly after 10 o'clock that Monday morning, his father called from Chapel Hill, North Carolina.

"So there goes your day off, eh?" his father said.

"What do you mean?"

"There's this big shooting at Virginia Tech."

Most days, Brenner walked to the *Post*. This day, he drove.

In the suburbs, Ian Shapira, a young Metro reporter, had taken a call on his way to work at the Prince William County bureau. An editor, Nick Anderson, told him to get to Virginia Tech. There had been a murder on campus. As Shapira headed south and west, his father called from Kentucky.

"Did you know," Harry Shapira said, "that five people were killed at Virginia Tech today?"

"What?" his son said.

Both hands on the steering wheel in strong cross-winds, cell phone in the crook of his neck, eyes on the interstate, attention being paid to his editor in his ear, Shapira pushed his little black car to maybe seventy-five miles per hour and would have gone faster—he had the speeding tickets to prove it—except "being inside my Honda felt like being inside the fuselage of an airplane hurtling through bad weather."

Instead of a casual morning drive to the bureau office in Manassas, he was hustling to Virginia Tech, four hours away. He was small and slight, twenty-nine years old, articulate, confident, a Princeton graduate. His primary beat was Prince William's educational system. But bureau reporters are always on call. He once did a story on a man who accidentally killed himself. As the man tried to beat his dog with the butt end of a shotgun, the gun discharged. Shapira wrote, "The police know this much: The dog didn't do it." A rueful smile here, and Shapira said, "The desk rewrote it for me."

As he drove south along the eastern slope of the Appalachians, Shapira listened to radio reports and spoke to *Post* editors by phone. The number of dead rose from five to nine to a dozen. Other reporters were on the way. This would be a flood-the-zone story, every available reporter working, the kind of story that newspapers with money and ambition do. In the Fifteenth Street newsroom, religion writer Michelle Boorstein, once a wire-service reporter in the world's trouble spots, told an editor, "If you need help . . ." She was dispatched to Blacksburg and told she might be gone four days; she stopped at home for a change of clothes.

At Washingtonpost.com's offices in Arlington, executive editor Jim Brady had broken off a senior staff meeting. "Like, in a half hour, the number went from two to thirty," he said. Two videographers were dispatched to Blacksburg. For the first time, Brady used a live-blogging tool that enabled Washingtonpost.com to publish in ten seconds rather than five minutes. The *Post*'s newsroom always had been reluctant to move so quickly. But this was a new world. Brady persuaded Len Downie they could not wait: "If it's out there—The Smoking Gun had a story that we couldn't confirm—you must say it's out there. Otherwise, you look old and out of step."

Just after noon, Shapira reached the Inn at Virginia Tech, a Gothic building long familiar as a celebratory gathering place for the Tech community.

There he saw a tableau serene and sad.

It was a college campus, abloom in the spring.

There were people huddled and weeping together.

When you arrive in the midst of grieving, and the job is to ask questions, if you're Ian Shapira you stand aside, wondering, "How do I approach these people?" Of course you'll do it. It's what made you a reporter, the need to be where it's happening when it's happening. What you do is wait until someone sees you. Go to eye contact. Be courteous. *Tell me*, you say. *Tell me what's happening.* The dance has a delicate balance, giving people their space even while sliding into it, and yet you know that if you wait, you may have missed your only chance.

By 2 o'clock that afternoon, the Virginia Tech campus was under a media siege. Trucks rolled in with their communication dishes aimed at satellites twenty-five thousand miles high. Producers, photographers, makeup artists, boom mikes, lights, those tall canvasback chairs on the lawns as perches for the talent. CBS procured a private room for Katie Couric's interviews. Throughout the transformation of the campus into a television studio, Ian Shapira, newspaper guy, was put off by "television's theatrical faux sympathy."

And then he saw a scrum of reporters around a young man, no doubt a student, probably an eyewitness, at which point the reporter's body made a decision for him.

"My legs revved into motion," Shapira said.

As Brenner and Shapira hurried to work, Len Downie remembered the newspaper lessons of 9/11. On that morning almost six years earlier, his assistant, Pat O'Shea, called him from home. She had never before done that. As Downie walked into the *Post* building after his Tuesday breakfast with publisher Bo Jones, the editor heard O'Shea say, "Did you know that a plane hit the World Trade Center? I'm getting dressed and I just saw it on televison."

Downie arrived on the fifth floor in time to see a plane explode against the second tower. Within minutes, he said, "this wonderful thing that happens in newsrooms—it began." Editors and reporters called in and came in from everywhere. Fashion columnist Robin Givhan and sports columnist Sally Jenkins, both in New York, headed for the disaster scene. Marcia Kramer, the Metro copy desk chief, came to the newsroom with a broken arm in a sling (left humerus, rollerblading). Because Kramer couldn't drive, a neighbor delivered her. She called her people who were off that day: Chris

Hopfensperger was already in; Jeff Baron would be on his way; and Nathan Willis, hired after a summer's internship, "was already thinking like a newspaper person; though it was his day off, he showed up to work," Kramer said.

That afternoon, as in days long gone when newspapers were most people's single source of information, the *Post* rushed into print a new edition, an "extra." Downie said, "We took every story out of the morning's A-section and replaced them with whatever we could get on what we then realized was a terrorist attack."

Steve Coll produced the extra. Only forty-two years old, he was in his third year as Downie's managing editor. Coll, first a writer, took the number two management job believing he could help build a newspaper that published brilliant writing. While Downie's instincts that day ran to asking for investigative reporting on airport security and counterterrorism, Coll would want a narrative.

He wanted David Maraniss to write it. A *Post* lifer and Pulitzer Prize winner for his coverage of Bill Clinton's first presidential campaign, Maraniss was a bestselling author still under contract as an editor and writer of big-theme stories for the newspaper. Downie said, "So that's when I called Maraniss. And he devised a method that he would use again. He asked for copies of everything that anybody filed, not only what was in the paper, but notes that went to other reporters, everything. Then he would sift through that to create his narrative and pick out characters that he would then reinterview himself."

That was Tuesday morning. For Sunday's paper, five days later, Maraniss delivered five thousand words on 9/11.

Now Downie called on Virginia Tech.

It was midafternoon.

In the third-floor bedroom of his home in northwest Washington, Maraniss heard the phone ring and knew what it was about. After a few words with Downie—"I'm on my way"—he walked to his office to pick up an egg timer. The trinket was an inch and a half in diameter, shaped like a June bug in colors of orange, yellow, and black. The old baseball radio broadcaster Red Barber set an egg timer by his microphone as a reminder to give the game score at least once every three minutes. Maraniss needed his timer because he had undergone hip-replacement surgery two weeks earlier and wasn't supposed to sit more than forty minutes. His wife, Linda, knowing her man, bought the bug to wake him from his writing trances. June bug in hand, Maraniss moved carefully down the stairs.

When he left home, the number of dead was set at thirty-two.

Downie wanted a narrative done as Maraniss had done 9/11. Only this time he wanted it sooner. "Five days now," he said of the new media world, "is like a year."

If you're Ian Shapira, newspaper guy, your legs run, they do not walk, to the young man. You've already missed what the kid said to dozens of reporters from—where? Richmond, Roanoke, the school paper, maybe the *New York Times*.

"Alec Calhoun," the kid said. "A junior, Waynesboro, Virginia." The other reporters had stopped him and his parents on the way to their car. They got the spelling of the name. They got the hometown. They begged his pardon if he had already told the story, but they had just arrived and, if you would . . .

Calhoun said he had been in room 204 in Norris Hall just before the gunman entered. He said students pulled screens away and pushed windows open. "Then people started jumping."

"You leapt out?" Shapira said.

"I didn't just leap. I hung from the ledge and dropped. Anybody who made it out was fine. I fell and I hit a bush to cushion my fall. It knocked the wind out of me. I don't remember running."

And Ian Shapira wrote it all down.

Calhoun's escape appeared in the twenty-fourth paragraph of Shapira's front-page story Tuesday morning. Shapira had filed by laptop, by e-mail, and by dictation to rewrite man Tom Jackman. With line-editing touches by Virginia editor Mike Semel, the lead-all story began:

> An outburst of gunfire at a Virginia Tech dormitory,
> followed two hours later by a ruthless string of attacks at a
> classroom building, killed 32 students, faculty and staff and

left about 30 others injured yesterday in the deadliest shooting rampage in the nation's history.

The shooter, whose name was not released last night, wore blue jeans, a blue jacket and a vest holding ammunition, witnesses said. He carried a 9mm semiautomatic and a .22-caliber handgun, both with the serial numbers obliterated, federal law enforcement officials said. Witnesses described the shooter as a young man of Asian descent—a silent killer who was calm and showed no expression as he pursued and shot his victims. He killed himself as police closed in.

Done with the day's work, Shapira drove ten miles to Radford in search of a Wal-Mart. He had left home without toothpaste. The *Post*'s six reporters in Blacksburg met for dinner that night at an Indian restaurant. Michelle Boorstein placed her cell phone in the center of the table so everyone could hear a call from Semel.

"There's six of you," the Virginia editor said, "and you've been phoning in feeds all day, so I just want to let you know . . ."

They all loved Semel, an old-school newspaperman who demanded good work, a hard case when necessary, but laughing most of the time.

". . . that we've managed to squeeze in a graf of your stuff."

He was busting their chops. He followed with laughter.

"No, no," he said, "the package is full of the feeds. Outstanding work, every one of you. The North Wall is pleased, and that is a very good thing."

The North Wall was home to the big offices of Downie and his number two, Phil Bennett.

Reporters at a big story will tell you it was fun to work the thing, the bigger the story the more fun, and for many reporters there was never a bigger story than Virginia Tech. "You hate to say it," Boorstein said. "But it's true." This, at Blacksburg, was fun. It wasn't joy. It was the rush of your heart pumping, adrenaline running, your senses sharp, clear, focused. You're inside the event, and nothing outside matters.

So Ian Shapira was back on the Virginia Tech campus Tuesday morning. He knew the *New York Times* would be there, Katie Couric, probably even Geraldo. From the second-floor windows of the gunman's Harper Hall dormitory, students looked out on the crowd. Reporters shouted questions—except for Shapira. The newspaper guy out of Princeton was smartly competitive. No need to hand the *Times* your questions, let alone answers. Instead, he shouted out his cell number.

A student, Brian Winthrop, called and said it was "creepy" to know he lived in the same building with someone—now identified as Cho Seung Hui—plotting mass murder. Police stood guard at Harper Hall, keeping reporters out. Shapira said, "Brian, go to Cho's room for me, and memorize everything you see. Pretend you're a video camera. If it's a bag of Doritos on the floor, tell me about it."

BrianCam didn't see much, maybe a pizza box.

"Brian, is there a back way in?" Which is how the *Post* reporter came to walk into the killer's suite—only to find that Brian's report had been on target: the usual dorm debris, a crushed soda box, crumpled newspapers.

Then a resident adviser asked Shapira, "Who are you?"

"A friend of Brian's."

"Are you a member of the media?"

Game over.

Too many reporters, too little access, television ruining everything—Shapira was on the phone explaining the difficulties, but Mike Semel wanted to hear no complaints. "Ian, come on. Today, this is the biggest story in the world—and it's local to us. Right now we're not getting a lot out of you."

Uh-oh.

"You cannot get nothing."

Oh, man.

"You need to do a better job."

Oh, man.

"Ian, failure is not an option."

Shapira had been reluctant to do reporting based on the shooter's Asian heritage. He said it felt intrusive, discomfiting. But an earful from an editor is often a curative for that condition, as it was in this case, when Shapiro bumped into an Asian who gave him the phone number of a friend in an English class with Cho. From a phone interview, Shapira then drew the first tracings of the shooter's dark profile. Paul Kim said he sat across from Cho, but never made eye contact. "He never looked up," Kim said. "He never spoke a word. Even when the professor asked questions, he never spoke. He constantly looked physically and emotionally down, like he was depressed. I had a strong feeling to talk to him on the first day of class, but I didn't get to talk to him because he sat right beside the door, and as soon as class was over, he left." Then he vanished. "For the past month, he stopped coming."

And Shapira wrote it down.

Maraniss was in the newsroom from 4 to 9 p.m. Monday and another fourteen hours Tuesday. R. B. Brenner, in addition to overseeing all of Metro's coverage, organized the movement of news, notes, and information to him. Wednesday, Maraniss woke up at 5:30 a.m. He wrote three paragraphs. It was a habit of his. He called it "writing in my subconscious." Overnight, it happens. "Then I get up and write out what came to me in my sleep."

Those paragraphs:

The roommates crossed paths near the bathroom door at 5 in the morning. In the Monday darkness, another school week at Virginia Tech was about to begin. Karan Grewal had pulled an all-nighter to finish his accounting paper. His eyes were bleary as he saw Cho Seung Hui, in boxer shorts and T-shirt, moving around him to get into the bathroom. No words were exchanged, but that is how it always was with Cho, the silent stranger among six guys in Suite 2121 at Harper Hall. Cho, or Seung as his suitemates called him, never looked you in the eye, rarely changed expression, would just walk right on by.

Grewal returned to his room and collapsed on his bed, falling into a deep sleep. He would not stir until mid-morning, awakened by an uncommon sound on campus, the wail of sirens.

Cho left the bathroom, got dressed, pulled a stocking cap over his head, and set out from the dorm on his way to kill thirty-two students and teachers and then himself in the bloodiest mass murder by a lone gunman in American history.

Maraniss wrote from his own reporting and from files provided by ten reporters in Blacksburg, seven more in the newsroom, and three researchers. Before it was over, the *Post* had assigned seventy-five reporters to the story. "Everything we did on 9/11 and learned through after-action reports on that one," Len Downie said, "we used on Virginia Tech."

The image that appears and vanishes throughout the Maraniss narrative is of Cho materializing in doorways, silent, no life behind those eyes, ominous in a black vest with ammunition clips in it, a gun in his hand, killing without expression, moving silently in the screaming, and then gone only to reshape himself in another place. "Life is mundane," Maraniss wrote of ordinary people on an ordinary morning, arguing football, talking television, "until it is not, and then the mundane can look serene."

There were thirty shots fired in Room 206 of Norris Hall, and Maraniss wrote of a student there, "His mind raced to his mother and what she would go through when she heard he was dead." Survivors' voices: "That was the desk I chose to die under." "They stared at each other until the gunman left." Another voice—whose? No one knew. The gunman's? Saying, "It's okay. It's going to be okay. They will be here soon." Soon, thirty-two dead. And the shooter dead, by his own gun, his face blown away.

Maraniss, again:

It was not until 9:06 that night—when Virginia State Police investigators knocked on the door at Suite 2121 in Harper Hall—that Karan Grewal realized that the roommate he had last seen in boxers and T-shirt 16 hours earlier was the cause of all the horror. The investigators interviewed Grewal and the four other roommates. No, they had not seen guns around the suite, but Cho was a strange guy. Wouldn't talk. Played the same songs over and over on his laptop. Didn't like to turn the light off in his room. Had a bike that he rode around campus late at night. Would not go out with them, except one rare time when they got him drinking at a party and he said he had an imaginary girlfriend who called him Spanky. Never saw him with a girl, though, or any friends whatsoever. Before spring break, he had seemed to get obsessed with a few women. Had been stalking them on his computer, and sometimes in person. The cops were called twice. Once he was sent to counseling and said he might as well kill himself. He started shaving his head down to a fuzz cut. Wore contact lenses. Used something for his acne. Was working out at the campus gym. Had been getting up really early recently.

The Maraniss story on 9/11 ran five days after.
This one, three days.

It cannot be said that Ian Shapira came to know Katie Couric. But he did offer to share dinner with her.

One evening at Blacksburg, the CBS network anchor came into the media building. She cast a star's cold eye on the place and said to a minion, "That's all we have to eat, a brownie?"

Shapira sat cross-legged on the floor. Beside him were the cold, gray, greasy-limp remains of one more newspaper-guy-on-deadline meal.

"Katie," he said brightly, "want a piece of pizza?"

She opted for the brownie.

9.

ANTHONY SHADID

From a cardboard box on the floor of his apartment in Boston, Anthony Shadid pulled out one of the notebooks that he had shipped home from Baghdad. On its cover he had labeled it "Iraq (War) April 9." That would have been April of 2003, his first year as a foreign correspondent for the *Post*. He had worked for the Associated Press and the *Boston Globe* throughout the Middle East before being hired by the *Post* to cover the coming war in Iraq.

At the top of the notebook's first page was the date: "4-9." Below it, the first of Shadid's notes on the day that American forces pulled down a giant statue of Saddam Hussein.

Signs of collapse of auth
running red lights
no traffic cops
no BP - the face of gov't in streets
driving wrong way

"These were signs of collapse of authority," Shadid said. He traced a finger across the notes. "Cars were running red lights because there were no longer any traffic cops. Saddam's Baathist Party militiamen had patrolled the city's streets—now they were gone. Their uniforms and boots were dumped where they had put on civilian clothes to avoid being identified."

I first saw Shadid's byline the day the war began. From Baghdad he wrote, "At 5:34 a.m. explosions thundered over a city still asleep." Every morning without fail, his stuff was reporting and writing so rare as to be his alone. Thirty-eight years old, an Oklahoman of Lebanese descent, Shadid looked like the elegant little man on a wedding cake, provided that man had a full head of salt-and-pepper hair with a matching beard neatly trimmed. His manner was soft, his voice gentle as it danced along on light laughter.

That day in April 2003, reporting on American troops in Baghdad, Shadid went downtown to Firdaus Square. Now, in Boston, he flipped pages in that day's notebook and relived the scene as he had recorded it in a reporter's clipped notes.

1st threw rocks
statue
sledge hammer to the purple stand
noose ard his neck
6 pm M-88 arrives
love machine
6:35 ard rt leg, then both legs
i'm 49 nvr lvd single day only now

Those notes became part of Shadid's page-one story on the chaos in the streets that culminated when an American M-88 tank recovery vehicle—"Love Machine" painted on its side—used cables around the statue's legs to pull it down. He wrote: "They threw a heavy rope tied like a noose around its neck. Many hurled rocks at it. A few minutes later, someone in the crowd showed up with a sledgehammer, and residents took turns pummeling the purple granite at its base. 'Scum, son of scum,' shouted Yusuf Abed Kadhim, as he swung at the pedestal. 'I'm 49, but I never lived a single day. Only now will I start living,' he said."

Two hours later, at dusk, the statue fell.

"A seminal moment," Shadid said.

That was why he did the work. To be there when history was made, when a statue falls, when a dictatorship falls. It made it worthwhile. Not that he expected to change the minds of people who thought he was crazy to subject himself to the dangers and deprivations of doing journalism in a war zone. But those were the moments a foreign correspondent lived for.

Those moments could get you killed.

Until the Israeli sniper shot him, it had been a good day. Shadid's notebook was full because he had been eyewitness to a drama that was a perfect metaphor for the latest Israeli-Palestinian conflict. He started a long walk back to the hotel. There he would write for his newspaper, the *Boston Globe*. He was looking at his notes when he realized that his body was falling. He was halfway to the ground before he heard the gunshot.

It was March 31, 2002. Shadid remembered the sky over Ramallah as cemetery gray. Once the bustling hub of a new Palestine, the city was cloaked in silence. War in its third day had emptied the streets. That day, as on all days, Shadid was driven by a reporter's questions: Why? How do I put the pieces of the puzzle together? Here in Ramallah, why did Israel's army wage war against civilians when the nation's prime minister said the objective was to eliminate a "terrorist infrastructure"?

Shadid had gone to Ramallah Hospital to interview doctors, nurses, ambulance drivers, and humanitarian workers. He wanted to talk to people who had found themselves in harm's way by leading their everyday lives. As he arrived, so did the roar of war. A tank rolled up, and two armored personnel carriers unloaded soldiers. The soldiers rushed toward the hospital with rifles leveled on people who had come outside. Someone said, "This is a hospital!" The soldiers, seemingly in search of an enemy, shouted, "Everyone back, everybody inside!"

Shadid saw it all. The scene spoke to the asymmetry of the conflict. Here were doctors in white smocks facing soldiers with M-16s. As an Israeli lieutenant talked to the hospital chief, Shadid listened. In their confrontation, he saw the war. For him the lieutenant symbolized an army that had to search among civilians for the enemy, and in the hospital chief he saw Ramallah, powerless against power.

"The doctor and this Israeli were face to face and they were yelling at each other," Shadid said. "I'm standing right next to them. And I'm writing down every word. This was one of those moments. Through it, I could tell the entire story of this fifty-year conflict. I was so excited. This is it. You could see how the entire story would be structured. So excited."

When a peaceful compromise was made, Shadid headed back to his hotel with a colleague, Said al-Ghazali. They walked in the middle of the street lest they raise suspicion by moving along walls. Both wore white flak jackets with "TV" marked on the back in red tape, the best-known symbol for international press. He had his notebook in his hands, flipping pages to read notes.

Then he was falling before he heard the gunshot. "It was deafening, like they shot next to my ear," he said. "Probably twenty-five feet away." On the street, he couldn't move. He first thought someone had thrown a stun grenade, a weapon that momentarily paralyzes its target. Then he felt pain on his spine. "Said," he said to his friend, "I think I was shot."

Al-Ghazali was down on the pavement with Shadid, searching for blood. "I don't see anything," he said. Shadid now reached under his flak jacket and brought back a bloody hand. He thought to tell his wife and infant daughter good-bye. He thought of ambulances that couldn't move on Ramallah's streets. He also thought, *I'll die if I wait for help.*

Al-Ghazali carried him twenty yards before they fell. "Journalists!" Al-Ghazali shouted. "Help! Bring us a car!" There was no one in the street, no one could hear them, no one except perhaps the Israeli who had shot him. Shadid thought that man might now be watching him struggle toward a vehicle in the street ahead.

"He's wounded!" al-Ghazali shouted.

An Israeli said, "Show us!"

Al-Ghazali turned Shadid so the soldier could see the white flak jacket red with blood. The bullet had passed through Shadid's left shoulder, sheared off part of a spinal column vertebra, and burst through his right shoulder, a classic M-16 wound: tiny on entry, huge on exit. Twelve pieces of shrapnel remained inside the reporter's back.

In his Boston apartment years later, I asked Shadid, "Did the guy intend to shoot you?"

"There were rumors that Palestinians were posing as Red Cross workers and journalists. I don't think if they knew I was an American journalist that I'd have been shot. They might have, who knows? They can be rough on journalists. I think they wanted to teach a lesson. 'Here's what we're going to do to people acting as journalists.'"

"God," I said.

"A cold-blooded execution."

"From point-blank range," I said.

"They were looking to kill me. Crazy, but reading my notes may have saved my life. I think they were aiming at my head, and I moved my head down looking at my notes."

"The M-16 wound makes you sure an Israeli did it?"

"Yes. And the Israelis were in complete control of that area that day."

He could have been dead. He could have been paralyzed. Instead, he was in a Ramallah hospital miles away from the one he had visited that day. From his bed, he called Boston and told his editor what happened. He also said, "I got this great story. I think I can still write it." And the editor said, "If you think you can do it, we'll take it."

Before Shadid could get his laptop, common sense, in league with morphine, prevailed against the idea. Besides, he hadn't been in the hospital an hour when here came more Israeli soldiers, guns drawn, entering his room and shouting something in Hebrew, a language he did not understand. He said, "Back off. I'm an American journalist." They answered, "Get your hands up"—as if he could. He was mummified in bandages around his chest and shoulders. He raised his forearms.

Later that night, an Israeli army officer stopped by. "If we shot you," he said, "I apologize on behalf of the army." Then he shrugged. "But you know, you were in a war zone."

Shadid's notebooks were tangible evidence of a reporter's adrenaline rush. Well formed and orderly notes suddenly skittered across the pages and landed wherever there was white space. Sometimes he even made space by turning the notebook sideways to write along what used to be margins of the page. We were in Boston looking at notes made years before, notes of events so vivid that he still could translate the scribblings.

He kept the apartment to be near his daughter, Laila. She lived with her mother, a doctor who had loved Shadid but not his work. When it was clear to both the husband and wife that the man and the work were inseparable, they divorced. He said, "That combination of altruism and ambition that makes reporters who we are— sometimes I wonder if only journalists understand that. You think you're doing something good, something worthwhile, and you like doing it."

He loved the Iraq story in 2003 and 2004, Lebanon in 2006. "You basically lose yourself in it. You take a deep breath and sink into it. The story becomes you. It defines your life in a way I've never experienced elsewhere. The downside to that is, it takes a bit of your soul away. You're thinking about the story constantly. How do I understand that story, how do I put the pieces of the puzzle together?"

"And you're thinking of that," I said, "instead of playing Scrabble with your daughter?"

"Afraid so. This will sound cheesy, but it is an overwhelming experience when you're defined by a story to that degree. And that's when journalism can really be great, when that's who you are, you're here to report that story."

The old general assignment reporter Don Graham knew that about newspaper people. He told staffers in Iraq, "No story is worth your life." Shadid disagreed, almost. "Some are really important. It's worth taking a risk to stay in Baghdad. This is a seminal moment in our country's history and to not have someone in Baghdad for *The Washington Post*—that wouldn't make a lot of sense."

I said, "So you say to your wife, 'I need to do this,' and she says, 'Anthony, you can make a living doing something else.' "

"In some ways, that's why our marriage dissolved. It was a choice of how we were going to live our lives. Her contention was I just should have never put myself in a position where I could get shot, that I brought it on myself."

———

George W. Bush's vice president had promised that American troops would be celebrated as liberators in Iraq. To understand how mistaken a notion that was, I needed only one source of information in Baghdad. That source was Anthony Shadid, who did in the *Post* every day what American political leaders never did. Because he spoke Arabic, he talked with Iraqis. Because he cared about them, he listened. He reported that while Iraqis despised Saddam Hussein, they preferred tyranny over a superpower's invasion that would kill tens of thousands of innocents and unleash anarchy in a country forever near civil war. Iraqis asked Shadid, Why are the Americans doing this?

"Shadid is simply the best foreign correspondent working for any English-language newspaper or magazine," the freelance foreign correspondent/photographer Mitch Prothero said. I had asked him for twenty-five words on his friend. He e-mailed seven hundred. "Anyone can learn to speak Arabic or push themselves harder through fatigue or dangerous working conditions, but I doubt very much anyone can learn to listen to people with the skill and grace of Shadid. It's not just that phony crap reporters always pull out—particularly in the Arab world—where they condescendingly nod their heads as someone explains what it feels like to be humiliated, to lose a loved one, to be oppressed and afraid, or to be so enraged and alienated as to take up violence. Enough with the callow head-bobbing. Anthony, on the other hand, sits there and listens, asks some questions, and everyone just loves him." Prothero then wrote, "To conclude this nearly nauseating tongue-bath, he's funny, humble, hard-working and never obnoxiously self-loving like so many of his colleagues and peers at the *Post* or the *New York Times*. And I'm pretty sure he beats his maid, tortures neighborhood pets, and sacrifices babies to the devil."

Anthony Shadid found the quiet places inside war, and no place was quieter than the simple cement and cinder-block home of a man named Salem Kerbul. It was the quiet of heartbreak.

This was in the desert oasis town of Thuluya, ninety minutes north of Baghdad. A month before, four thousand American soldiers moving by helicopter gunships and armored vehicles had swept down on Thuluya. They took away four hundred insurgents, as identified by informers in the town. One informer had been recognized by villagers despite covering his face with a burlap mask. That man wore distinctive yellow sandals. That man had a mutilated right thumb, severed long before in an accident. That man was Salem Kerbul's son.

Because Kerbul's son was also blamed for the deaths of three villagers in the raid, and because tribal customs demanded vengeance, the informer's family was told it must kill him—or they would be killed in his place. The execution had, in fact, taken place. With the help of his Iraqi driver/fixer Nasir Mehdawi, Shadid learned that Sabah Kerbul had been killed by his brother and father, both using AK-47s.

"Then I said, 'I gotta talk to the father,' " Shadid said. "Everybody told me, 'They'll kill you if you go to the father.' I didn't believe that. And I had to try. Better hearing no than not knowing. And he actually let us in. He knew we were journalists, but he brought us into the house."

And so, in the house of a man said to have killed his own son for the treachery of informing on village neighbors, Shadid sat with Salem Kerbul. They sipped tea. The father sat cross-legged on the floor against yellow walls with green trim. He smoked a cigarette and rubbed his thumbs restlessly against black prayer beads. Two overhead fans turned against the desert heat. Shadid had done this work for twenty years, but he had never asked this question.

"The father knew why we were there," Shadid said, "but I kept thinking, 'How do I bring this up?' We were skirting around the question in a very Middle Eastern way. You don't go for the jugular. You dance around the edges. But, finally, it came to a point where all the questions had been asked and I needed to say, 'Did you kill your son?' "

He didn't say it.

Couldn't say it.

"I decided, 'I've got the story, I can write.' I just didn't want to hear him say yes. There had to be some dignity. I didn't want him to be humiliated again. I didn't want to see him cry. For him to cry would have been to lose every shred of dignity. So I said something much looser, like 'How did you feel after your son died?' "

The light caught the glimmer of a welling up in Salem Kerbul's eyes. He spoke softly, a whisper of grief. "I have the heart of a father, and he's my son." Then he cast his eyes down. "Even the prophet Abraham didn't have to kill his son."

Shadid called those last words the most chilling he ever heard. "I'd never come across anything so devastating. A bombing is one thing. You see body parts. It's traumatic. I still have dreams of it. But this, where you catch your breath and have an emptiness in your gut—I'd never had that kind of reaction to any story. It told me, again, that this place, Iraq, is just fucked up. A brutal place. Thuluya is not even a footnote in this war's military history. But American troops set into motion events that ended up as this biblical moment. A father had to kill his son. This is the detritus of military intervention."

Soon after, Shadid took leave to do a book about his family's ancestral home in southern Lebanon. Then, restored by the time away, he was eager to again be part of what he called the story of a lifetime. "The idea that Iraq has fallen off the front pages of America's newspapers because of a lack of commitment is breathtaking," he said. "That's why I want to go back." Then, early in 2009, he sent me an e-mail from Baghdad:

> When I asked two colleagues to join me in Baghdad, they politely refused. When I asked why, my fiancee answered for them. "They've moved on," she said. I guess I haven't. I can't say that Iraq was my favorite story. Although I adore Baghdad and cherish its memory, it is not my favorite city. But something feels undone here. It still feels like there's work to do. Before I left in 2002, I told my editor that I thought Iraq would be the most important work I did in my career. I still feel that way. And at a time when the country is more complicated and more ambiguous, I'm wondering if

that work hasn't just begun. My first impression when I returned was that it felt like 2003. No one then really knew what was ahead in those tumultuous months after Saddam's fall. It still feels like 2003 to me.

Shadid intended to be in Baghdad for the *Post* through all of 2009.

Part III

"THE GREATEST DAY IN THE HISTORY OF *THE WASHINGTON POST*"

10.

MISTAKE ON THE EASTERN SHORE

The powerful exposé by Priest and Hull, Weingarten's magic, the family's agony described by Shadid, the Virginia Tech coverage—in five years would that kind of reporting still be done? Would any news organization pay for the people, time, and resources? The answers seemed to be no. If newspapers went away, 90 percent of revenue would disappear and with it would go the ability to do that work. Like every major American newspaper, the *Post* had no idea what to do next.

It reminded Bob Woodward of the Bush White House. "Here is the question for newspapers, twofold," he said. "One, when was 'strategic warning' issued? Like when that famous top-secret presidential daily brief of August 6, 2001, went to Bush. It said, 'Bin Laden determined to strike in U.S.' George Tenet, the CIA director, came down the month before and said, 'We've got all this intelligence.' His counterintelligence chief, Cofer Black, came down. But Bush didn't get it. Condi Rice didn't get it."

Now, he said, newspaper publishers had failed to act on strategic warnings given them by the Internet's repeated, unmistakable threats. "One thing you learn in reporting on national security and war is that hope is not a strategy. You gotta say this is what we're going to do. Don Graham and other publishers said, 'We're losing ad revenue in print and we're gaining ad revenue online—and we hope online will make up the difference.' But it never did. And it got worse. The question now is, 'Can they fix it?' So far, no."

To all this, I had a sportswriter's questions. What was the turning point? When was the game lost? What was the moment of truth? The answer usually was a shrug, as if no one could know. Then someone said I should find out why Steve Coll left the paper.

Coll had been a wunderkind at the *Post*, a Pulitzer winner, managing editor at age thirty-nine, and next in line as executive editor. He saw the future, he was the future—and then he was gone. No one understood how the paper could lose a top editor who in 1999 had written an essay that began:

> A new era for newspapers is emerging as Internet use spreads and deepens. New competitors, new audiences, and new pathways for distribution already are reshaping life in The Post's newsroom. For reporters and editors the greatest challenge involves adapting our work to World Wide Web formats that emphasize speed, active interaction with readers, and a new synthesis of words, pictures, and sound. Compared to earlier arrivals of radio, television, and cable as news and information sources, the Web's format is in many ways friendlier to a newspaper's journalistic strengths and ambitions.

The essay ran under the headline "Can Newspapers Thrive in a Digital World?" Coll's answer was an enthusiastic yes.

> The Post can innovate and experiment on the Web, bolstered by confidence in its old-fashioned journalistic values— accuracy, independence, completeness, honesty, depth, and a commitment to holding government and public institutions accountable. In the Internet era, we believe these bedrock journalistic values will be as important—and as rewarded by readers—as they were in every previous era of technological change. If not more so: The chaotic explosion of channels

made possible by the Web is driving online audiences increasingly toward credible and reliable news outlets.

The revolution had started. Don Graham had signed on. Chief political reporter Dan Balz said, "Don told me he had stopped being publisher [in 2000] because he wanted to understand what the hell the Web was about." After hearing Bob Kaiser's fable of the boiling frogs, Graham committed tens of millions of dollars to online operations. As early as 1997, Kaiser's unlikely partner in revolution, Mark Potts, sent his *Post* bosses a memo predicting a future of "light, easily portable, wireless computing/communication devices that can do everything our current desktop PCs can do and more." When those devices arrived, Potts wrote, "Some newspapers will survive—after all, you still can take horse-and-buggy rides and buy vinyl LPs. But I think portable electronic information devices will essentially kill the printed newspaper—within our lifetime."

Unlike many newspaper people, Coll bought into the revolution completely. He asked his people to produce content for Washington post.com. Union rules made it all but impossible for management to order it. And the odds were against the troops volunteering to do pro bono work for a multibillion-dollar company. But Coll thought he might seduce them with futuristic tech-savvy talk. On October 20, 1999, he wrote, "Reporters will be wandering into the streets not only with notebooks in their pockets, but occasionally, with little video cameras in their hats. A great way to cover a riot, for instance."

At this point, grumps in the *Post* newsroom likely had three questions.

Cameras? Hats? Riots?

The hat-cam concept tickled David Carr of the *Washington City Paper*. The alternative weekly's media critic imagined "a fleet of electronic chapeaued Max Headrooms who will mix it up with angst-ridden hoi polloi and beam digitized mayhem back to the screens of people killing time between check-ins on the progress of their stock portfolios."

Carr's joke was built on the idea that the *Post* needed no change.

The Len Downie/Steve Coll newsroom rocked with nine hundred people. It had thirty bureaus around the world. An investigative unit with a dozen reporters did long, Pulitzer-winning projects. Other departments, even sports, had their own snoops whose bylines appeared maybe twice a year. The *Post* was the newspaper of an idealistic editor's most extravagant imaginings. The paper made a 20 percent profit some years. No one much worried that such a paper was an aberration. But Graham knew it, and that's why he had gambled all that money on the Web. Coll knew it, too, and told me, "It was never going to last forever." But preparing the *Post* for a future that depended on the website was easy only in theory. The website people were kids from a computer culture of video, audio, databases, photo galleries, interactivity—all those gadgets that were alien to the veterans in the Fifteenth Street newsroom. "Even the most creative of us," Coll said, "were imprisoned by our inherited newspaper assumptions."

Trying to break people out, Coll went cubicle to cubicle recruiting the reluctant with scare statistics that underlined the need to make the website more valuable. "My pitch was, 'This is your future, own it,'" he said.

Coll also came to believe that Graham's decision to separate the print and website operations—editorially and in business as well as physically—had outlived its usefulness. At the start, it allowed the website to become "whatever it was going to be without forcing it into the newspaper," Coll said. The *Post* had been hurt because it was allowed to "operate as if we were only to decline at two percent a year for the next twenty years. So we could afford not to deal with this coming reality. If the newsroom had been forced to become faster, smarter, and more digital earlier, that wouldn't change the business equation, but we'd be further along to the newsroom required to succeed in the new era."

With each year, the business equation became more problematic. Even with the newspaper's financials going south and the website making double-digit gains in revenue, the *Post* still brought in ten times more money than Washingtonpost.com. And the suits in the corporate offices seemed to have no idea how to change that ratio.

Coll yielded to his betters on all financial chatter.

But he did have an editorial idea that, if executed well, might make a significant difference financially.

Ever notice how Hollywood portrays *Washington Post* reporters?

Coll did.

"They were usually like ex-Rangers with the moral system of Jesus—the complete romanticization of the Woodward and Bernstein narrative," he said. They were men of integrity, square-jawed action heroes, each moving with Harrison Ford's certainty of purpose. "And it was lovely."

Coll himself favored a boyish intellectual look, Harry Potter with a reporter's notebook. He came to the newsroom's number two job as a representative of two eras. He was an old-school wordsmith and a twenty-first-century techie. On May 20, 2003, he unveiled an ambitious plan that married the newspaper's mythic history with a future it could shape.

At the annual off-site meeting of top editors, Coll cast reporters as superheroes. "Let's not disabuse everybody of their beliefs in *The Washington Post*! Let's market it!" His plan was to sell the *Post*'s extraordinary journalism everywhere. That would be done, as always, in the newspaper and now, more than ever, on Washingtonpost.com. He called the project "Beyond Washington."

Even in its infancy, the website's reporting had a long reach. In 1999 the Nobel Peace Prize winner José Ramos-Horta came to the *Post* newsroom. His country, East Timor, had declared independence from Indonesia. The invader's troops then went on a killing rampage. When someone at the *Post* asked how many Timorese were killed, Ramos-Horta said, "I will know that when I read Keith Richburg's reporting on your *Washington Post* website."

Don Graham's deep-pockets commitment to the website was proof that he believed online success was critical to his company's long-term health. Now, in support of that commitment, Coll would show how Washingtonpost.com could conquer the world.

He had created a task force of senior editors in response to the *New York Times* squeezing the *Post* out of its ownership share in the *International Herald Tribune*. The IHT had given prominence to the *Post*'s foreign correspondents; it was often the only place an interview subject could read the correspondent's work. Coll called the loss of the IHT "a traumatic event in the newsroom." Once a foreign correspondent himself, he felt a need to restore morale.

Coll's task force asked questions: "Had we lost our ambition? Were we shrinking? Had we lost the competition with the *Times*? Who were we? What were our ambitions outside of the Washington area? Should we have any? Did we have any? Did we have a real global strategy? Should we have one? What was it? Did we have a national strategy? If we had one, what was it? Should we think about a print strategy outside of the Washington, D.C., area? What was the *Times* doing? What was the *Wall Street Journal* doing? Were we really their competitor?"

The task force studied the national strategies of the *Times*, the *Wall Street Journal,* and *USA Today*. It examined data about the *Washington Post Weekly Edition*. Advertising and marketing people from both the paper and website produced demographics and analytics on readers, users, and advertisers. An assistant managing editor, Jill Drew of Financial, said, "I would walk on water for Len Downie. But we all were from Steve's generation. This was an incredibly exciting project, and we believed in him."

After six months, the task force decided on its message to Graham. First, the newsroom agreed it made no sense to pursue a national distribution strategy, as the *Times* did. Nor did the newsroom want an international edition to replace the *Herald Tribune*. Instead, the idea was all digital, all in line with Graham's push to make the website meaningful and profitable.

"For me," Coll said, "the headline was: 'The newsroom now understands that a print strategy outside of Washington is a loser.' So this whole mythology that had been built up all these years, people wanting a national edition—let's put that to rest. It's not a business for us. What is a business for us is a somewhat more aggressive national and global Web strategy. And here's why. Look at the audience that's come to us accidentally: six million people have gathered outside of our window unbidden. We haven't spent a dime asking them to come. They're just standing there looking up at us—'Give us something.' Don't we want to do something about this?"

Assorted editors spoke during a ninety-minute PowerPoint presentation. Then, Coll said, "There was a grand summary, stating, 'And we think that in the world after *Herald Tribune*, we ought to embrace those audiences that are out there. We think this is the answer.' The fact that we wanted to spend a little money to market to them was really incidental. I mean, ten million dollars? That's like nothing."

The managing editor said he expected Graham's response "to come with this headline: 'Newsroom abandons long-held desire to have national print edition, which I opposed. Instead, newsroom has been co-opted into my own belief that the website, which is relatively cheap, ought to be the basis of our strategy.' "

The meeting took place at the Inn at Perry Cabin, a resort on Maryland's Eastern Shore. Forty editors and business executives sat at two parallel tables with Coll between them at the slide projector. He believed the task force had created a win—win deal: "To me, there was going to be really no resistance to this. It was another way to get the newsroom pouring stories at the website. And there was a national and global component to it."

Then Graham rose and spoke. In a five-minute soliloquy, the CEO rejected the task force's six months of work.

To quote one witness, "Don got up and machine-gunned the room."

Another said, "I felt the oxygen being sucked out of the room." And, "We got Coll killed."

Still another murmured, "Oh my God, Steve's out the door."

Jill Drew said Graham spoke "eloquently and passionately" about the character of his newspaper. "His paper was 'local,' " she said. "It was about firefighters and teachers and police and everybody that is the community that is greater Washington. To go beyond Washington we necessarily would be skewing our journalism to an elite audience. He said that what we were describing was elitism—'and elitism is death.' "

Coll told me, "Don's message was 'You people are in danger of losing contact with your regional mission, your local news mission, and that's everything.' Don said we ought to be worrying about why the Prince William County fireman doesn't read the paper as much as he used to."

Instead of thinking globally, the boss wanted his people thinking locally. It was nice, yes, that a Nobel laureate in East Timor reads Keith Richburg for a report on mass murder. But it was better that a butcher in Bladensburg reads the school board briefs in his zoned edition. When I asked Graham much later if he had brushed aside Coll's proposal, he said, "I did say, 'Yes, Washingtonpost.com is a very successful site with a subculture of users who use the site very intensely around the country and the world, and we would be crazy not to exploit that to the most we can. But the people in the local area, who are fifteen percent of the users, maybe a little less, account for two-thirds of the advertising revenue. It helps to be number one somewhere, and we're number one locally.'"

Coll believed the *Post* newsroom had done well locally. "Local strategies, regional strategies, the zoned editions, millions of focus groups with marginal readers thinking through their needs, commuter traffic reports, weather, sports—hey, we're all about the Redskins. But we could never do enough to prove that we were committed enough to the last marginal reader."

In five years as managing editor, he learned there was no limit to the website's reach.

"We've got these six million people on Washingtonpost.com, eighty-five percent from far outside our area, and we can do more for them. Even without changing our content, we can attract a bigger audience. We're all about the journalism. We should be excited that it matters in Jakarta now. In the middle of a revolution, people are reading the *Washington Post* to understand their own national events. That's gotta be good, isn't it?"

Everyone at the meeting knew of Coll's argument that the *Post* should strive to create America's number one newspaper website. "So it came across to the room as more of a repudiation of me than Don intended it to be," Coll said. "It was a repudiation of all the ambitious, high-church newsroom characteristics of the globalized, rootless cosmopolitans of the newsroom who were not 'local' enough."

The website's chief executive, Chris Schroeder, understood Graham's concern that a national/global strategy would be a distraction. "But I never thought of it as a zero-sum game. We didn't have to lose the Prince William fireman to gain a reader somewhere else. We could do both." Schroeder said the bottom line was that Graham knew he had a local business, could only guess there might be a national business, and in any case didn't think the return would be worth the investment.

Drew said of that day on the Eastern Shore, "We had Steve, ambitious, brilliant, and exciting, advocating, with all kinds of backup, his vision of a national and global presence for our *Washington Post* journalism. Just as brilliant, as visionary, and wise, Don simply says, 'That is not who we are.' And he owns the paper. Everybody left the room stunned into silence."

Coll left disheartened. His online ambition reached past survival to domination. He believed that in the ferociously competitive news media world, there would rise one major newspaper website. He wanted it to be the *Post*. That was his ambition—right up to the moment that Don Graham said no.

Anyone counting the episode as a pivotal moment in *Post* history could argue that it stopped momentum on the Web, changed the newsroom's leadership, and for the first time announced limits on the newspaper's ambitions. There had been a day when Katharine Graham said to Bob Woodward, "Never? Don't tell me never." Woodward came to believe that meant he should use all of the newspaper's resources. Now along came Kay Graham's son telling Coll he should use only some of those resources.

Coll had promised Downie five years on the job. He had done the five and now felt he had been ordered on a fool's errand chasing the marginal reader who had decided he no longer wanted to read anything, let alone the *Post*. "Chris Schroeder called me on my cell as I was driving home and said, 'Okay, I'm printing up my résumé,'" Coll said. "Colleagues called that evening and said, 'Don't quit.' I said, 'I'm not going to quit.' But it was a turning point in thinking about my own future."

He considered himself first a reporter and writer, and only later a manager, now a manager in circumstances he could not control.

"It was an important event for me. It wasn't decisive. I had a thousand questions. What about my writing? My body of work? But, to me, the reason for staying always sounded like 'If we're going to grow, if we're going to get big, if this is going to be more

complicated, more expansive, more creative, more challenging—
then maybe the management side will be appealing.' Managing
growth and risk and complexity and aspiration, I'm all about that.
But if you tell me what we're really doing is managing decline and
that the strategy we have is the only strategy that's permissible and
it's all about the marginal reader, then that's Don's decision to
make, absolutely. And it doesn't anger me that that is what he
decided. But it's clarifying because that's for somebody else to do.
That's not for me."

Coll resigned as managing editor at the end of 2004 and stayed
on as an associate editor and writer at large. On April 4, 2005, he
won a second Pulitzer, this one for his book *Ghost Wars*. Five
months later, he left the *Post* for *The New Yorker*.

It was impossible to know if Coll's ideas would have survived the
economic calamities to come. Nor could anyone say his national
and global ambitions would have resulted in more revenue for the
company. Still, there was no doubt that his leaving was a step back-
ward when the future, if any, belonged to the bold. Don Graham's
mistake on the Eastern Shore cost the *Post* newsroom a brilliant
writer, thinker, and true believer in the future of journalism
online.

For Coll, talk of that future came naturally, as if it were his
native language. On a day two years and more after Coll left the
paper, Len Downie talked the same talk and with passion. But for
him, it was a second, learned language. Listening to Downie, I
thought of Edward Bennett Williams.

11

HOWDY DOODY TIME

When Ed Williams bought the Baltimore Orioles baseball team in the late 1970s, I wrote a column suggesting that the man doth protest too much. The hot gossip was that Williams would move the team to Washington, thirty miles away. In reporting that possibility, I pointed out that trial lawyers of EBW's stature were actors who practiced their art before a thousand juries. Now, having heard his thunderous and repeated denials that he would never, never, not ever leave Baltimore in favor of his hometown, I wrote that EBW was due an Oscar.

Well. That wasn't smart of me. The EBW legend included the Jimmy Hoffa tale. Bobby Kennedy was so certain he had finally cornered Hoffa that he promised to jump off the Capitol dome if the Teamsters thug were acquitted. Well. That wasn't smart, either. After winning acquittal for Hoffa, Williams sent the president's kid brother a parachute. Naturally, EBW took offense at my implication that he had been disingenuous in denying any plan to rob Baltimore of its beloved birds. But all he ever said was "Wrong, kiddo." And, in fact, the Orioles never moved.

I remembered EBW's gentle chiding as I listened to Len Downie on November 5, 2007, the first Tuesday of the month, precisely a year out from the presidential election. As I had been skeptical of Williams's promises, now I wondered if Downie believed what he was saying.

He spoke to a group that called itself the E Streeters at an annual luncheon started by Kay Graham for old pros who had worked in the *Post*'s original building. Gathered in the newspaper's first-floor auditorium, they talked about the bad old days. Lawrence Laurent said, "In 1952 or '53, they began thinking television would be important and wanted me to cover it. But they didn't have a single TV and no money for one. I asked, 'How do you cover TV if you don't have a TV?' I bought my own. Thirty dollars."

The E Streeters' chairman was a ninety-five-year-old pepper pot, Al Manolo, who in 1946 had been an assistant news editor. He knew Eugene Meyer well enough to call the distinguished millionaire "Butch" and invite him into newsroom craps games. Newspapermen of any age, especially those almost a century in the making, can feel deadlines coming, as Manolo then proved by saying, "We usually have a moment of silence for our members no longer with us. But we're a little bit pressed for time here today."

Skipping the silence, he introduced Downie. "He supervised the *Post*'s Watergate coverage," Manolo said before turning to the executive editor. "Who played you in that movie? Wasn't there somebody that played you?" Not waiting for an answer, Manolo hurried on: "He spent a year on leave on an Alicia Patterson Foundation Fellowship, studying urban problems in the United States and Europe." To Downie again: "And I hate to say this, but you sure didn't solve them." Finishing up: "He's the author of four books whose names I will not give you, but he will if you want them. Len, you're on."

Downie delivered to the white-haired crowd the same message he carried to his newsroom. "This is a really exciting time at *The Washington Post*," he said. "It is a daunting time, a challenging time, a scary time, and also really exciting, full of opportunity— because we are changing more in these last few years and the next few years ahead of us than I think we changed in all of the forty-three previous years that I've been at the newspaper." Downie said the best news was that *Post* reporters now embraced change. "It's not just a print-newspaper newsroom anymore. In fact, we have many, many more readers on Washingtonpost.com now"—ten million some days—"than we have of the printed *Washington Post*."

He hoped the E Streeters had seen "Left of Boom," a *Post* series on IEDs, the improvised explosive devices that were the al-Qaeda in Iraq insurgents' most effective weapon against U.S. troops. The project had been done by a Pulitzer winner, Rick Atkinson. "In the newspaper, it was a conventional series, a lot of stories, photographs, graphics. On the Web, all of that was accompanied by videos that Rick himself made in Iraq." Atkinson's videos included interviews with army generals and a tour of a Humvee. "It was a really lively package of multimedia presentation that hundreds of thousands of people read online, which five years ago wouldn't have existed," Downie said. "That's what makes this really exciting, what we're embarking on now."

His excitement was a reporter's. If these were the changes necessary for survival, Downie could make those changes. They gave everyone more ways to tell stories. Reporters covering "this amazing political campaign" went online with blogs constantly updated with inside-politics information. The new National staff boss, Susan Glasser, created "The Trail," items contributed throughout the day by campaign reporters. A "Fact Checker" blog awarded from one to four Pinocchios to politicians whose words strayed from the truth. Newsrooms had never been busier. Reporters had never seen more reaction from readers. There had never been more creative ways for journalists to work.

Yet the more Downie talked about the "really exciting" times "full of opportunity," the more I wondered if he truly understood the revolution in his business. The game-changing editor in the twenty-first century would understand instinctively, without intellectualizing it, that a website was not a newspaper with audio and video bells and whistles. That editor would know it was a different animal altogether that demanded different ways of thinking. He would know the Web the way Len Downie knew newspapers.

On the fifth floor that day, the *Post* geared up for the campaign. I stood at the door to David Broder's cluttered office. Though the campaign already had a marathon feel, Broder was ready for more. He would do the campaign the way he had done them all since 1960, two or three columns a week, a news story when he found it.

"David does whatever David wants to do," Downie said. Broder intended to knock on doors because talking to folks taught him what he needed to know. The first important dates were the Iowa caucuses January 3 and the February 5 Super Tuesday primaries. Those events figured to identify the presidential candidates.

"It'll be Clinton and McCain," he said. The Arizona senator's name was a surprise in that all reports had his campaign dead. "I say McCain because the Republicans always come back to who they feel comfortable with."

Among newsroom contemporaries, Broder had earned distinction for a minor set-to with that major character of the 1970s, Henry Kissinger. As the secretary of state scolded Broder for something he had written, the columnist did what reporters do. He wrote it all down.

"What are you doing?" Kissinger said.

"Taking notes," Broder said.

"This is not an interview. I invited you over here because I respect your work and I want you to understand what really happened."

"That's very flattering, Mr. Secretary," Broder said, "but you and I have no private or personal relationship. You invited me over here because of what I wrote about you. You tell me it was wrong. If it was wrong, or if you think I was wrong, I want to share those arguments with the people who read the column."

"If I cannot talk to you on background," Kissinger said, "then this conversation cannot continue."

"I guess it cannot continue," Broder said, and he left, not meeting Kissinger again until two years later, when the secretary of state thought to introduce a companion. He said, "This is David Broder of *The Washington Post*. He walked out on me when I stopped his taking notes."

Broder thought, *By God, I got to him. It still rankles the so-and-so. That's what I'd like on my tombstone: He walked out on Kissinger.*

Now, for a thirteenth presidential campaign, Broder was eager to walk into the snows of Iowa, where he had celebrated so many New Year's Days waiting for the heartland folks to tell him about the next president.

"Yes!" he said. "New Year's Eve in Des Moines!"

If Broder could pass as the newsroom's wise and wizened Yoda, next door I met Luke Skywalker. He came to our planet disguised as a tall, trim, dark-haired political junkie using the alias Chris Cillizza. Every week he pounded out ten thousand words on "The Fix," his Washingtonpost.com blog. He worked in print, television, radio, video. Perpetually ebullient, Cillizza said, "Clinton's the nominee! But if Obama or Edwards wins in Iowa, she's no longer invincible! On the other side, McCain, Huckabee, Thompson, Romney, and Giuliani! A political junkie's dream!"

Cillizza came from Connecticut to Georgetown University, contracted Potomac Fever, and stayed, first with the *Cook Political Report* and then *Roll Call*. He joined Washingtonpost.com in 2006. He said, "We are in the process of building a community of people who have an unhealthy interest in politics!"

The mayor of that community could be Dan Balz. The *Post*'s chief political correspondent was sixty-one years old. He favored a stubble of beard, coming in white, that when left untrimmed for two or three days gave his thin face a Don Quixote look, as if he were about to tilt at windmills—which he would do for the next year covering his fifth presidential campaign.

"Corny, but what I like is the old 'first rough draft of history' thing," he said. (The "rough draft" line came from a Phil Graham speech to *Newsweek* reporters in the last year of his life.) "The candidates are making their cases, and the country is trying to understand the issues, and we, the press, are reporting it as it happens. It's just always a great, human story. There's not anything like a presidential campaign because it gives the country, every four years, the chance to collectively say who we are, what our hopes and dreams are. As a reporter, covering the intersection of candidates and voters is very challenging."

He had been on the Obama trail from the start. "I didn't know where he'd announce, but I knew I'd go wherever it was. At that point, Obama was a great story even though he was the clear underdog. That's the kind of event, if you're a political reporter, you want to be there. No matter what happened, the story of Obama in '07 and '08 would be compelling. For presidential campaigns, particularly one like Obama's, you want to see the launch. You want to see how they do it, hear it, feel it. You want to experience it at the moment."

The difference in how they did it was telling: Mitt Romney stood with cars in Detroit. Rudy Giuliani announced on a Fox TV talk show. John McCain did it before a listless group in New Hampshire. Hillary Clinton put two words on her website: "I'm in."

Barack Obama reached out to Abraham Lincoln by going to the Old State Capitol building in Springfield, Illinois. That's where Lincoln, accepting the Republican nomination for the U.S. Senate in 1858, made his "House Divided" speech prophetic of the Civil War. Obama spoke outside the building to accommodate a crowd estimated at fifteen thousand. Balz had grown up in northern Illinois, at Freeport, so he came with his winter wardrobe. The temperature was sixteen degrees with a windchill of five. Ink froze in reporters' pens. It was a brilliant morning of blue sky and bright sunshine. More than five hundred journalists were there. Van Halen's "Right Now" staged a full assault against icy eardrums.

"Let me begin," Obama said, "by saying thanks to all of you who've traveled from far and wide to brave the cold today. I know it's a little chilly."

His speech sounded themes of change, hope, and common purpose. "By ourselves," he said, "this change will not happen. Divided, we are bound to fail. But the life of a tall, gangly, self-made Springfield lawyer tells us that a different future is possible. He tells us that there is power in words. He tells us that there is power in conviction. That beneath all the differences of race and region, faith and station, we are one people. He tells us that there is power in hope. As Lincoln organized the forces arrayed against slavery, he was heard to say: 'Of strange, discordant, and even hostile elements, we gathered from the four winds, and formed and fought to battle through.' This is our purpose here today. That's why I'm in this race."

Balz worked the crowd, talking to people "who'd brought their little kids and driven a couple hundred miles in some cases. One woman, who had a daughter in Springfield, had driven in from Kansas City. They had a sense that this was a moment in history that they wanted to see and have their kids see. It was really extraordinary to get their sense of it. And you don't get that by covering the speech on TV. Just to be out there, to absorb it all, was valuable."

Balz laughed. "Fun, also!"

It helped to know the tricks of the trade, as he explained in revealing how he and colleague Anne Kornblut arranged an in-the-bus interview with Hillary Clinton that made unique audio available on Washingtonpost.com. The clever duo used an old journalistic technique with the candidate's handlers, probably perfected in Lincoln's time.

"We whined," Balz said.

"For a long time," he added.

The *Post* would cover the campaign completely. Bill Hamilton, a National editor, called the coverage "a matter of survival," and by that he meant the very life of the newspaper. Downie said, "We will own the campaign." He also said, "And we will be ready for something to happen because something always happens. A terrorist attack. God forbid, assassination. A Fred Thompson campaign that takes off like a Reagan rocket. We will be ready."

Downie sat in his North Wall office, feet propped on a coffee table, his back to the *Post* newsroom visible behind floor-to-ceiling glass. Except for one mystery—the *Post*'s future—he was happily comfortable. He was sixty-five and had been the *Post*'s executive editor almost seventeen years. He had no plans to retire. Ben Bradlee did the job twenty-six years and retired at seventy. "Between now and seventy," Downie said, "we'll see how it goes year to year."

His reporters and photographers had won nineteen Pulitzer Prizes, a total matched by no other editor. With a $100 million newsroom budget, he had staffed the *Post* with stars in every discipline. One reporter said, "He has the talent of a field general. I've never found him remotely inspiring, but you always assume he is making the right decision. And you always trust that, even if it was the wrong decision, it was being made because he thought it was right. It's an irreplaceable quality."

Some saw a future of revolution for the *Post* while others

thought of the change as only transitional. Downie admitted his own confusion. "I never would have dreamed that these years of my tenure would be what they are now," he said. "You ask what will it be in five, ten years? I don't know. I say, 'Look back five, ten years, and what could you have predicted about what's going on now?' The answer is, very little."

Monopoly newspapers had been money machines. They survived competition from magazines, radio, and television to make the 1980s and '90s the most profitable decades in their history. But those days ended when the Internet established an ethos of information delivered instantly and for free. Newspapers created online presences in self-defense but soon learned they could not charge even the pocket change they asked for their papers at street-corner news boxes. Then along came Craigslist, a classified ad service that was raw, crude, even amateurish—but free. This creation of a techno-dweeb named Craig Newmark eviscerated the classifieds that had produced 40 percent of a big-time newspaper's revenue.

"With all that change, there's going to be that much more in the next five, ten years," Downie said, "because the Internet now is roughly where television was when Howdy Doody was on the air."

The next day, Downie returned to the first-floor auditorium for a quarterly staff meeting. As three hundred staffers filed in, he waved a hand toward empty seats in the first two rows and said, "Anyone who sits down here will still have jobs when the meeting is over." A couple dozen people hustled down, laughing as they played along with the joke. As he had done with the E Streeters, Downie presented the glass as half full. "In the twenty-five to thirty-four age bracket, we're stronger than most major papers," he said. "We're not going to kiss those people good-bye. At the other end, our core readership of older people is not going to die off tomorrow. So that gives us ten, twenty, maybe more, years of figuring out what our course is."

Wait.

Did he say ten or twenty years?

It had been fifteen years since Bob Kaiser's boiling frog memo and eleven years since Don Graham began spending tens of millions of dollars on the Internet. Now, in 2007, Downie talked of getting it figured out . . . someday? News cycles were no longer measured in days but in hours, if not minutes. Years were for dinosaurs. A newspaper losing circulation and revenue every year could hardly sustain ever-increasing losses for another decade, let alone two.

The veteran copy editor Tony Reid said, "Hell, I dunno. You listen to Downie, everything's fine. You listen to Don, everything's great. But Downie can't answer the big questions about layoffs or buyouts because, he said, he doesn't know what's gonna happen. And he totally blows off the morale questions. Of course, newsroom morale almost always sucks, but ever since these cuts have started and people have gone from being cranky to being confused and frightened, he hasn't done anything to salve anyone's fear. Not his personality, he says. Which means maybe he's the wrong guy for the job at this point."

Besides, Reid said, "Len Downie's sixty-six on May 1. Seems to me he'll call it quits after the election."

Graham and Downie had worked together so long at the *Post* that media critic Jack Shafer, in *Slate* magazine, wrote, "Like an old married couple, they had begun to look like each other." Now, with both men over sixty years old, there was, for the first time, uncertainty about their roles in the newspaper's future.

On November 10, 2007, evidence of that uncertainty made its way into the headlines.

12.

TAHITIAN LOINCLOTH

Late in 2007, times had changed in such dramatic ways that Don Graham, a private man, became a public figure in his own newspaper. He made two stock transactions that required public announcement. One dealing transferred family-held stock to public shares; the other gave $77 million worth of that stock to his wife, Mary. "And then not a day went by," the *Post* business reporter Frank Ahrens told me, "without somebody asking, 'Is Don getting a divorce?'" Both sixty-two years old, the Grahams had been married forty years and had four grown children. Ahrens said, "I called people close to Don and asked the divorce question. One said, 'You can't say anything now, but it's the beginning of a separation of assets.' I told my source that I respect Don, I love Don, and I'll sit on it, but I don't want the *Post* to be embarrassed by being beat on the story. I'm no media adviser, but it seems to me he should get out in front of this."

On November 9, Graham released a statement that Ahrens included in a short piece published the next day on an inside page of the business section. The story said:

Donald E. Graham, chairman and chief executive of The Washington Post Co., is separating from his wife of 40 years, Mary Wissler Graham, he said yesterday.

No comment was given on whether the two will seek a

divorce. Mary Graham has divided her time between Washington, New York and Boston; Donald Graham continues to live in Washington.

In a one-paragraph statement, Graham called the separation amicable and said, "There will be no further comment from the company or the Graham family."

Phil Graham's ambition moved him to become a king-maker, and Katharine Graham created a queen's court. Their son rode the subway to work.

Chief executive officer of a multibillion-dollar company that operated one of the world's most famous newspapers, Don Graham avoided a *Forbes* magazine interview by saying, "I'm not the center of the story." To see him in a rumpled brown sweater under a charcoal gray suit coat a half size too big and hanging askew on his shoulders was to believe that this extraordinary man with extraordinary wealth went an extraordinary distance to be ordinary. He was one of America's rare practitioners of conspicuous nonconsumption.

Graham, this man who gave humility a good name, once said, "You know, Levey, how I start my day?"

Bob Levey, then a *Post* columnist, had come to pick up his daughter from a sleepover.

"No, Don," he said, "I don't know how you start your day."

Graham said, "I go into the bathroom, look in the mirror, and say, 'Don't screw it up.' "

Was Graham's line to Levey evidence of a brilliant man's modesty? Or did it suggest the anxiety of an heir to empire? Or both? Len Downie called Graham "the most complex person I've ever known," and Pulitzer winner David Maraniss said, "You couldn't have a better newspaper owner, and I love him to death, but he's weird." A person determined to be opaque can avoid a meaningful psychological portrait. Graham's life could be seen only at its basic level, as a reaction and reflection of his parents' lives, the father charismatic and tragic, the mother as imperious as she once was shy.

Graham worked for his mother for decades, not always to good effect. On a winter day in 1992, heavy with snowfall, she was about to leave for a vacation in Hawaii—only to discover she didn't have a proper suitcase. She sent her driver into the weather to bring back a choice of suitcases. The driver trudged in from the snow lugging five suitcases and set them down for her inspection. She looked at each and said, "No, no, no," and sent the poor man out to get more. "Don turned to me," said a friend, "and said, 'Now you know what it was like to grow up here.' "

In a decision that Mrs. Graham called "the most painful thing to look back on," she left the country the day after her husband's funeral. She traveled with her daughter, Lally, and a friend, Luvie Pearson. To "get away from everything," she met her mother on a yacht at Istanbul. For reasons she couldn't articulate even thirty years later, she left her sons behind—Steve, Bill, and Don. In her autobiography, she wrote, "The decision may have been right for me, but it was so wrong for Bill and Steve, and even for Don—so wrong that I wonder how I could have made it."

Whatever damage may have come, time had done its repairs by the summer of 2001 when Mrs. Graham, eighty-four years old, suffered a probable stroke. A guest in the company of Warren Buffett, she collapsed during the annual Herb Allen gathering of media moguls in Sun Valley, Idaho. Don sat at his mother's bedside in a Boise hospital, distraught.

Buffett's biographer, Alice Schroeder, recorded the scene as the billionaire came to the hospital. His daughter, Susie Jr., led Buffett to an intensive care unit "where Don Graham, red-faced from weeping, was sitting alone with his mother. Kay, drained of color and unconscious, lay connected to monitoring devices that blinked little lights and made tiny noises. There was an oxygen mask over her mouth. Warren and Don clung to each other, sobbing."

Two days later, Mrs. Graham died.

The end of his father's life, especially in its public phases, was a dramatic piece of the continuing Washington saga. There was no record of Don Graham ever speaking of the death. His choice of privacy over celebrity was repeatedly affirmed by friends. A Harvard classmate who had introduced him to his future wife saw me approaching in an airport, leaped from his chair waving his hands as if I were a radioactive cloud to be dispersed, and said,

"No, no, I can't talk about Don." Later, a *Post* lifer said, "I wouldn't write about him, so why would I talk to you so you could write about him?"

So deeply ingrained was Graham's reluctance to be the center of any story that it gave rise to stories about that reluctance. Bob Woodward told one. At the chairman's sixtieth birthday party, Woodward remembered a day of golf with Graham and sports columnists Tony Kornheiser and Michael Wilbon.

"Don wore a pair of khaki pants that he probably got in Cambridge when he was an undergraduate," Woodward said, recounting his tale. "On about the sixth hole he was teeing off—and the pants split. A total wardrobe meltdown. All the thread, which was twenty or thirty years old, just evaporated. And it was like he was in pantaloons rather than pants. Instead of acknowledging it, he takes towels and tucks one in the front, the other in the back—like a Tahitian loincloth.

"Now, this would be the moment most people would fall apart on the golf course, right? Kornheiser, Wilbon, and I can hardly play. Don never says a word, just keeps playing. The more intense the pressure, the better he plays.

"When the drink-cart lady comes by, he takes her aside, and we see him peeling off a couple twenty-dollar bills, which is big money for Don. She leaves and comes back with two pair of Bermuda shorts. He goes behind a tree and changes out of his pantaloons and Tahitian loincloth into his new shorts—a total wardrobe upgrade. And he's back on the golf course. And never said a word to us."

The sportswriter Tom Boswell had seen reminders of the good schoolboy athlete Graham had been, rawboned and strong, six two, 180 pounds. Playing for the advertising team against the newsroom in the *Post*'s softball league, Graham hit a shot over the left fielder's head for a home run. "Next time, with the outfielders backed up, he went over their heads again, another home run," Boswell said. "Third time, the outfielders are clear out there under the trees. That one, he put in the treetops."

I asked the slugger about that day, and here, in its entirety, was his response, in this exact word: "Awww."

When Henry Allen, the veteran Style star, was diagnosed with prostate cancer in 2004, help came from an unexpected source. "I got a phone call saying, 'Mr. Graham would like to see you at your convenience,'" Allen said. Graham had undergone prostate surgery himself. "So I go up to his office and he waves to his secretary, 'Hold all my calls.' And this multibillionaire says, 'We're going to talk until you've said everything you want to say and asked everything you want to ask.' Well, he knew a lot about prostate cancer. Then he tells his secretary, 'Get Pat Walsh on the phone.'"

Walsh, a preeminent specialist in prostate treatment at Johns Hopkins, was on vacation. "Don told Walsh's receptionist, 'Don't interrupt his vacation, just ask him to call me when he returns. Two weeks is fine.'

"So I go back to my desk," Allen said, "and there's a note: 'Pat Walsh called, wants you to tell him when you can come in.' He wants *me* to tell *him* when I am available."

The people in the *Post* newsroom admired and respected Graham for many reasons but mostly for keeping the *Post* on the course set for it in the previous half century. Don had signaled his intentions early with what he often called the only important job a publisher had, the hiring of an executive editor. By choosing Downie over the Bradlee protégé, Shelby Coffey, Graham told editors and reporters that style was good, and there was a place for style, but the values of his newspaper would be based solely on substance. Even his "Donniegrams"—personalized notes of praise—came to newsroomers with more than simple hurrahs. Steve Coll said, "The notes were effective not because he wrote them but because he was reading my work the way I would wish it to be read and noting the things you wished people would value. That's a harder trick to pull off."

Coll set aside the puzzling aspects of Graham's personality. He admired what he was able to know. "To inherit what he inherited and to have the divergent paths available to him—he could run the newspaper or not run it, could have been anyone, lived whatever life he wanted—with all that, he chose a life of service. And he managed under extraordinarily intense pressure over a long period of time to get the balance right. He created a newsroom that was as good as it could be. The most amazing thing is, he intuitively understands where the talent is in the newsroom. All the people he really loved as reporters were in fact the very best. I mean, Kate Boo—a lot of colleagues admired Kate and respected Kate, but still wondered what the fuss was about. Don understood from the very first piece she published that she was a genius. She was interested in things that mattered." In 2000, at age thirty-five, Boo's work on neglect and abuse in D.C.'s group homes for the mentally retarded won the *Post* a Pulitzer gold medal for public service. Two years later, she won a MacArthur Foundation grant worth a half million dollars.

Graham also identified the sportswriter John Ed Bradley early. He even knocked on his door out in the boondocks. Bradley was an exotic character at the *Post* in the mid-1980s, a small-town curiosity out of the Deep South who had won a job by writing a letter to Ben Bradlee during a wee-hours shift as a night watchman. Strikingly good-looking with a slow, sweet drawl, twenty-four years old, tall and lean, he had been a center and captain on Louisiana State University football teams. He lived in Rectortown, a village in the Virginia countryside near the Grahams' estate, Glen Welby.

"One Sunday morning, there came a knocking at my door, and there he was. No messages, no calls," Bradley said. As they had coffee, Graham noticed train tracks behind the house and asked if he could bring his small son over. "So they came unannounced another time and stood on my deck for two hours. Lo and behold, with me feeling like it was my fault, the darn train never came that day."

That was Graham's last visit to Rectortown. "But one day somebody came to the door and said, 'Mr. Graham is inviting you to dinner at the house.' It was only the two of us, Don and me, in that big house, a house like you'd see in Italy or France." When Bradley asked directions to a toilet, Graham took him down a hallway. "He told me his father had committed suicide in the house." In fact, Phil Graham had died in a downstairs toilet.

It had all seemed odd, as if Graham were sad and lonely. "I told my girlfriend that he was a little goofy, maybe because he hadn't had a man in his life to model his behavior on or to emulate. That prince thing and there's no king to guide him. He seemed to want to be a regular guy, and maybe he saw me as a regular guy."

Later, like Boo, Bradley decided to leave the *Post*. Graham told him if he stayed he could do anything he wanted, but Bradley wanted something a newspaper couldn't offer. He wanted to be a novelist.

"As much as I admired Don, I felt sorry for him, too," Bradley said. "He really didn't have to become a cop to show that he was like everybody else. He must've been incredibly hard on himself."

Both parents gone, his marriage coming apart, and the *Post* in crisis, Graham added to the uncertainties of his life on December 5 by telling Wall Street analysts that he had redefined the nature of his company.

"In 2008 and going forward," Graham said, "*The Washington Post* is really going to be an education and media company." Frank Ahrens reported the announcement as a "rebranding" that marked "the rise" of Kaplan and "the decline" of the newspaper.

For Graham the newspaperman that must have hurt. It had been seventy-four years since the auction on E Street and fifty-three years since Eugene Meyer reckoned little Donnie would run the *Post* forever. Now the man who told his mirror, "Don't screw it up," came to say that on his watch the newspaper had fallen to dependency on an obscure education outfit created by a Belorussian immigrant's son during the Depression.

In fact, the most appropriate name for his company, the name best suited to attracting investors, would be the Kaplan Education Company. For the first time, Kaplan had produced more than 50 percent of the company's revenue (to the paper's 20 percent).

Graham downplayed it as old news. By financial measures, the newspaper had long been a tag-along to Kaplan. And he insisted that he still believed good journalism was good business; he just didn't know how it would be paid for in the near future. The best hope, he said that day, came in knowing that the *Post* website drew millions of users. Because "eighty percent of them are from outside Washington," he said the *Post* had "a very unusual opportunity" to find an audience at once local, national, and international.

He did not mention that four years earlier he had turned down Steve Coll's proposal to capitalize on that very audience.

Graham was often given credit for his foresight in acquiring Kaplan. In fact, he had nothing to do with it. Nor was Katharine Graham much interested. In 1984, when asked if she wanted to buy Kaplan, she said, "I don't give a shit about it."

But her new president did. Richard D. Simmons was eager to diversify the *Post*'s holdings, especially after taking a phone call from an old friend.

"Have I got a deal for you," said Bob Wallace, head of security at Dun & Bradstreet during Simmons's tenure as president.

"I'm listening," Simmons said.

"Stanley Kaplan."

"Who's that?"

"I'll tell you."

Stanley H. Kaplan's father, Julius, after arriving at Ellis Island, started a plumbing and heating business in Brooklyn. Stanley's mother, Ericka, the granddaughter of a rabbi in Prague, insisted on her son's education. At fourteen he first tutored a student in his basement, his fee twenty-five cents an hour. When he met Simmons a half century later, Kaplan operated seven hundred test-preparation centers with ninety-five thousand students paying him $35 million.

Kaplan had turned away suitors. But his financial adviser—a friend of Bob Wallace—"persisted in promoting a sale if the perfect partner could be located," Simmons wrote in an unpublished memoir. "Wallace believed the Post company under my leadership represented a near-perfect fit and due to Kaplan's highly developed ego might represent for him a level of recognition that had escaped him to date."

Theirs was a swift romance. Simmons had what Kaplan wanted, nearly limitless capital to drive growth around the world. And Kaplan had what Simmons wanted, a company with nearly limitless upside potential. But Mrs. Graham balked.

"To say that Kay had but little interest would probably be an overstatement," Simmons wrote. "'A test preparation company? Who's ever heard of it?' The 'who' in that last sentence really referred to her peer group of media executives whose approval she continued to seek and covet." But he had a plan to persuade her that a test-prep company was just the thing her company needed. His plan, simple and direct, would be critical to the company, to the newspaper itself, and to thousands of employees for decades to come. His plan was to whisper in Warren Buffett's ear.

"One thing I had learned in my almost three years on the job," Simmons wrote, "was that if Warren supported a concept, Kay not only blessed it but usually became an advocate."

In preparation, Simmons sent a lieutenant, Alan Spoon, to Omaha with the Kaplan financial data. On August 20, 1984, Graham called Buffett. "After favorable introductory remarks about the financial strength of the proposed acquisition, Warren opined that Stanley reminded him of Mrs. B., the by-then legendary operator of the Nebraska Furniture Mart."

Mrs. B. was Rose Blumkin, who moved from Russia to the United States at age twenty-four. At ninety, she sold a two-thirds interest in her megastore to Buffett for $67 million. Buffett's connection of Mrs. B. and Kaplan "sewed up the deal," Simmons wrote.

The Post's annual report for 1984 showed no record of the purchase price. Nor did Simmons reveal it, other than to write, "That amount, including some reserved for an earn-out payment based on profits over the ensuing three-year period, was approximately $40 million. In 1985 the Kaplan profit was $8 million, or a 19-cent-per-share positive contribution to our earnings. No media related purchase could conceivably have done so well so fast."

Simmons was the Post president ten years. In that time the company stock price rose from $27 to $245. After Simmons left the president's job, Kaplan languished for a decade before becoming a $2 billion a year business returning profits that reached $150 million a year. Don Graham had shuffled through a series of CEOs for Kaplan before finding Jonathan Grayer on Newsweek's business side. As Kaplan grew, it was Graham who approved acquisitions. And it was Don Graham who now came to New York to say out loud—with the Post in trouble—what he otherwise might have whispered.

After Graham's announcement of the *Post*'s status as a Kaplan subsidiary—to be unkindly accurate about it—I sought out a man whose business it was to know the *Post*'s business.

I asked, "Without Kaplan, where would the *Post* be?"

"Dead," he said.

In addition to the Internet's arrival and the economy's collapse, he said the *Post*'s problem was that "an entire generation and a half between the ages of eighteen and the low thirties simply does not read newspapers." He believed small, local papers would continue to do well because they supply unique information. As for major metropolitan papers, he was less sanguine. He did find comfort for the *Post* in two realities. The first was Kaplan's phenomenal growth. Second, this: "The *Post* is lucky enough, thanks to Kay Graham's father, to be located in the nation's capital and, thanks to Kay and Don, still be relevant. That means the paper will continue to have readership."

Also, he said, "Don recognized early on that the Internet was here to stay, and if he did not do something fast, it would take away his automobile and real estate advertising, which together represent a significant piece of all *Post* advertising revenue. Don really got on board, and Washingtonpost.com, which once lost $30 million a year, has made respectable if modest profits."

The businessman thought the *Post* had started a long slide away from the everyday reader with Ben Bradlee's retirement in 1991. Too many investigative projects, blown out into ten-thousand-word, five-part series with photographs and graphics, seemed designed primarily to win journalism prizes. And though buyouts reduced the newsroom population, he argued that the remaining five hundred were "still way, way, way too many. Good for the journalistic ego, not the bottom line."

I asked how the *Post* might regain favor with everyday readers.

The wise man laughed and said, "Beats the shit out of me."

A month later, on January 21, 2008, photographer Matt Mendelsohn prepared to shoot a formal portrait of an old friend who didn't want the word to get around.

She came to his studio in Alexandria, Virginia, just across the

Potomac from Washington. They had met ten years earlier in a Georgetown dog park. Now she was about to get a new job and needed a nice photograph. She asked him to keep it quiet because the promotion wouldn't be announced until February 7.

Her uncle had decided it was time for her to move into the most important job in her family's oldest business.

Katharine Weymouth would become the *Post*'s publisher.

13.

"SAVE THE PAPER"

It was Thursday, January 31, when Len Downie's assistant, Pat O'Shea, reminded him of a 5 o'clock meeting in Bo Jones's office on the seventh floor.

At sixty-five, Downie still moved with the chin-up swagger of a young editor on the make and worked with the confidence of a master. Even Ben Bradlee's admirers admitted that under Downie the newspaper had become more sophisticated, focused, and dependable. He also had reshaped the newsroom to produce the paper even as it helped Washingtonpost.com create video, audio, and multimedia reports available 24/7. All of it was evidence of Downie's new-age mantra: "We must be platform-agnostic."

Still, he was a newspaperman. "Every day's paper was Len's way of judging himself," one of his lieutenants said. "His thinking was that if he put out the best paper possible every day, the future would take care of itself." But these were revolutionary times. Early in 2008, the newsroom was made uneasy by a sense of unknowable change coming. There would be a third round of buyouts, maybe soon. Bill Keller, Downie's opposite number at the *Times*, had made a crack about *The Washington Post* being an education company that happened to own a newspaper. The apparent end of Don Graham's marriage was a reminder, as if one were needed, that nothing was forever. "So much is happening, we're all hiding under our desks," Gene Weingarten said.

Downie wondered what Jones could want on a Thursday in his office. They met every Tuesday for breakfast. If the publisher wanted to talk at other times, he stopped by the editor's office. In Jones's eight years on the job, Downie had never before been asked to come upstairs. But even as he thought, *Something's up,* he had no idea what.

Downie walked to a stairwell that led to the seventh floor. A man trying to lose weight—"It's all those damn birthday cakes in the newsroom"—needed to climb the two flights to Jones's office. He had reached the stairwell's sixth-floor landing when he stopped. Suddenly, he connected the dots. There, in that silent, sterile space, he thought, *My God, they may want me to retire.*

Bradlee had gone to seventy, and Don Graham had given Downie no sign that he would expect him to retire any sooner. But now, without warning, this. "Like I'd been punched in the gut," Downie told a friend later. It got no better in Jones's office. The publisher was Graham's lifelong friend and business associate, both men reserved and shy. Jones was so uncomfortable delivering the news that he later told Downie's wife, "It made me sick."

He had blurted out the messages. Katharine Weymouth would become publisher. He would move up to the ninth-floor corporate suite as vice chairman of the company. "And they want you," he told Downie, "to take the buyout."

It was neither a negotiation nor a recommendation. It was an order. Jones didn't say who "they" were. Maybe Weymouth had pressed for the change. But it would not have been done unless Graham signed off on it. For Downie, the ache of losing his job was compounded by hearing the news from someone other than Graham.

Back in his office, Downie reached Graham by phone.

"Bo has talked to me," he said. "Can we talk?"

As part of the separation settlement with his wife, Graham had given her the house they shared for much of their marriage. That afternoon he was moving into a townhouse in the downtown DuPont Circle neighborhood. Shortly after 6 o'clock, with a storm bringing icy rain toward Washington, Graham walked among the sofas, tables, and chairs still covered with sheets.

He said, "Do you want to see me in the office or come over here?"

Downie drove over. With nowhere else to sit, the men went to a second-floor bedroom and used the only uncovered chairs in the house. Their talk was stilted, things half said, thoughts unfinished, all awkward. Downie hadn't come to argue. Intellectually, he understood the decision; emotionally, it hurt. He wanted to ask, *Why?* And, *Why, Don, didn't you tell me yourself?*

Graham said he had given the publisher's job to Weymouth "because, to save the paper, she will do things I wouldn't do." He didn't define those things. But Downie knew Weymouth had argued that it was time to merge the website and newspaper newsrooms. He also knew there was more downsizing to do on Fifteenth Street, even beyond a third buyout.

Their shared history made it impossible for Graham to tell Downie the harsher truth, that it was time for an editor more suited to the media revolution. A merger of newsrooms, a new executive editor, a new direction—these decisions would shape the *Post* for years to come. Graham had passed the decisions on to his niece. To save the paper, he had let go of it. For both men, it was a wrenching moment. The future, once theirs, now belonged to others. They wept.

A week later, at 11 o'clock on the morning of February 7, Bo Jones rose to speak at the annual "State of the *Post*" meeting in the newspaper's auditorium. In his twenty-eight years at the *Post*, as counsel, vice president, and publisher, Jones had earned the admiration reflected in the warm greeting from the crowd of four hundred staffers. His people liked him and felt an empathy for the fix he and the paper found themselves in.

That made the day no easier for him. Jones again had to tell people there would be a buyout, that some of them would be out of the job that had defined their lives. Details of the third Voluntary Retirement Incentive Program would be announced soon. Then, in his last act as publisher, he invited Don Graham to the microphone. To the surprise of those in the room, Graham said that Jones, his friend from St. Albans through Harvard and the *Post*, would move from the seventh floor to the ninth floor's corporate suite. The chairman said the Post Company had become such a complicated business that he needed Jones at his side. People had barely sorted through the implications of that graceful kick upstairs before Graham answered the obvious question.

From notes he had written for the moment, Graham read the first sentence in a playful voice: "Our rate of success with publishers named Katharine has been outstanding." Before he could go on, applause again rang through the room, only this time it happened so suddenly as to carry the energy of celebration.

"Katharine Weymouth is a member of my family, of Eugene Meyer's family, the daughter of my stalwart sister, Lally," Graham said. "But her family status is not why Katharine is getting a new responsibility . . . She is, to begin with, the only member of management who has worked for years in the top jobs with both the newspaper and the digital company, which is such a huge part of our future. And her work at the demanding job of vice president of advertising has shown everyone that she is smart, hardworking, modest, tireless, and gutsy. She listens, she learns from people, and people like her."

The critical word in those lines was the coarsest. Gutsy. If she were to "save the paper," as Graham had told Downie the week before, he knew the necessity of courage and perseverance. Now he said, "There is no misunderstanding in this room about how hard her job—which is our job—will be. As you have always done for Kay Graham, for me, and for Bo, this room will help her find a way."

Only two months before, Graham told Wall Street that his flagship newspaper ran a distant second in revenue, and was losing ground, to his Kaplan education division. Now, for the first time since Meyer bought the bankrupt rag from the playboy fool Ned McLean in 1933, a change of publishers came with a sense of urgency. Mrs. Graham, Don, and then Jones had moved into the job as routine steps of succession. But Graham had decided that business as usual would not work in this unusual time. Even people who expected him to promote Weymouth had not expected the move so soon.

"Don cannot hold back the sea," said David Von Drehle of *Time* magazine, a former *Post* editor and writer. "He has to act, and this—Katharine—is great news. She is bright as hell and fearless."

Ben Bradlee put a tight, bright lead on the story: "She's got the goods." Mary Jordan, a *Post* reporter, said Weymouth loved being a mom for her three children, had a big dog named Maxine, favored pizza joints over fancy French restaurants, and once dressed for Halloween in a white wig and black witch's pointy hat. "She's wickedly smart, she's direct, and she's determined," Jordan said. They had met twenty years earlier when Mrs. Graham asked the reporter to show her granddaughter around town. "Mrs. Graham wanted her to be happy in D.C. so she'd stay. They became really really close. I can't imagine how proud Mrs. Graham would be that Katharine has decided to take this on. And we're so lucky she has."

Mrs. Graham and her granddaughter had been together at the *Post* in 1975 when management did the work of striking press-room employees. In her autobiography, Mrs. Graham wrote of her daughter Lally pitching in: "Lally came down from New York with my granddaughter Katharine, then nine years old, who stood on a box one Saturday night in the mailroom, helping to wrap papers."

Now, in that same building, Katharine made one promise. As publisher of the *Post* as well as CEO of Washington Post Media— a new division reflecting a planned print-website merger—she said, "We will transform what used to be solely a print business in order to meet the needs of generations of readers to come. With your help, I will do my absolute best to hold up the mission that my great-grandfather started, and the Graham family has continued, to produce outstanding journalism supported by a top-notch business operation . . . Don gave me a piece of advice I've never forgotten. He said, 'Katharine, you don't have to be the smartest person in the room. You just have to surround yourself with the smartest people in the room. And then listen to them.' And that is exactly what I intend to do."

On this day, she wore her grandmother's pearl necklace and told one Kay Graham story.

A friend had once stopped by Weymouth's office and asked if she noticed that the elevators open on the lobby floor even when no one has pressed the lobby button. The doors open and no one gets off. That, she said, is Mrs. Graham getting on.

"I got chills when she told me that," Weymouth said. "And this morning, that happened for me. I was riding up from the garage level, a nervous wreck. And the elevator stopped on the lobby floor, the doors opened, and no one got on."

A week later, his own forced retirement still a secret, Downie came to the auditorium to announce buyout details. He said more than one hundred staffers would be notified that they were eligible. As Downie spoke, Henry Allen whispered, "And the *Times* is cutting a hundred jobs today."

I asked, "When was that announced?"

"Twenty minutes ago."

Here were America's two best newspapers telling two hundred big-time talents to retire. Allen later e-mailed me saying the news carried "the attar of failure, the crumbling of edifices that for a brief moment seemed to us to be a fourth wing of government, superior to the rest, and accountable to none of them, while they, of course, were accountable to us. The arrogance was spectacular twenty years ago. And now . . ." Now, calamity everywhere. Now four hundred journalists sat in the *Post*'s auditorium, dispirited.

Downie tried to be optimistic: "Don Graham believes we're one of the best-positioned news organizations in the country to survive . . ."

The sentence went on, but nothing else mattered after the chilling thought that Don Graham himself saw the *Post* in a fight for its life.

"We're doing better," Downie said, "with less." He named twenty-two staffers up for journalism's highest prizes, including the Pulitzers to be announced in April. Among the nominees: Dana Priest and Anne Hull for Walter Reed, the Metro staff for Virginia Tech, Peter Baker on the Bush administration, Steve Fainaru on private security in Iraq, Eli Saslow on sports competition, Gene Weingarten on Joshua Bell, Marc Fisher for commentary, Ann Hornaday for criticism, Ruth Marcus and David Ignatius for editorials, Bart Gellman and Jo Becker on Dick Cheney.

Nothing could be much more distasteful for a big-time editor than advising staffers that a buyout was a good deal. And how unpleasant it would be to make that pitch when you have been ordered to take the buyout yourself. Yet Downie went on: "I really do not expect another opportunity like this to come along again." For the folks in the room, "opportunity" sounded disingenuous. An opportunity? To end my career? To leave a great newspaper at age fifty and look for work?

Downie closed by adding that it was long past time for everyone to adapt to newspapers' new environment. "It means not just accepting accelerating change but helping to initiate it." Those staffers eager to adapt would be given training, support, and encouragement in learning the skill sets necessary in a multimedia news organization. For those unable or unwilling to leave the past and move toward the future, Downie had a stern message: "People who are fighting adapting, who don't like it, who think it's wrong—they really ought to go."

One listener piped up, "It's like, adapt or die?"

Downie responded with a wry smile and said, "There's life beyond *The Washington Post.*"

Later that day, a lifer e-mailed me: "Downie handled it all ham-handedly. The room is in a state of fear about these buyouts and the possibility of layoffs, partly because we're in a recession or nearly in one, and partly because there seem to be no chances to get jobs. And he dealt with buyouts so cavalierly. Remarkable that a guy who has been here 43 years had the balls to say there's life beyond *The Washington Post.*"

It would be months before the newsroom learned that Downie already had lost his job. But old hands would not be surprised. They figured that Weymouth's to-do list would begin with what her uncle called a publisher's only real job in the newsroom, the hiring of an executive editor. They knew that Phil Graham immediately hired Russ Wiggins from the *New York Times.* Katharine Graham's first major decision brought in Bradlee, and Don chose Downie. Now it was Weymouth's turn.

14.

GOD LOVES JOURNALISTS

Chris Cillizza sat clean-shaven in a downtown Starbucks. For months the *Post*'s young political junkie, who wrote "The Fix" column online, had cultivated what he called his Caucus Beard. He had resolved to keep it until the parties had chosen their presidential candidates. McCain was in, but as the Obama-Clinton war of attrition went on, the beard's future became more tenuous. As Cillizza put it, "Mrs. Fix began to sour on it." So, fresh-faced, Cillizza sipped tea, checked his BlackBerry, and nodded toward a table outside. There was a man at ease, handsome, elegantly groomed, sitting by himself and reading.

Cillizza asked, "Is that Rick Atkinson?"

"That's him," I said.

"That's the life. Sitting at a sidewalk café. Reading." A pause. "He's written two books on World War II already. One more for his 'Liberation Trilogy.' Genius, just genius."

Then Cillizza nudged me. "Look. There's who he's waiting for."

It was Katharine Weymouth.

Because neither Weymouth nor Downie had disputed news reports that she would hire a new executive editor, speculators offered up candidates, among them Rick Atkinson. And there they were, chatting in public. Sure, why not him? Impeccable *Post* credentials: twenty years at the paper, newsroom management experience, a Pulitzer-winning reporter and author.

There was another, less dramatic possibility. Maybe in the interests of due diligence, the publisher wanted Atkinson's opinions and advice. It was even possible she wanted the sun on her face as she shared an afternoon latte with an old friend.

In any case, we didn't pay much attention, mostly because of the twenty-first-century journalist's enslavement by the BlackBerry. Cillizza scrolled through e-mail arrivals, clicked on news headlines, thumbed messages to campaign aides. Every thirty seconds, "The Fix" needed a CrackBerry fix. He wrote thousands of words weekly, updating his column throughout the day and night, and yet he spoke in awed tones of the workload shouldered by the *Post*'s chief political reporter, Dan Balz.

"Covering this campaign, traveling, doing lead-alls, writing a take for 'The Trail' every day—and he's doing a book on the campaign," Cillizza said. "Dan Balz is God."

And he said, "Hillary's gone negative. Okay, but you can't go negative on 'hopes and dreams.' That's why 'the 3 a.m. phone call' works. It's an issue for Obama. Is he ready? But not on 'hopes and dreams.' "

I said, "She can't win. She ought to quit now."

"If she doesn't quit, this could go on into June, to the last primary, Puerto Rico. But who's going to tell her to quit? There's one éminence grise in the Democratic Party. And it isn't Al Gore. It's her husband. Is he going to tell her?"

As we left Starbucks, Weymouth and Atkinson were still talking.

Someday this tumult would reach Dan Balz. But while corporate types do their corporate things, reporters report. Six weeks after Weymouth's promotion, Balz was less interested in corporate intrigue than in finding out what time Amtrak left Union Station for Philadelphia. Barack Obama would make a major speech there. With eight months to go, Pincus may have thought the campaign hadn't started yet, but Balz believed this speech on race could win or lose it for Obama. Any newspaper that would own the campaign had to be there. And if that newspaper wanted to stay alive in the nation's capital, its ace political reporter damn well better be on the first train north.

Balz left home before dawn to catch the 7 a.m. Metroliner. The man never slept. No time for such foolishness. Cillizza could tell you that about him. Five days a week, Balz wrote an opinion/analysis piece for Washingtonpost.com and did the occasional video report. Whenever events demanded, he wrote for the newspaper. By plane, train, automobile, and bus, he chased what he called "the most fascinating presidential campaign ever." Through it all, he did reporting for the book on the campaign that he was coauthoring with a former *Post* star, Haynes Johnson. He did that work in his spare time. Sources said his spare time occurred every day between 2:47 a.m. and 4:12 a.m.

Like Balz, op-ed columnist Gene Robinson had not planned to work that Tuesday. But a newspaperman's life belongs more to events than to himself. The night of March 17, like Balz, he read the speech Obama would deliver at the National Constitution Center. It would take on the Reverend Jeremiah Wright problem. When Robinson decided the speech was by-damn brilliant, here's what he said, almost laughing:

"Oh, shit."

He also said:

"Now I'm going to have to write a column."

God loves journalists. Immediately following that decision, Robinson's phone rang. Caller ID flashed a Chicago area code. Earlier, Robinson had called the candidate's Chicago office with his usual pro forma interview request. Seeing the area code, he thought, *Better answer that one, Gene.* Obama's press guy asked if Robinson would like to speak to the senator after the Philadelphia speech. That night Eugene Robinson slept the good sleep of a columnist who knows at bedtime that tomorrow's column will divide the house, some for, some against, everyone paying attention.

For some people, the presidential campaign seemed long past its sell-by date. Yes, all the great themes were there—sex, race, religion, taxes. But did they have to be there every minute? If Balz had his way, yes. Obama's advisers had described the speech as "a major address on race, politics, and unifying our country." Balz would be there, just steps from the Liberty Bell, near Independence Hall.

In a small hall with an audience of maybe two hundred people, Obama stood at a plain wooden lectern and spoke plainly. His voice was a smooth, silver stream designed to move listeners from confusion to understanding. Balz sat in a press row at the rear of the small room. Television and still photographers worked from risers behind him. He sensed improvisation, the hall rented at the last moment, the speech written in answer to the previous week's controversies raised by the Reverend Wright, Obama's longtime pastor in Chicago.

Balz thought the speech's tone, flat and unemotional, was chosen by Obama not to arouse passion but to rescue himself politically. For fifteen minutes, the invited guests sat quietly, perhaps, Balz thought, made uncomfortable by Obama's examination of race. He wondered when, and if, applause would interrupt the candidate. At home, watching on television, Gene Robinson thought, *Just the right pacing, just the right tone, very much in control of himself as an orator.* He also thought, *God, he's a smart guy.* To ignore race, Obama said, would be the same mistake Reverend Wright made, "to simplify and stereotype and amplify the negative to the point that it distorts reality . . . And if we walk away now, if we simply retreat into our respective corners, we will never be able to come together and solve challenges like health care or education or the need to find good jobs for every American. Understanding . . ."

Then, for the first time, but not the last, listeners applauded.

Soon after the speech, Robinson's phone rang again, this time with Obama on the line. "My goal," the candidate told the columnist, "was to try to lift up some truth that people talk about privately but don't always talk about publicly between the races." He also told Robinson it had been his decision not to run from the Wright firestorm but to deal with it directly: "What was fascinating over the last three or four days was to see how Reverend Wright's admittedly offensive comments were packaged in sound bites in a way that didn't contribute to understanding between black and white Americans but only expanded the chasm between them. I thought it was both a challenge and an opportunity to use this moment to describe, to black and white, why there is this chasm."

This was one of those wonderful days when a columnist runs to the typing machine, and here's how Robinson started:

"Once again, the conventional wisdom proved stunningly unwise. Barack Obama was supposed to be on his heels, forced into a backpedaling, defensive crouch after racially charged remarks by his former pastor, delivered from the pulpit years ago, suddenly became the hottest story of the presidential campaign. But instead of running away, Obama issued a challenge to those who would exploit the issue of race: Bring it on."

Balz wrote that the speech "was remarkable: ambitious, lofty, gritty, honest and unnerving. In tone and substance, and in the challenge he laid down to the country about the need to somehow move beyond the racial stalemate, it was the kind of speech Americans should expect of a presidential candidate or a president."

On that Tuesday, Balz got back home at midnight, one more eighteen-hour day in a newspaperman's life.

Last time I asked, Sally Jenkins said Hillary Clinton was driving her nuts—not the candidate herself, the problems in doing the profile. Of course, a reporter going crazy is a good thing. Only those writers married to the craft care enough to be completely loony. Jenkins was one of America's best sportswriters. She occasionally wrote for the National staff as well. She was stressing out even though Clinton's man in Washington, Phillip Reines, had arranged a phone interview with the candidate, giving Jenkins fifteen minutes. That's four days short of the time necessary to do a decent job on the Redskins' left tackle. But reporters know that fifteen minutes is better than fourteen and fourteen is better than getting stiffed. So they go in with their best stuff. Which was why Sally Jenkins said, "Senator, how'd you learn to hit a curve ball?"

Curve ball? No way would Jenkins finagle an angle that allowed her to write about a "new" Clinton. She did the more difficult thing. She presented Clinton as a real person, even likable. Who knew? All it took for Jenkins to find that real person was imagination, perseverance, and a trek through the fallow fields of Iowa, which came in for four paragraphs near the end of the profile:

The Iowa that Hillary Clinton campaigns through is furrowed as far as the eye can see, an ocean of corduroyed yellow-stubble fields under a robin's-egg-blue winter sky. Her motorcade glides past clapboard farmhouses, listing barns and fat rolls of gray-yellow hay that sit in the harrowed fields like sluggish animals.

She is heading toward Correctionville.

"Prepare to Meet Your God," declares a sign posted in a vacant field brown as aged parchment.

At local halls and county fire stations, she invokes her conservative Midwestern past to people in workaday clothes sitting in folding metal chairs. With her buff-colored hair and narrow shoulders in a brown suit, she blends with the landscape. In a flat accent, she echoes all that she heard at the dinner table, talking about "American innovation" and "good jobs with rising income!" She intends to "restore the habits of our parents and grandparents" and says, "Everything I've put forward, I've said how I would pay for it."

Covering Clinton, Jenkins rode between cornfields in a van with the *Post* political reporter Anne Kornblut. The city girls saw really big farm machinery.

Jenkins: "That a combine?"

Kornblut: "Dinosaur."

They stalked the candidate from fire station to town hall. They heard the stump speech, they heard Iowans quiz Clinton. And Jenkins wrote it down.

The curve-ball question came up because Jenkins had paid close attention to baseball's minor role in Clinton's memoir. At age ten, Clinton was a tomboy who played ball in the streets of her Chicago suburb, Park Ridge. Now here came a reporter from *The Washington Post* who did not ask about Iraq or Obama. The reporter asked about hitting a curve ball, and Sally Jenkins remembered what happened then.

"She burst out laughing," Jenkins said, and the fifteen minutes were wonderful. Hugh Rodham, Clinton's father, had taught her to hit the curve. "He showed her the backspin of a fastball and the ducking topspin of a curve, and he trained her to be patient, to wait for pitches over the center of the plate and judge the break of the ball before swinging. 'It's not only a true story, but a good metaphor,' she says."

Back in New York, in her apartment, alone, Sally Jenkins approached the presidential candidate profile with all the grace, élan, and confidence of an uptown girl driving really big farm machinery down Fifth Avenue "I don't think I showered for three days," she said. "I just wrote and printed out drafts, and then cut and revised, and printed out new drafts."

No new Hillary Clinton. The one who wanted to be president was the same one who had listened to her mother and father debate politics across the dinner table, Hugh Rodham the conservative, Dorothy Rodham liberal, their daughter agreeing with each side at one point or another, even then tending to the reasonable center of every issue. Jenkins found Clinton's oldest friend, Betsy Ebeling, who said of the candidate's centrism, "It's that Midwestern thing, cheesy or all-encompassing as that sounds. You can't remove it from her fabric . . . She's triangulated, if you will."

Jenkins was happy to be done with the profile. "I didn't mean to say it wasn't fun," she said immediately after saying it wasn't fun. "But it was 'fun' like jumping off something really high is fun. And then it was really fun being finished. I thought, 'Great. Now I don't ever have to do that again, ever.'"

Readers who get stuff like this from Balz, Robinson, and Jenkins are readers who soon know what's good and what's not. If those readers are really lucky, they will find a newspaper and a website that also gives them the nakedly provocative Gene Weingarten. On a Saturday afternoon in April of 2008, two days before the Pulitzer Prizes were announced, Weingarten sent me an e-mail.

15.

"HOW IRONIC! HOW GLORIOUS!"

The Pulitzer prize judges always finish their work on a Friday night with the results to be announced the next Monday morning. But word gets out. Weingarten's e-mail to me arrived at 3:31:33 p.m. on Saturday, April 5, 2008. It came in the lowercase style that newspaper people use in casual typing.

In the subject-line box was:

"you are . . ."

And in the text box . . .

"one lucky motherfucker."

I wrote back, "if you mean what i think you mean, congratulations."

GW: "i mean that i think the pulitzer results are gonna help you explain your book. the rumor is that we are winning many. many many . . . in other words, you are lucky in that the highly erratic and crapshooty pulitzer process has coalesced somehow into a fabulous confirmation of the thesis of your book, that this is the best newspaper in america, in the final years of newspapering."

I wrote, "i've heard 6 finalists—you, fainaru, priest/hull, va tech, pearlstein, gellman. nice number, 6, but 3'd be good."

GW: "the current rumor—this could be wrong—is that we won them all."

"holy shit."

Some smart guys read about the Pulitzers and go, "Oh, whoop

dee doo." Even the best sportswriter ever, Red Smith, made light of winning one. After receiving the award for commentary in the *New York Times*, he told his pal, Tom Callahan, "At the *Times*, if you haven't won at least two of the things, you're considered a slacker." Callahan later helped Red's widow gather memories; he went to a ramshackle outbuilding that Red used as an office, and there on the floor of a closet, thrown in with fishing gear, was the Pulitzer certificate. It had been smudged by a worm.

Jack Shafer of *Slate* wrote, "Outside of a couple thousand journalists working at the top-tier newspapers that stand a chance of winning one, does anybody really care about the Pulitzer Prizes for journalism? . . . As Alexander Cockburn theorized in a 1984 *Wall Street Journal* column, the Pulitzers are a kind of show business, a 'self-validating ritual whereby journalists give each other prizes and then boast to the public about them.' "

Shafer suggested the Pulitzers could be front-page news as an honest inventory of journalism. "I'd give awards to the Worst Editorial Page, the Most Compromised Local Paper, the Most Predictable Critic, and the Most Tractable White House Reporter. Rent out Lincoln Center, trot the finalists down the red carpet, and televise the event. 'Now accepting the award for Most Pliant Reporter on the Weapons of Mass Destruction Beat, Judith Miller.' "

Okay, okay, enough. It's intramural, it's unfair to little papers, it's the blowfish of the journalism establishment puffing themselves up to within a breath of messy explosion, and, yes, on top of all that, it's crapshooty. Okay. Still, when Jim Murray, another sportswriter and Pulitzer winner, heard about Red's certificate sitting in barn dust, he said, "Mine's going to be on the roof of my house, in a spotlight."

Whatever else they may be, the Pulitzers are symbols of what a jury of journalists perceived to be the best American newspaper work done during the previous year. That was why, from his office on the morning of April 7, Downie called home to his wife, Janice.

"I have something to tell you," he said.

"Yes?"

"We've won some Pulitzers."

"Great," she said. "One, two?"

"I hear we won six," he said.

"Oh, my . . ."

"All right. I have to go. Bye."

When the good news reached Pat O'Shea, Downie's assistant, she thought, *How ironic! How glorious!* She knew the bad news that had been delivered to her boss by Bo Jones two months earlier—news still held secret while Katharine Weymouth settled into the publisher's job.

That morning, David Maraniss came smiling into the Caribou coffee shop at Fifteenth and M. He had been an invisible hand in the Walter Reed series, editing Anne Hull as always and working for the first time with Dana Priest. On another story, the Virginia Tech horror, Maraniss's five-thousand-word narrative had raised the coverage from flood-the-zone excellence to a masterwork of breaking news. When I said, "A good day coming," he responded, "The greatest day in the history of *The Washington Post*."

In her office, *Post* ombudsman Deborah Howell said, "It's fucking unbelievable."

I said, "Six?"

"Yes, six. The only time any paper's won more is the *Times* with seven. And that was after 9/11. This is different. The *Post* won in features, commentary, breaking news. Everything. Every discipline. Classic journalism."

I quoted Pincus to Howell. "Walter says the paper has lost one hundred thirty thousand readers, which he attributes, in some ways, to the newsroom chasing prizes. Which would you want, the hundred thirty thousand readers or six Pulitzers?"

"Readers!"

Not knowing Downie's future already had been decided, she said, "There are now two schools of thought on Len. One, it's the perfect time to go. Two, they couldn't make him go. Even if I didn't feel Katharine breathing down my neck, I'd go—now! You get a feeling. You know when your time is done. Len's still good at what he does. But! It! Is! Time! Wait six weeks, give her time to get a new editor ready, take the buyout."

In Ben Bradlee's twenty-six years running the newsroom, the *Post*'s news staff won twelve Pulitzers. In Downie's seventeen years, it now had won twenty-five. Maybe, as critics have said, the prizes are traded politically among elite journalistic tribes. With fewer newspapers doing long, hard, expensive stories, competition seemed limited to the *Times*, the *Post*, the *Wall Street Journal*, and the *Los Angeles Times*. And priorities are out of order if papers allot resources to prize-winning projects rather than the daily news that matters in readers' lives. But only the harshest critic would argue against the substance of the winning entries and the talents of the journalists who produced them. For good reasons, editors and reporters considered Pulitzers the ultimate validation of their work.

At 3:11 p.m., Downie stood outside his office facing maybe three hundred people gathered in the newsroom. Don Graham took up his customary Pulitzer-day place, in the middle of all those people, leaning against a pillar, silent, almost out of sight. "This is a historic day for our newsroom," Downie said. "*The Washington Post* has won six Pulitzer prizes."

To successive rounds of sustained applause, shouts, and hurrahs, he began, "Anne Hull and Dana Priest, with photographer Michel DuCille, have won the Pulitzer Gold Medal for Public Service for their articles exposing the mistreatment of severely wounded soldiers at Walter Reed hospital." And then he named the metropolitan staff for local coverage of breaking news on the Virginia Tech shootings . . . Bart Gellman and Jo Becker for national affairs reporting on Vice President Dick Cheney . . . Steve Fainaru for international affairs reporting on the private war being waged in Iraq by armed security forces . . . Gene Weingarten for feature writing on violin virtuoso Joshua Bell's performance at a Metro subway stop, and Steve Pearlstein for commentary in columns foreshadowing the collapse of the American economy.

For an hour and a half, the winners took bows.

It was wonderful.

And yet . . .

Even the celebrants knew the glory was ephemeral. When Priest spoke of the lessons of the Walter Reed reporting, she had fun with the image of Anne Hull—the writerly half of the team—"set like a cat ready to pounce on my dull verbs and predictable adjectives." Then she said, "The lesson that remains foremost in my mind is that investigative reporting and the whole very imprecise thing that we do here every day is essential to the kind of country that we are and we cannot be thrown off the course by layoffs or early retirements or the uncertainty of where or how our revelations are going to reach readers. And we have to stay focused, especially reporters. If we forsake the responsibility given to us in the Constitution, then people that we write about, people like the army specialist who lived with the cockroaches and the mold in Building 18, will go unnoticed and unhelped."

Hull wished her mother could have been with her on such a happy day. Victoria Desmond Hull, her daughter's constant reader, died of an aneurysm in 1995 while Hull was at Harvard on a Nieman Fellowship. "My mom would have said today"—laughing now—"'Anne, just please brush your hair.'" And Hull nodded to the silent man by the newsroom pillar: "Don, thanks for keeping the lights on for as long as possible. Please, keep them on."

After his first stint in Iraq, Fainaru told the crowd, he thought a long while before agreeing to go back. When he said yes, managing editor Phil Bennett responded, "Great. You're sick." Fainaru said, "I thought, 'Thanks a lot for rolling out the welcome wagon.' And Phil said, 'No, no, I mean that's totally sick, like the kids say.'" News of his Pulitzer reached Fainaru at the funeral of a mercenary he had written about; that man and four others had been kidnapped, tortured, and killed, though the bodies were discovered only in the last month. After the ceremony, Fainaru told me he was not going to Iraq again. "I'm done there," he said.

Gene Weingarten did a comic routine on his Joshua Bell piece. He said that Bell, on their first meeting, had asked what could go wrong at such a stunt. Well, Weingarten told him, we can't assure crowd control, and it is possible "your three-million-dollar Stradivarius could wind up in pieces no larger than the human pinkie toenail." More likely, though, the writer told the virtuoso, he would "suffer the most humiliating hour of his life," as harried commuters at L'Enfant Plaza hurried past him to their governmental cubicles without recognizing the beauty of his music.

"And though he would try to forget it," Weingarten said, "the rejection would remain in his brain like this pulsating nugget of self-doubt that would haunt him for the rest of his life. It would be there at every performance until critics began to notice that something indefinable was missing from the great Joshua Bell. And, his self-confidence totally eroded, his career would collapse like a soufflé in an earthquake. Eventually he'd find himself back at L'Enfant Plaza—with a bottle of gin in his pants—and a sign that says, 'Will play for food.'

"So Josh looked at me and said, 'Sounds like fun. What the hell.'"

On a historic day, there was still the sense that the moment, affirming and thrilling, was yet only a moment, soon gone. Maybe Don Graham recognized that more profoundly than anyone else. He did not speak to the crowd during the fifth-floor ceremony. As always, he leaned against that pillar and gave the Pulitzer stage to the people who did the work. Now, in his ninth-floor office, he sat briefly for an interview but said little beyond "Terrific day, terrific . . ." And, in a knowing nod to his friend, added, "a wonderful day for Len Downie."

When better than in a happy time to ask the hard question? So I said, "Is the paper in a struggle to survive?"

Graham said, "What do you mean?"

"It's not news that newspapers everywhere are in a bad way," I said. "Like, when is anyone going to figure out how to make money online?"

Graham quoted Warren Buffett's right-hand man. "Charlie Munger says he has learned not to waste his time on things he can't know."

I moved on. "Bart Gellman, thanking everyone for his Pulitzer, quoted a colleague as saying, 'The Grahams have operated this paper as an act of patriotism.' Do you feel that way?"

Graham sat in silence for ten seconds.

"This," he said, "is a business."

A long pause.

"It's a business, and it's something more."

"What's the 'more'?"

Without answering, he bounced up from his chair because his sister, Lally Weymouth, Katharine's mother, had entered the room. "Lally!" he said. Graham hugged her and they made small talk. I said my thanks and started to walk back to the party. As I left,

I heard the chairman say, "Oh, that's all right, Lally, I was only maintaining my reputation as a terrible interview."

That day, between the champagne and strawberries, Deborah Howell said an intriguing thing about Katharine Weymouth. "Bo Jones is cautious," he said. "Katharine, less so." Barely had the echoes of celebration died away before Weymouth confirmed Howell's judgment.

Part IV

"DUDE! COOL!"

16.

"HONORED, FLATTERED . . .
AND TERRIFIED"

Weymouth and Downie answered media queries about the executive editor's job by saying they were, quote, discussing the future,
unquote. As deceptions go, this one lacked only a loudspeaker on
the side of a van bellowing, "DOWNIE'S GONE!"

It was not as if Weymouth needed time to think about it. The
publisher's job had long been hers. Friends knew it as early as the
summer of 2007. "And we really knew ten years before that, if you
know what I mean," one said. Weymouth quit the law then for the
Post. In the men-only world of the 1950s, her mother, Lally, had
been shunted aside in favor of the first-born son, Don. His four
children never showed an interest in the family businesses. That
left Don and Katharine as the last Grahams at the *Post*.

Weymouth's job in selecting a new editor would be more difficult than either her grandmother's or Don's. Kay Graham knew of
her husband's admiration for Ben Bradlee, and she moved quickly
to get him back at the newspaper. Don's appointment of Downie
was a logical step in their partnership. But it was no longer so simple. An editor's primary responsibility was no longer the production of holy-shit newspaper stories. Now it was about survival, and
survival depended less on journalism than on mastery of the
Internet.

The week after the Pulitzer party, Weymouth began her search.

The next week, with the American Society of Newspaper Editors convening in Washington, she interviewed possibilities. Then, on April 22, Rupert Murdoch, the new owner of the *Wall Street Journal*, accepted the resignation of his managing editor, Marcus Brauchli. Don Graham called Brauchli's predecessor, Paul Steiger, for a scouting report that he passed on to his niece.

While real-news publications quoted the discussing-the-future diversion, the *Onion* pushed up against the truth. The *Onion* was a parody of newspapers. It was printed under contract by the *Post* and was there for the taking on a rack at the fifth-floor newsroom entrance. The month after the Pulitzers, reporters and editors coming to work saw this headline:

DYING NEWSPAPER TREND BUYS NATION'S NEWSPAPERS THREE MORE WEEKS

The *Onion* reported that so many features had been written on the demise of newspapers that "the outmoded form of media" would live another twenty-one days. Downie was quoted saying, "People really seem to identify with these moving, 'end-of-an-era'-type pieces. It's nice to see that the printed word is still, at least for now, the most powerful medium for reporting on the death of the printed word." The story's last sentence was "Downie added that the poignant farewell Op-Ed he recently penned was so well received that he will be able to hold onto his job for up to six more days."

Wrong—but only by a month. On June 23, Downie resigned. By then, Weymouth already had chatted up one candidate in a venue aptly chosen for a private meeting of journalists—the Off the Record bar in the Hay-Adams Hotel. There she met Marcus Brauchli.

Graham was no longer a young man. If he intended for the family to retain control of the *Post*, it was time to test Weymouth. Near her desk, draped over a chair, was a pink sweatshirt that was once her grandmother's. It bore the legend "Presidents Come & Go, But the Post is Here to Stay." If Weymouth did well, the company's CEO chair would someday be hers. The test was: Save the paper.

For the first time since Ned McLean was locked away in a psychiatric hospital, the *Post* faced a financial crisis that threatened its existence. As bad as 2007 had been for the *Post*—a 2 percent profit—2008 figured to be its first money-losing year since the company went public in 1971. The first time we met, I asked Weymouth, "Did Don literally say 'save the paper'?"

She replied carefully. "Umm, that's probably a translation. Don's charge to me is more comparable to something my grandmother said: 'In order to do good, you need to do well.' Our goal is to remain profitable so we can support the kind of news gathering that we traditionally have done. That is the mission he has assigned me."

And how did she feel about it?

"Honored, flattered . . ."

A small smile.

"And terrified."

She had reason to be anxious. Her uncle was a newspaper person, she was not. He could have waltzed into the executive suite; instead, he did the grunt work of reporting and editing for three years. By moving through every production and business department, he gained credibility, earned standing, and learned the way newspaper people think. He didn't have to be a cop, not in a violent city, but he did it to understand the city his newspaper served. In the doing, he had heard all the questions and knew where to find answers. But Weymouth, a neophyte, had not yet learned even the questions. She didn't know what she didn't know.

Almost twenty years before, she had decided against working as a reporter. Reporting "didn't feel right to me," Weymouth told me. "Who am I to pretend I can write? And Don said it's not required." Yet she had no shortage of opinions on the *Post*'s news operation. A former *Post* reporter, Lloyd Grove, doing a profile of Weymouth for *Portfolio* magazine, was with her on a get-acquainted meeting with the Style staff. To a reporter who said a front page filled with politics and government was boring, Weymouth responded, "I think the evidence will tell us you're right. There are days when I look at the front page and think we've done a better job, and there are days that I think, 'You must be kidding me!'" And: "There are days on Saturday that I think maybe somebody is trying to not have people buy the paper."

She had contemplated moving her office to the fifth-floor newsroom, against the advice of her predecessor, Bo Jones. "Bo hates my idea," she said, adding, "I don't know how many of you have been to the official publisher's office on the seventh floor. It's like a dreadful funeral coffin." Grove also quoted Don Graham as being in favor of a move to the newsroom. "Katharine came up on the business side," he said, "but she loves the newsroom and the people in it, and by being in the middle of it, she'll learn a lot, and they'll learn a lot about her."

Presumably, they would learn what she liked. "Do you remember the rural-dentist photo, a month ago or whatever?" she asked the Style folks. "There was that elderly woman with, like, no teeth, dying in bed, and he was treating her? That was a good story, and I'm sorry to be so horrible—I'm hoping it was no one in the room who picked the photo—but there were better photos! I went on the website and—not to do a Sam Zell thing—they have the same dentist with a beautiful old-fashioned truck and, no kidding, a dalmatian on the hood!"

Grove also quoted Weymouth on Zell. The billionaire owner of the Tribune Company had snapped, "Fuck you," to a photographer who said Zell would prefer stories about puppy dogs to reports from Iraq. "Sam Zell may be a loon with Tourette's syndrome," Weymouth said, laughing, "but he's not crazy. To some degree, it is puppies and Iraq."

None of this could have been encouraging to reporters, editors, and photographers accustomed to *Post* business executives minding their own business. I was not there, and I found no one who would talk about the meeting. For Weymouth, the day was part of a honeymoon period during which the newsrooms had reason to hope for the best from a woman who was a Harvard graduate and number two in her class at Stanford Law. She first worked in Washington at Williams & Connolly, long the *Post*'s law firm of choice. From there, she moved to the newspaper and website. She said the publisher's job came to her by evolution, perhaps finally decided by her insistence on merging print and online.

She said, "Don felt, because of my experience on both sides of the river, as well as my perceived neutrality—I'm in the family, I'm not a print girl, I'm not an online girl—everybody would understand I'm somebody who wants everybody to win."

She gave the newspaper its due, but her praise sounded leaden. "One million people read the daily newspaper, two million on Sundays. Print will be around a long time because you can carry it, you can fold it, you can cut it out. It's a package of 'Here's everything you need to know that happened yesterday.'"

That came off so totally yesterday, especially when her voice rose with enthusiasm as she said, "Online is an integral and critical part of our future. The Web gives us specific information, like with Cars.com, Wikipedia, restaurants, movies, what's happening in town right now, all the breaking news. As a news organization, we need to think of ourselves as a 24/7 operation because we're in an era when we can't hold a story for tomorrow's paper. Get it out on the Web now, get it to mobile devices, to iTouch and Kindle or whatever device they come up with next. Then run a story with analysis in the next day's paper. That's the world our readers are in."

Ben Bradlee, the editor hired by Weymouth's grandmother thirty-three years earlier, had been out of the office for almost three weeks. That was unusual. Since his retirement in 1991, he had missed one day's scheduled work with a cold. But now he walked slowly, leaning on a cane. "Hi, pal," he said, and the words were an effort, spoken with his head down and his eyes turned up to see me. Suddenly, he was an old man.

"It's the first time he's ever been really sick," said Carol Leggett, his assistant. He had undergone emergency gallbladder surgery two weeks before and had been in the hospital nine days. Then he developed an infection that put him back in the hospital. "Now," Leggett said, "he's impatient with how slowly he's recovering." Downie had seen him that morning. "He looked bad. He has never been worried about his health. Now he is."

Bradlee said he had suffered a "tremendous gut ache," which turned out to be the bad gallbladder. "Got a big scar there now."

I asked, "How'd you get it infected?"

"I misbehaved."

Surgery at eighty-seven is a good reason to stay home, but he had come to work. Two nights later, the University of Illinois was to honor his life in journalism.

"You going to that dinner?" I asked.

"Sure," he said.

Two nights later there he was—the self-assured, sexy Benjamin Crowninshield Bradlee walking in the ocean surf, wind tousling his hair, his silky white shirt falling open to show his bronzed chest. It was an Annie Leibovitz photograph projected onto a huge screen at the dinner. It showed Bradlee as a younger man—only eighty-three.

During the evening, the dinner guests saw Bradlee in photographs as a dashing young naval officer, friend of Kennedys, and journalist interviewing Castro. From the lectern came talk of history and newspapers and Bradlee's place in both. Bob Woodward said Jason Robards read for the Bradlee role in *All the President's Men*, only to say of the script, "I can't do this. Did you read this? All this guy ever says is 'Where's the fucking story?'" Until, finally, Robards boiled the role down to finding different and elegant ways to say, "Where's the fucking story?!?" He won an Oscar.

In her turn, Weymouth spoke of her grandmother's first big hire. "In the best decision of her life, she made Ben Bradlee her editor." And not only that, the new publisher said, "I believe she let him keep his left one."

At evening's end, Bradlee rose to thank each speaker with a hug and a smile. He spoke only briefly but his voice was strong. "I love this business," he said. "Of course, I love the *Post*."

Then he said, "My God."

And walked back to his seat.

He did not use a cane.

Even before Downie announced his retirement on June 23, a dozen editors' names had been in the rumor mill. As evidence that the decision would be Weymouth's, word was she had bypassed two candidates who had Graham as their longtime patron—Phil Bennett and op-ed columnist David Ignatius.

Rick Atkinson told her no, perhaps that afternoon when Chris Cillizza saw them at Starbucks. The *New York Times* Washington bureau chief, Dean Baquet, wasn't interested. *Newsweek*'s Jon Meacham never fit her idea of the necessary visionary newspaperman. She spoke with Steve Coll, who said no; at the urging of friends, he reconsidered, only to pass again.

That left two candidates. One was Jonathan Landman, a deputy managing editor running the *New York Times* website. ("Kicking our ass online," Weymouth told a friend.) The other was the Off the Record man, Marcus Brauchli.

I asked Weymouth what she wanted in an editor.

"Four things. One clearly is the intellectual capacity, the journalistic experience, credibility in the field. That's a given. We want to maintain our standards and our journalistic expertise.

"Two, a leadership ability, a charisma, an ability to communicate well with the troops. That is in many ways more important than it ever has been because a lot of what we're doing is hard and you need somebody who's going to say, 'We're going to take this hill, and here's how we're going to do it.'

"Three, the editor has to be someone who isn't exclusively focused on putting out tomorrow's paper—someone at the executive level who thinks of us as a news organization that uses the Web, provides news to mobile devices, someone who isn't exclusively focused on putting out tomorrow's paper but is thinking about the whole.

"Finally, that person also must have an ability to think strategically. In a world of diminishing resources, how do we best allocate our resources? That's something I'm not sure was required in the past. Tomorrow's paper is incredibly important, but we need someone who's really thinking, 'Let's make sure we get this up on the Web now,' 'Let's get it out on mobile.' We need someone who's thinking about the whole."

As Weymouth spoke, I thought of Downie. He made her grandmother's paper better than it had ever been. And now—now it's Web this, iPhone that, and, oh, yes, you bet, tomorrow's paper is really really really important, in fact it's so important that we'll get to it right after we do these four-line iTouch abstracts.

So I said, "Where did Len fail on those things?"

"I don't ..." She paused, then said, "He is amazing, and so I think it would make more sense for me . . ." Another pause. "We have been doing all of those things, frankly, and Len has been doing all those things. He has taken the newsroom from nine hundred-ish people to seven hundred-ish with most of our readers recognizing no detrimental impact on the newspaper. Most don't even know that we've done that. And he's managed to maintain, for the most part, morale in the newsroom. And obviously main tain our standards. In a year when you cut back on resources and you win six Pulitzer prizes, that's pretty impressive. So I'm not sure Len failed on any of them . . . It's less about where Len failed and more about what are the strengths that are going to be really important going forward."

She remembered an online piece written by Metro columnist Marc Fisher. "There's a quote about Len. Let me find it." At her computer, Weymouth printed out a Fisher tribute to his old boss and read aloud: " 'The work of reporting the news is not terribly complicated. But it requires an editor of unbending spine to send the message to reporters and subeditors that we are here to speak truth to power, to comfort the afflicted and afflict the comfortable.' " She read those last seven words as if they were italicized. "A ter-rific quote," she said.

I was confounded by two pieces of our conversation. First, it was remarkable to hear the publisher of *The Washington Post* say she believed "most of our readers" did not notice the decline in qual-ity that came with staff reductions. The readers a publisher should most value, the loyal subscribers re-upping for years, certainly would notice the paper gone limp. Second, she seemed to believe the afflict-the-comfortable line was original to Marc Fisher. The words were written by Finley Peter Dunne almost a century ago. Old news to people who know newspapers.

On July 7, Weymouth announced Brauchli's hiring. There was no hoorah in the *Post* newsroom. Not so much because staffers doubted Brauchli's ability; he was a veteran foreign correspondent who had reported from twenty countries in fifteen years and in six years had risen quickly through management ranks at the *Wall Street Journal* to reach the top newsroom job in 2005. But the problems were so complex that had Herbert Bayard Swope materialized at Weymouth's side, the reaction likely would have been "Poor Herb, such a mess he has to straighten out." Also, for the first time in forty-three years, the *Post*'s executive editor would come from outside the company because, Weymouth said, "I thought that we could benefit from someone who would come in and look at what we do with fresh eyes."

Brauchli arrived as partially damaged goods, the latest in a long string of good newspaper people bruised by contact with Murdoch. A condition of the *Journal*'s sale had been the creation of a five-person committee designed to protect the paper's integrity against the new owner's habitual editorial intrusions. But rather than con-test Murdoch's immediate intervention—he gave a News Corp. executive, Robert Thomson, last say in the newsroom—Brauchli left the *Journal* quietly. The *New York Times* reported that he left with as much as $3 million in severance pay. Brauchli said only, "I have come to believe the new owners should have a managing edi-tor of their choosing." *Slate*'s Jack Shafer dipped his pen in an astringent before writing a paragraph of advice to the *Post*'s new editor:

> Unless you want your staff to think of you as the guy who zipped his lips for $3 million, may I suggest that you say what Harold Evans and every other editor swindled by Murdoch has ultimately said: I knew Murdoch was capable of lies, monstrous lies, heinous lies, but I thought it would be different with me. I was naive, which is hard for a journalist to admit. I don't want the Murdoch blood money to jinx me, so I'm giving all $3 million of it to my alma mater, Columbia, to endow a chair in his name in the psychology department to study congenital liars.

A former colleague, Dean Starkman, also questioned Brauchli's surrender to Murdoch. Starkman wrote an essay for the *Columbia Journalism Review* in which he asked, "Had News Corp. taken over Washington Post Co. under the same terms and moved Thomson into the newsroom, would Downie have handed over control of the *Post*'s legacy without recourse to a committee that was put in place to protect his autonomy? Or would he have stood up to Murdoch? How about Ben Bradlee?"

Soon after Brauchli did a get-to-know-you tour of the newsroom, Henry Allen e-mailed me a reaction:

> Brauchli seems to be a very smart, funny, and confident man who does not commit the old senior Posties' error of confusing himself with a cabinet secretary. It struck me that he's interested in being custodian of a media organization, not a myth. He also has the wry alertness to the ways of the sophisticated world that was one of the better aspects of the Bradlee years. At no time did I catch a whiff of that arrogance from him, that post-Watergate triumphalism of the Times and The Post. It's possible that The Wall Street Journal didn't share in it, and he never picked it up.

I was never an editor or a publisher. I was a reporter. At this melancholy moment in the newspaper revolution, I wanted to know what old reporters felt when they were told it was time to go away. I also wanted to know what young reporters felt when they had no idea what was next. I talked to Annie Groer, Tony Reid, Eli Saslow, Rachel Beckman, James Hohmann, and Len Downie. They told me.

17.

ANNIE, TONY, ELI, RACHEL, JAMES, AND LEN

Annie Groer didn't want to leave the only work she had ever done, but she was fifty-five and Weymouth frightened her with one line in a memo on the *Post*'s third round of buyouts. "I am sorry to say," the publisher wrote, "that we cannot rule out layoffs." After talking to her editors in the Home section, Groer went to Downie. Glumly, she reported, "Nobody threw themselves on the floor and said, 'Please, please, Annie, don't go.'"

The question for her became elemental: Should she take the buyout with its generous benefits or risk it all by staying? She had seen public hangings in which reporters were reassigned to jobs designed to make them so miserable they quit. "I'm way too old for night police in Loudoun County," Groer said. Or she could simply be laid off. Either way, she would lose the buyout program's pension enhancement, health coverage, and lump-sum payout. In the end, she recognized the cold truth. "There was nothing really 'voluntary' about the buyout."

She would go.

Tony Reid might welcome the buyout. At fifty-one, the copy editor was no longer the bright young man on the way up, and he considered the possibility that he had become a grump with enemies. It was bad enough that he had been passed over for newsroom jobs he wanted. Worse, he was bored in the one he had. He imagined reinventing himself as "an itinerant William Zinsser, teaching college kids to write." If he stayed at the paper, he could slog it out to a real retirement age. But Weymouth's L-word played in his brain, too.

Reid thought he would go.

Then came a day when Reid told me, "Got the package." He meant the data on payouts. "But they had to recalculate everyone's lump sum because the number was too low—which, if you're recalculating, is better than having to adjust the other way and facing threats to burn down the building." Reid missed qualifying for his full pension by a year and would petition for a break. "If they'll give me the year," he said, "I'll probably go, and I may go, anyway." With the full pension, it would be easier to get a job in the real world. "So I don't know what the hell to do. But I really want to get out of here, and that'll probably sway it in the end."

A month later, there were dozens of empty desks throughout the newsrooms on the fourth and fifth floors. "A wasteland," Frank Ahrens said. Through the first half of the year, the *Post*'s newspaper division lost $15.7 million—a steep fall from the $32.7 million profit in the same six months of 2007. Groer hadn't finished packing when Bo Jones stopped by on his morning send-off rounds. She described a "sweetly awkward conversation" that devolved into how hard it is to get rid of books; she later wrote, "People, well, that's another story." Managing editor Phil Bennett did his own farewell circuit. "You all right?" he said, and Groer lied, "I'm okay." The ME said, "You've been a huge part of this place." He shook her hand, and then moved on, all in under ten seconds.

An invitation showed up that day, announcing a party at Stoney's bar: "They Took the Cash, Now Watch Them Get Smashed." Groer called the buyout "the sweetest get-the-hell-out retirement deal in American journalism today." The package was financed by a *Post* pension fund that long ago invested in Warren Buffett's Berkshire Hathaway and was now worth more than $1.8 billion. Still, the get-the-hell-out part left the crowd uncertain if they should celebrate or commiserate. "The noise level made real conversation impossible," Groer wrote, "but that was not the point of this gathering, where from 6:30 p.m. until after midnight, the smartass journalist's facade we wear so casually gave way to unabashed mush."

Tony Reid worked his way through the overheated crush to the back of the room in search of relief. He said, "It was like a sauna up there, and kinda sloppy. People spilling their sweat and their drinks. I think I had as much vodka on my right wrist as I did in my mouth." He found colleagues Andy Mosher, Bill O'Brian, and Don Beard, all copy editors at one time or another. "I came to think in my time at the *Post* that people like us made the difference—we were as good at our jobs as the best reporters and writers were at theirs, and I don't think that's true at lesser papers. And here we were now, loud, drunk, stunned, and pouring out decades of emotion." At night's end, Reid said, "As afraid as most of us were about the uncertain future, and as sad as we were to leave, we felt worse for the people who had to walk back into the building on Monday. There was a lot of talk about that at the Stoney's party—because the party at the *Post* was, more clearly than ever, over."

In a way, it was over for Don Graham, too, though he would be going nowhere. He knew what the newsroom staff did not yet know, that Len Downie would be among those bought out. This buyout cut deeper into the group of editors and reporters of Graham's generation—so much so that he opened wide his arms to the crowd and declared, "These are my people." He did it with tears in his eyes.

The little girl Annie Groer had ridden her bicycle to deliver the *Washington Daily News*. Now, for the first time since then, she went three days without touching a newspaper. Each morning the *Post* came to her apartment door. She brought it in, but did not unfold it, read it, or look at it. The *Post* had asked her to get the hell out. "Most of us think of newspapers as a calling instead of a job," she said. "I don't know if I'm ready to go over to the dark side." The dark side, for newspaper people, is the world outside a newsroom. "But then I say, 'Don't be an idiot! You're a writer, write!' Will write for lunch!"

She fell in love with journalism when she realized that working on the college newspaper got you a parking spot and empowered you to ask important people important questions. "I was alight with idealism and enthusiasm," she said. "I'd discovered a profession where you could be a snoop and get paid for it."

She sat at her kitchen table, the floor covered with boxes. In those boxes were scraps of paper, the debris of a newspaper life. "Looks like I've been doing tax returns for the Seven Dwarfs," she said. She was a case, Annie Groer. Talked in laugh lines, wrote that way when she and Ann Gerhart teamed up for the *Post*'s gossip column, "The Reliable Source." "We called it 'investigative gossip,'" she said. "We had two rules. It's gotta be true. And it's gotta be dishy."

Don Graham had a habit of introducing her by saying, "This is Annie Groer, she does 'The Reliable Source,' and she knows everything!" "At those moments," she said, "I'd think, 'No, but you do know everything and if you'd spill, we wouldn't have to do a lick of work for months.'"

A sigh here. "But that wasn't going to happen."

Then a sly smile. "His mother, on the other hand, was ever so helpful."

Many a time, when Kay Graham was offended by the behavior of a Washington panjandrum, she invited Groer and Gerhart to her finely appointed private luncheon room. The "Reliable Source" tandem, if not precisely fish out of water, noticed a class distinction in Mrs. Graham's presence. "We looked like unmade beds," Groer said, such being a reporter's natural state, the tatters more obvious alongside Mrs. Graham's haute couture. "And she had a tendency to view us as the hired help."

How perfect for gossipmongers that the most powerful woman in American newspaper history should find their work both entertaining and useful. Groer and Gerhart feasted on "the rampant bad behavior of people in power." A wicked laugh now in remembrance of how they wrote the column: "Rather than a bazooka, we used the stiletto. That, or an ivory-handled ice pick."

On March 25, 1998, a simple fact was weapon enough to cause trembling in high places. "Leaving No Tome Unturned," said the headline running with "The Reliable Source." The Groer/Gerhart lead went, "Is independent counsel Ken Starr interested in Monica Lewinsky's taste in literature?" The columnists reported that Starr, then investigating the Clinton-Lewinsky shenanigans, had demanded that a Washington bookstore, Kramerbooks & Afterwords, turn over its records of purchases by Lewinsky, the former White House intern then enamored of the president.

They wrote, "One of several books Lewinsky bought there is 'Vox,' Nicholson Baker's 1992 novel of yuppie phone sex between a man in a Western city and a woman in the East." Groer and Gerhart identified no source for their reporting. "Somebody I knew," Groer said, "and whose word I could take to the bank." (Hello, Mrs. Graham?)

Starr's people were furious at the leak, booksellers claimed sales were privileged information, civil libertarians rose up in defense of privacy. Even the *Post*'s managing editor was upset. Steve Coll thought Groer and Gerhart should give the story to National, then panting in pursuit of any Lewinsky-Clinton connection.

Groer said, "It was three o'clock in the afternoon when I got Coll's call. When he said he really wanted it, I said no. His people would have called all over hell and the story would have been lost to somebody else. 'So you're using it?' he said, and I told him, 'You bet. In our column tomorrow.'"

Next, Groer and Gerhart tracked down the *Vox* author, Nicholson Baker. They quoted him dutifully and with absolute glee. "Starr should get down on his kneepads," Baker said, "and beg the country's pardon for undermining the Constitution in this way."

Groer had come to the *Post* in July of 1995 after twenty-one years as a Washington correspondent for the *Orlando Sentinel*. She had sat through enough committee hearings on urban blight to say, "One more, I'd kill myself." She met Gerhart at a get-to-know-you dinner. Groer said, "When Ann ordered gin and a rare steak, I thought, 'Ah, a woman of appetites. This is excellent.'"

For ten years, they did the column five times a week. Groer loved the work until she had been to too many parties under too many deadlines. She moved to the Home section, content until the third round of buyouts. Not long after taking the buyout, she sat at her kitchen table and gently rubbed her hands against her cheeks. Even as she ached from leaving the paper, she found no fault in Don Graham. She had seen his tears. She knew he did what he had to do. "I hope, whatever happens," she said, "that Don finds a way that *The Washington Post* can always be *The Washington Post*."

In the meantime, she had learned one valuable lesson working in the Home section.

"If you want to sell an old house," she said, "you gotta renovate it, refurbish it."

Yes?

"So the first thing I did with the buyout cash was get a face lift."

She laughed and she smiled, raising her chin a click. She was ready for the real world.

The two kids weren't going anywhere. Eli Saslow and Rachel Beckman even got married.

Saslow wrote features in National, Beckman did general assignments in Style. They first spoke at Syracuse University when he signaled his interest by charging her two dollars instead of three to attend a kegger. Then, for a couple of years in Washington, poor Eli, clueless as any young man ever was, missed all of Rachel's hints that he should propose. On Valentine's Day, 2007, he did a candle-lit dinner. She wore a black party dress (over items of red lace).

"Presents?" Rachel said.

She gave him a bag of chocolate-covered espresso beans. He gave her . . . a gift certificate for a hot stone massage. Rachel stared at the certificate. She looked at Eli. She waited for the moment. She hoped he would drop to one knee. Eli looked at her, confused by her silence.

That's when she started crying.

On June 15th, she followed a cheerful trail of red carnations leading to their apartment door. This time she wore a white University of Oregon hoodie. Eli poured her a glass of wine and said, "I was going to do this during dessert, but I couldn't wait." He held a small box in his trembling hand as he got down on a knee.

"I love you so much," he said. "And I was just wondering if maybe you might want to marry me?"

So dreary were the industry prospects, of course, that the poor souls working at newspapers couldn't be sure they'd have a paper to work for the next morning. The rabbi conducting their marriage ceremony understood that and understood reporters. With Rachel and Eli under the huppah, Rabbi Ariel Stone said, "The two of you share a wonderful passion for *tikkun olam*, the 'repair of the world's brokenness.' You also share a determination to celebrate possibility and to create it out of uncertainty. That you have a certain tolerance for uncertainty is clear enough from your choice of vocation! Where so many see only the uncertainty of the future of newspapers, you have both plunged in, with all the passion for justice that you share, because you are both convinced that through journalism you will realize your own potential to make the world a better place. May each of you find your own power to act in the world enhanced and strengthened because you are in it together. May you always share your passion for justice, may you always see hope in the uncertainty of the future."

After a honeymoon, Mr. and Mrs. Saslow returned to the *Post* to work forever. Or until further notice, whichever came first.

After breakfast one morning, Walter Pincus said, "Hohmann."

As we stood in the middle of Fifteenth Street, cars materialized from both directions and seemed to accelerate once they determined we were geezer jaywalkers.

"What?" I said.

"James."

However many times for however many years Pincus had negotiated this perilous passage from the Madison Hotel to the *Post*, I hoped for one more.

"He's the future," Pincus said.

The great man then led me through the traffic.

The Saslows, man and wife, had chosen reporting's future because, like Bob Woodward, they couldn't imagine anything better. Now James Hohmann had to decide.

The erstwhile precocious publisher of the *Hohmann Times*, now twenty years old and a rising senior at Stanford University, understood the history of newspapers as well as today's sorry state of the business. History suggested that no one ever sought out newspaper work to get rich. That was still true, though newspapers added a twist of the knife: they can make you poor. They could eliminate your job, lay you off, buy you out, and generally demonstrate that journalism was comatose, kaput, dead, and -30-. Even the *Doonesbury* cartoon strip's redoubtable newspaper reporter, Rick Redfern of *The*

Washington Post, had the dreaded uh-oh moment. He was told, "Grab the buyout! You can re-invent yourself!! Rick Redfern, blogger!!!"

Garry Trudeau's chronicler at the *Post*, the redoubtable Gene Weingarten, had considered taking the current buyout himself. Like Annie Groer and Tony Reid, he was fiftysomething. He was both energetic and ambitious enough to think of doing books, screenplays, even a comic strip in partnership with his son. But when the *Post* did some financial juggling for him, Weingarten decided to stay. "I feel good about it," he said at the time. "I doubt if I made the fiscally prudent decision, but I'm happy with it. I never really wanted to leave."

So, with a lifetime to go and journalism circling the drain, what was a bright, ambitious young man to do?

James Hohmann said, "I've got millions of options, I guess."

"Such as?" I said.

"Lawyer, probably, or an academic."

Good. Be a lawyer and get rich. But does a lawyer get to fly out his door at 7 a.m. on a Sunday and drive one hundred miles through labyrinthine streets to four apartments (one twice), a hospital (twice), and a jail? Does he do a bootlegger's turn at a McDonald's to grab six chunks of alleged chicken (with barbecue sauce), medium fries, and a medium Diet Coke? Then eat in the car en route to a jailhouse press conference?

That day, Hohmann forgot to eat again. He spoke by cell phone with five different editors, four other reporters, and a researcher— eleven people working a story about a teenager who had killed a Prince George's County police officer by running him down with a stolen pickup truck. Hohmann finished in the *Post*'s downtown newsroom at 10 that night.

It was his day off.

Lawyers may want a day off. Not a kid reporter on a story that had earned him his first front-page byline. Only two days earlier, with Aaron C. Davis and Ovetta Wiggins, he reported the policeman's death. Now, after a young man had been arrested for the killing, Hohmann volunteered to do a follow-up. An editor asked him to be at the suspect's apartment by 8 o'clock Sunday morning on the chance the family would talk.

At the eighteen-unit apartment complex, Hohmann did the shoe-leather thing of going door to door, knocking, not expecting an answer, hoping to get lucky and find the one cousin, or somebody, who knew everything. It happens. But Hohmann's persistence had gained him nothing when his cell phone rang.

It was an editor with news and orders. In the dead officer's own county jail, the suspect had been found unconscious under bizarre circumstances. It was less than thirty-six hours after his arrest. There was no trauma, no suggestion of suicide. Ronnie L. White had been pronounced dead at the Prince George's Hospital Center. He seemed to have died sitting on the floor by his cell bed. He was nineteen years old.

"Get to the hospital," the editor told Hohmann

The story, already good, had changed dramatically, even mysteriously.

The reporter jumped in his car, shoving the McDonald's trash over.

His heart was alive, adrenaline at high tide, fingertips tingling.

"It was really fun, just really exciting, to be out there wandering around," he said.

Hohmann's tracks that day might have been a diagram for a Boy Scout's clove hitch knot. From the first set of apartments, he headed for the hospital only to twist back for a jailhouse press conference before turning toward another apartment and getting back on the road to the hospital, where, once inside and doing the reporter's thing of looking like he belonged in a place even when he knew he didn't belong, he asked a security guard, "Hey, where's the White family?"

The guard said, "Why, who you with?"

"I'm a reporter for *The Washington Post*," Hohmann said.

The guard said, "You can't be here."

"I'd really like to talk to the family about Ronnie."

"You'll have to leave."

The guard went with him, to make sure. But then, as they passed a window, the guard whispered to Hohmann, "That's them in the parking lot."

Which led to the fifth paragraph of a 1,161-word front-page story the next morning: "Ten members of White's family who gathered in the hospital's parking lot yesterday evening were visibly angry and said they were suspicious of authorities' explanations. Angela White, Ronnie White's mother, declined to comment, saying she wanted to consult a lawyer."

All that hustle for forty words, two sentences, one graf. Not much in the big universe of journalism. In an intern's small world, sweet.

Hohmann's was the second name in the story's three-man byline. He finished work in the Fifteenth Street newsroom at 10 o'clock. On the newsroom's internal computer system, he studied the editing of the story. The finished story would go up on Washington post.com at one minute after midnight.

At 12:02 a.m. James Hohmann logged on to read it.

Through the summer of 2008, Hohmann occasionally drove downtown just to walk into the building. "For a taste of the big newsroom," he said. He saw Dana Priest at her desk, Bob Kaiser in a tiny office just off National, Walter Pincus all but hidden by towers of government documents rising alongside his desk. Woodward and Bernstein had worked there for Ben Bradlee. Downie's men won all those Pulitzers there.

One night a week, Hohmann attended a Stanford in Washington class taught by Pincus. At breakfast now and then he heard the griot's stories about the *Post* and heard Pincus says it's a journalist's job to make government better and that it is his ambition, still, after all these years, to do work that changes the world.

"Walter makes you want to go into newspapers," Hohmann said. "I love the public service aspect of it. That sounds corny to people not in journalism. Even to some in it, it sounds fake. But I believe in the line 'afflict the comfortable, comfort the afflicted.'"

By late September, Hohmann had come to two conclusions. One, the *Post* was unique. He had done internships at the *Los Angeles Times* and *Dallas Morning News* along with school-year weekend work commuting from Stanford to the *San Jose Mercury News*. Nice newspapers. But not the *Post*, not in resources or ambition. He believed the *Post* was foremost a reflection of Don Graham. "He sends Donniegrams even to the interns," Hohmann said. "He stood up at a welcome for interns and gave an impassioned speech on how the paper could do better online and how he really wanted to hear ideas from us. He challenged all of us—interns!—to come up with ideas for the future of online and the paper. There is a certain humility in that kind of solicitousness. He made it feel like a family, not a big corporation."

Hohmann's second conclusion was no surprise. He had decided to be a reporter.

"What do you like about the work?" I asked.

His voice danced. "I love telling stories that aren't scripted. I love it when there are people who have the truth and don't want it to get out, and you can report that truth. That's such an exciting thing, and it's a feeling you don't get anywhere else."

Newspapers were groping for a future that enabled them to do the good and important work they saw as their reason for being. There was no guarantee that newspapers would find that bright future. As Hohmann himself put it, "I'm not 'cautiously optimistic' about the future. I'm definitely anxious."

So, James Hohmann, why journalism, why now?

"I'm gambling a lot of my future that something will come together," he said. But he considered that risk a small price to pay for the satisfactions of the work. "For me, it's a lifestyle choice. You never turn off being a reporter. Every day, something new is happening. And you get to be there and learn about it and you get to ask questions. It's not working, it's fun."

After graduation in the spring of 2009, Hohmann hoped to retrace his journey across the country, this time to stay at the *Post*. He had seen the past in the proud old dinosaur Walter Pincus and he had divined the future through a summer's romance. He wanted it never to end.

For Len Downie, it ended too soon.

The third iteration of the *Post*'s Voluntary Retirement Incentive Program document ran to nineteen pages. Appendix A listed 271 eligible employees. They were identified only by position and age. Thirteen people listed as "janitor" ranged in age from fifty-one to sixty-five. There was a listing for "VP & Executive Editor." There was one such employee.

On June 23, 2008, a note had gone out on the newsroom's

message system about an important gathering in the room at 3:30 that day. Bob Kaiser was there and this time he was not sliding across a desk to upstage his ambitious rival. He was crying. "Ben created the *Post*," Kaiser said. "Len perfected it." It had been five months since Downie stood alone in that sixth-floor stairwell knowing he would be asked to leave. Five months since he went to Graham's home and left unsatisfied. He had not come to a full measure of peace with any of it. That was clear in his turn to speak.

Without preamble, he read his speech: "On June 22, 1964— forty-four years ago yesterday—I came to work in the newsroom of *The Washington Post* as a summer intern. I was hired full-time at the end of that summer. I was twenty-two."

In that summer of 1964, Ben Bradlee was at *Newsweek*, Don Graham at Harvard, Katharine Weymouth yet unborn. American bombers struck North Vietnam. Ed Sullivan paid the Beatles $2,400, not enough to buy an Oldsmobile ($3,495). The Dow Jones hit 891. *Peyton Place* played twice a week on prime-time television, and man had not been to the moon. Bob Kaiser used a black Royal typewriter that made sweet clattering music. At forty-seven, Katharine Graham had been a widow less than a year.

The newsroom knew, the way newsrooms know, that Downie had been told to go just as the paper had told hundreds of others it could no longer afford them. In a time of profound uncertainty, an inexperienced publisher had made it her first piece of business to force the retirement of an editor whose people had won twenty-five Pulitzers in seventeen years. Why not wait through the last four months of a historic presidential campaign? As if tone deaf to the nuances of the trade or, worse, indifferent to them, Weymouth had removed an editor who lived for big-story moments.

Because she did not immediately name a new editor, newsroomers reckoned she had passed over Downie's number two, Phil Bennett, and would go outside the building. That raised a new level of concern. Besides the announced merging of the print and website operations, what was her vision for the *Post*? One old hand, the art critic Paul Richard, confessed to bewilderment: "I began in 1963 when the paper was shit. Before Bradlee, before Kay. And saw it rise to become a giant. Now, this. Now, Downie gone. Another buyout. My God, all my friends are dead! Where's the paper going?"

Downie stood near his North Wall office, continuing to read: "I wrote obituaries, covered night police, and filled in at the local court on weekends."

It was odd, Downie reading aloud. He noted that he did investigative stories on bail bondsmen, perpetrators of home mortgage fraud, slum landlords. Worked as an editor on the city desk, "where one of my reporters was a promising young journalist named Donald Graham." Twenty years later, on June 20, 1991, Graham gave Downie the editor's job. "These seventeen years have been full of accomplishment, challenge, and change."

And now, he said, "A new, young publisher needs a new, younger editor. I am now sixty-six years old. After forty-four rewarding years in the newsroom, it is time for me to retire as executive editor, which I will do on September 8."

Then I realized why he read his speech. He didn't trust himself to remain unemotional. Near the conclusion, he mentioned his wife. "As Janice and the six children in our blended family know all too well, this newsroom has been more than a home away from home for me. I love all of you—and I love our newspaper. I will always cherish . . ."

On "cherish," he stopped, just for a heartbeat. Between the moment he saw the word on the paper and the moment he said it, he felt it.

". . . what we have accomplished together. To everyone standing here before me and listening to me elsewhere—and everyone who worked with us over the years—I simply want to say, thank you, thank you very, very much for the experience of a lifetime."

Then applause from a couple hundred people washed over him. Don Graham said, "How great an editor is he? . . . The right way to judge an editor—to put this in an old-fashioned way—is by the day-by-day quality of the paper because every paper matters and every story. In the second half of the twentieth century, I believe I speak for all of us in saying: we worked with the best in the business."

The men embraced, tears in their eyes, again, and the room's applause ended only when Downie said, "Thank you, thank you very, very, very much. I'll never forget this moment. I love you very much.

"Now, get back to work!"

Downie believed he had succeeded in the job he had been hired to do, but had failed to see the job that the executive editor now needed to do.

"The important question I'm going to have to answer for myself," he said, "is whether I was not strategic enough in the last few years in this job, as the world changed about me, because I'm so hands-on as a journalist. That's my focus. And probably the answer is, I should've been more strategic and pulled back from the journalism. But it just wasn't my nature.

"The journalism was great. The Pulitzers show it, and our overall performance shows it. But the newsroom was not as prepared for what was going on as it might have been—which is why I welcome Marcus. That's the way he thinks. He's not going to get overly involved in journalism. He'll be a stronger advocate for what the relationship ought to be between the newsrooms. I did make great progress on politics on the website, but that was because of the journalism. I wasn't thinking hard enough—or sometimes at all—about the internal structure of the newsroom. I'd been talking about handheld devices for quite a while. In fact, I'd like to think that part of Katharine's focus on it comes from our early discussions when she was running advertising. But I didn't have enough of a vision of the whole newspaper that I could go to Don and say, 'This is what we ought to do.'"

Now, like Bradlee, a vice president at large, Downie would have one more night in the newsroom. Brauchli asked him to work the presidential election. He would sit at the news desk, as always. He would make the calls on projected winners in each state. His wife knew he'd love that. "When there's a breaking story, he's like a little kid," Janice Downie said. "For him, it is sheer joy."

Downie had worked at the *Post* 16,148 days. In that time, twelve men walked on the moon, a president resigned, an actor became president, the Beatles broke up, Elvis died, the United States twice went to war in Iraq, the Dow Jones climbed past 14,000 and fell off a cliff, reporters thumbed silently on BlackBerries, Katharine Graham died, and Katharine Weymouth was born.

Throughout the historic presidential campaign, Downie's people had done the work a great newspaper does. Now, near the end, Sally Jenkins went to Alaska, Bob Kaiser flew with McCain, and Dan Balz accompanied Obama, on the campaign's last night, from Virginia to Chicago.

18.

"AN EXTRAORDINARY RIDE"

Three weeks after the Republican national convention, while political pundits in the Lower Forty-Eight were still trying to figure out where this Sarah Palin character came from, the *Post* sent Sally Jenkins to tell them. The sportswriter went north to Alaska, to the candidate's hometown of Wasilla, "this crazy little town with one hotel open." The others were closed against winter's coming. "The hotel had antlers all over the walls. You couldn't go to your room without practically catching your sleeve on a caribou spike." And what a trip. "You have no idea how far away Alaska is! It's far! And it's BIG! It took forever to get there. And I gotta tell you, you can't understand Sarah Palin until you go there. It's damn near another country!" And it's gorgeous. "Outside the hotel window were these magnificent gray-wreathed mountains studded with white-gold aspen trees, and it was so quiet that off in the distance you could hear a train going, 'hoooo-hooooo.'"

The *Post*'s financials continued their free fall in a 2008 disaster that would be the newspaper's first-ever year in the red. As reported by Frank Ahrens in the *Post* business pages, the company's newspaper division lost $192.7 million in 2008. It was "scary and desperately sad," to quote the old Postie, *Time*'s David Von Drehle, as the newspaper's army of political reporters continued their long march to November. The money would, or would not, take care of itself, but for newshounds such as Bob Woodward there was a simpler question to be answered, and it had to do with coverage of the candidates: "Did the *Post* get to the bottom of who these people are?"

Jenkins quickly learned who Sarah Palin was. She was Chuck and Sally's Wild West Wasilla daughter.

"It was impossible," Jenkins said, "not to have a good time with Palin's parents, who were so funny and unaffected." Chuck Heath was a retired public school science teacher and lifelong naturalist. Sally Heath was an outdoorswoman of deep religious conviction. The extent of Jenkins's search for the Heaths was that on arrival in Wasilla she opened a phone book, found their name, and called them.

Next thing she knew, she was at the Heaths' kitchen counter. "Her mother made me a grilled cheese sandwich and a caribou hot dog, and set a glass of milk on the counter in front of me. For the whole first half of the interview, I barely took notes. I was too busy staring at the stuffed wolverine hanging over my head, looking like it was ready to pounce." She also saw Chuck's garage, "filled, floor to ceiling, with jars of things he collects, beautiful fishing lures and buoys, which he had sorted and arranged in rainbow colors."

Out in the front yard, Jenkins saw art of an odd sort. She wrote, "A towering sculpture of bleached antlers sits by the driveway. Bright buoys and fishing lures dangle from silver birch trees." And in the house: "Fox pelts. Orca teeth. Bear fangs. Owl wings. A brown, bony thing with a huge span occupies the living room wall."

And the brown, bony thing would be . . . ?

"A walrus scapula," Chuck Heath said brightly.

Because the vice-presidential debate would be that night, the father told a story about his daughter's ability to handle herself in tough situations. She had taken her husband's fishing boat onto Bristol Bay, where she and her father were caught in a storm. "It was the toughest work I've ever done," Chuck Heath said, "and it wasn't only hard, it was dangerous." At day's end, in waves that crashed against the boat, they had to get it out of the churning water and onto a trailer.

"I'm not doing that," he said.

"Get out of the way," Palin said. "I'll do it."

She did.

All the Heaths' stories with a Self-Reliant Sarah theme came with heavy emphasis on standing up against all opponents, be they on a basketball court or in the woods. They said Sarah was one of four children crowded into a small cabin's attic bedroom, out of reach of the heat from a wood-burning stove, huddled under quilts, their breath floating on the air. With their neighbors, the Carters, the Heaths counted on one moose to provide the families' meals for a winter. At age ten, Sarah began shooting game for dinner, first rabbits and ptarmigan, later duck, moose, and caribou. As a senior on the high school basketball team, hobbled by a sprained ankle most of the game, she scored Wasilla's last point to secure victory and the state championship.

"I just really enjoyed talking with Chuck and Sally," Jenkins said. "It was a totally genuine experience. Her dad said, 'I really like talking to you. You need to come back tomorrow.' So I said, 'Okay.' And I went back the next day and had an even better interview. It became obvious that's where Palin gets her wit, and her sense of, well, oddity. They were just very different people, very independent thinkers. Didn't give much of a rip what you or anyone else thought."

In his "Tuesdays with Moron" chats, Gene Weingarten often spoke of the potential vice president as if she were, say, a walrus scapula.

One reader who signed herself "Sorely Vexed" wrote to Weingarten, "I am one of those white midwestern, middle-aged women who is supposedly flocking to John McCain's campaign because I am totally dazzled by Caribou Barbie's ascension to the ticket. I am sickened by the very thought of those two being elected. Gene, please, please tell me that Americans are not that stupid."

GW: "I appear to be in a pretty small minority of the media that didn't think her convention speech was good. It was delivered spunky but it seemed small-minded, mean-spirited, sarcastic, and ultimately dumbed down. I just loved the online reaction to her snarky comment suggesting Obama's experience was pretty much limited to community activism: 'Hey, Sarah, Jesus was a community activist, Pilate was a governor.'"

From Alexandria, Virginia: "So, Governor Palin did better in the debate than I expected, but what is with the winking? People are losing homes, jobs, life savings and their lives and she's WINKING at the camera. What is up with that?"

GW: "This is the inevitable endpoint of a TV-era presidential marketing process that for fifty years has been emphasizing style over substance and 'narrative' over experience. Actually, the same process gave us Barack Obama, I suppose, only we lucked out with that one. The disturbing thing about the Palin Pit Bull tour is the degree of angry nationalistic fervor. I will not make the fascism connection, I will leave that to others. I think it would be scary, but I think it is going to implode. I don't think we're that stupid."

And from Pal-o-ween: "So I'm a small brunette person with 'Tina Fey' glasses and sideswept bangs. Clearly, Palin is an awesome costume choice for me this Halloween. My question is on accessories—suggestions from you would be like gold."

GW: "You want to be dragging a moose carcass."

In the summer of 2008, under the headline "The Curious Mind of John McCain," Bob Kaiser decided, "McCain is a figure from an old-fashioned America that is out of fashion in our most cosmopolitan precincts—the America of 'Gunsmoke' and Gary Cooper, not 'The Daily Show' and George Clooney. For McCain, 'Duty, Honor, Country' isn't patriotic pablum but a credo to live by."

Kaiser remained an associate editor of the *Post* after leaving the managing editor's job in 1999. He wrote whatever caught his fancy—or nearly killed him, in the case of an aortic dissection that gave him reason to write five thousand harrowing words about the incident and his survival. For Washingtonpost.com, he conducted online chats throughout the campaign. Because he "long believed that a politician's intellect is one key to political character," he asked McCain's people if he might talk to the candidate. He wound up with McCain in the leather-covered first-class seats of his campaign plane.

He found an emotional man, harshly self-critical, given to seeing the simplicities of black and white where others might see the grays of nuance. Gary Hart, a McCain friend and former U.S. senator and twice a presidential candidate, told Kaiser, "I think his mind is visceral, driven less by thought and more by feelings. This doesn't mean he's totally reactive or without logic of thought processes; it just means he's a fighter pilot. He reacts to circumstances." In one of his autobiographical books, McCain admitted to lying in 2000 about the Confederate flag flying over the South Carolina capitol. To quell a controversy he had started by saying the flag was offensive, McCain read a prepared statement saying he actually saw it "as a symbol of heritage." To have lied that way, he wrote, "I had not just been dishonest, I had been a coward, and I had severed my own interests from my country's. That was what made the lie unforgivable."

He lied then to save his campaign, which he saw failing. And during their conversation on the plane eight years later, Kaiser sensed that McCain was again dispirited. He told me, "I was very struck by his fatalism, which I think is one of his strongest characteristics. I thought even then he knew he was going to lose; he realized that when his chance at the Big Casino finally arrived, the time was dreadful." The candidate at one point said, "I'm surprised that I am as close in the polls as I am right now. When you look at the fantastic campaign that Senator Obama has waged, it really is quite remarkable."

That fatalism, Kaiser wrote, became part of McCain's thinking at age thirteen when he read Ernest Hemingway's novel *For Whom the Bell Tolls*. Its protagonist is Robert Jordan, an American who fights with anti-fascists in the Spanish Civil War. Though Jordan finds love, he chooses to die for a cause he believes in. Kaiser asked McCain if he, like Jordan, was a romantic fatalist. "McCain answered quickly and forcefully: 'Yes, yes.' "

McCain's game plan since his days at the U.S. Naval Academy always included running for president. Kaiser came away suspecting that McCain now hated the process. In accepting as his vice president a woman unfit for the office—forced on him by political necessity if not by his party's conservative base—McCain might have felt as much the expedient coward as on that day in South

Carolina when he disavowed his own beliefs. "Part of me wonders," Kaiser said, "if he will write an honest book about it someday."

The old-fashioned America conjured by Kaiser was captured by Eli Saslow. The newlywed went to Findlay, Ohio, not to untangle lies and distortions about Barack Obama but to show their effects on voters. He saw the American flag rampant on College Street, a custom started by an air force veteran named Jim Peterman. "By 1980," Saslow wrote, "patriotic displays had grown into an unspoken contest of one-upmanship. Sixty flags planted in one yard on Memorial Day; a living-room window painted red, white, and blue . . . The entire block—and, soon, the entire town—shared in unabashed pride and gratefulness for the country that had given them this place. In 1968, a local congressman persuaded the House of Representatives to officially declare Findlay as Flag City, USA."

Saslow had gone to College Street and in David Broder fashion knocked on doors to ask for a couple minutes of the residents' time. That's how he met Peterman. The seventy-four-year-old retired tire company worker said he'd heard on the news that Obama was born in Hawaii and is a Christian family man with a record of public service. But he'd heard more often, from friends, neighbors, and family, that Obama is African, possibly gay, and a Muslim racist who refuses to recite the Pledge of Allegiance. Peterman told Saslow, "It makes it impossible to figure out what's true, or what you can believe . . . It's hard to ignore what you hear when everybody you know is saying it. These are good people, smart people, so can they really all be wrong?"

One neighbor said, "Obama would be a disaster . . . I understand he's from Africa, and that the first thing he's going to do if he gets into office is bring his family over here, illegally. He's got that racist [pastor] who practically raised him, and then there's the Muslim thing." Another: "He's a good speaker, but you've got to dig deeper than that for the truth. Politicians tell you anything. You have to look beyond the surface, and then there are some real lies." A third: "All I know for sure about Obama is that we're not ready for him."

On the morning of Monday, October 13, the eleven members of the *Post*'s editorial board met to decide on an endorsement for president. They met in a conference room hidden away in the rabbit hutch of editorialists' offices, which are separated, psychically and physically, from the newsroom. Fred Hiatt, the editorial page editor, presided over a discussion that wasn't so much about a choice between Obama and McCain. For the board members, that had become the easiest decision. They talked about issues to argue in the editorial. And in a nod to the new media world and changing habits of news consumers, Hiatt decided to publish the endorsement not in the Sunday newspaper but online on a Friday "when people were at work."

Hiatt was fifty-three years old, thoughtful and soft-spoken, a Harvard grad and lifer in the complexities of journalism. He started at the late, lamented *Washington Star* before joining the *Post*. His experience stretched from Virginia to Moscow, in politics, national security, and the military. Along the way he saw the Arizona senator John McCain move with grace and skill through confounding international issues. In this presidential campaign, Hiatt saw that version of McCain less often than he had hoped. As we sat in his office one day, Hiatt said, "This process makes it impossible for anybody to really be themselves." His tone was one of regret.

The editorial board's work habits included meeting three or four mornings a week with an agenda dictated by the day's news. "We'd talk about the campaign because we did a series of issues editorials," Hiatt said. "But we made a point of never talking in any direct way about who we'd wind up endorsing."

At the October 13 meeting, Don Graham sat in. Though the company CEO no longer had a newspaper title and only occasionally prowled through the newsroom, everyone on the fifth floor, in that newsroom and in the editorialists' cubbyholes, knew he was the ultimate decider on ultimate issues at the *Post*. Most every Thursday morning, he met Hiatt for breakfast. "I talked about it with Don as the campaign evolved," the editorial page boss said. "He spoke his piece at our meeting."

Tuesday, Hiatt wrote the editorial. Wednesday, he showed it to his deputy, Jackson Diehl.

Thursday, he showed it to Graham and to Katharine Weymouth. At 5 o'clock Thursday afternoon, the editorial went to copy editing "for a good scrubbing," as Hiatt put it, and at 8 o'clock that night it went up on Washingtonpost.com's home page. "By midnight," he said, "it had ninety thousand hits." Under the headline "Obama for President," the editorial began:

The nominating process this year produced two unusually talented and qualified presidential candidates. There are few public figures we have respected more over the years than Sen. John McCain. Yet it is without ambivalence that we endorse Sen. Barack Obama for president.

The choice is made easy in part by Mr. McCain's disappointing campaign, above all his irresponsible selection of a running mate who is not ready to be president. It is made easy in larger part, though, because of our admiration for Mr. Obama and the impressive qualities he has shown during this long race. Yes, we have reservations and concerns, almost inevitably, given Mr. Obama's relatively brief experience in national politics. But we also have enormous hopes.

Mr. Obama is a man of supple intelligence, with a nuanced grasp of complex issues and evident skill at conciliation and consensus-building. At home, we believe, he would respond to the economic crisis with a healthy respect for markets tempered by justified dismay over rising inequality and an understanding of the need for focused regulation. Abroad, the best evidence suggests that he would seek to maintain U.S. leadership and engagement, continue the fight against terrorists, and wage vigorous diplomacy on behalf of U.S. values and interests. Mr. Obama has the potential to become a great president. Given the enormous problems he would confront from his first day in office, and the damage wrought over the past eight years, we would settle for very good.

———

The night before the election, November 3, Barack Obama's embrace of symbolism led him to land that once trembled under the cannon fire of the Civil War's first major battle. Though outnumbered by the largest army ever assembled in North America, Confederate troops routed the Federals on July 21, 1861, and prepared to march on the nation's capital, twenty-five miles away. Almost a century and a half later, ninety thousand people came to the Prince William County fairgrounds in Manassas, Virginia. It was the last rally of Obama's campaign. Where men once owned black people and died to keep their property, the multitudes heard a black man tell his trusty campaign-speech story of the short lady in a big church hat who taught him to chant, "Fired up! Ready to go!"

About 10 o'clock, from the press tent at the back of the crowd, Dan Balz saw Obama onstage, enthusiastic in the twenty-second month of his campaign. The *Post*'s man moved to a press riser at the side of the stage to see the thousands gathered in a swale a hundred yards wide. Obama said, "You can keep your dignity, keep your decency, and still win." And at the end, in full cry, he said, "Virginians, your votes can change the world!"

It was after midnight on the chartered 757 taking Obama home to Chicago when he walked back into the plane's press section. Balz thought Obama more subdued than celebratory, grieving the death of his grandmother. The morning before, just after 8 o'clock, Obama had learned that Madelyn Dunham, who raised him in Hawaii, had died at age eighty-six. He moved down the aisle to thank reporters, photographers, television camera crews, and others in the media who had become familiar faces on the long campaign, some there from the beginning at a frozen dawn in Abraham Lincoln's town.

"Whatever happens tomorrow," Obama said, "it's extraordinary."

Then he said, "Okay, guys, let's go home."

As he headed back to the big swivel seat in the front cabin, Obama said, "It will be fun to see how the story ends."

After flying to Chicago with the candidate, Balz slept three hours before doing a 7 a.m. U-turn to Washington. On the flight home—

a political reporter's work never ends during a presidential campaign—he opened his laptop and wrote eight hundred words that
appeared on Washingtonpost.com under the headline "At the End
of an Extraordinary Ride." It was a summing up of what he had
seen, heard, and felt. Balz had covered too many politicians for too
many years to go all sentimental. Yet there was a wistfulness in
that little piece batted out on the plane ride home. He later said,
"My wife thinks this is slightly nuts, but after two years of this
campaign, you sorta don't want to see it end. It's just been such an
amazing journey in all sorts of ways, an amazing journalistic journey. It didn't matter who you wanted to win. You just knew you
weren't going to get another one like this to cover for a long time."

At home on the morning of Election Day, Dan Balz voted. Then
he went to the *Post* to write an ending to the story.

19.

"OBAMA MAKES HISTORY"

It was 6:30 p.m. on the first Tuesday following a Monday in November, Election Night in America. A familiar face had come to an unfamiliar place. From where she stood, Katharine Weymouth saw something she had never before seen. She saw the Fifteenth Street newsroom in full flight, carried along on the excitement of a big story, voices murmuring, quick movements crossing her field of vision. The new publisher said, "So much energy in this room."

Dan Balz was in. He had written the lead-all news story on the last four presidential elections, but this time would do an analysis of the campaign and the challenges ahead for the new president. "Obama's certainly going to win, so it's more relaxing than the usual election night," Balz said. "And the piece won't run until the second edition—when the winner officially has been decided—so I have plenty of time to write." He had been on the trail twenty-two months. He had seen Obama freeze in Illinois; he had written five times a week for a year, shaved his Quixote beard when he remembered to, wheedled for access—now he moved to his newsroom desk to write: "After a victory of historic importance . . ."

The warhorse Len Downie was in. He had worked on eleven presidential election nights, from LBJ in 1964 through Nixon, Carter, Reagan, Bush 41, Clinton, and Bush 43. Some vice presidents at large could pass on such a night's work, but not Downie. It was the end of a story he had framed two years earlier, the first presidential race in a half century without a candidate who had been president or vice president. He wouldn't run the paper this night, as he had for the last eight campaigns. But Brauchli had asked him to be part of the news crew; he would take reports from *Post* people in the field, check other media, and make the calls on winners. Downie himself had never voted, saying that as a newsman he needed to stay impartial lest his leanings influence his news judgment—but now, for the first time, he had registered to vote, so I asked if, in fact, he had voted.

"I did not," he said. "I'm making the calls."

He didn't smile. There was no irony in his tone. For his 16,149th day at the *Post*, he was seriously serious.

At 8:01 p.m. in the Washingtonpost.com newsroom across the river, Chris Cillizza looked into Camera 2 on a live webcast fed to ten newspaper websites in the United States, Canada, and Australia. He ran down the many states already called for Obama, then those few called for McCain. "The two key states to watch now," the Fix said, "are Pennsylvania and New Hampshire. These are really blue states. If McCain doesn't win either of them, he has to run the table on red ones."

Those blue ones, long Democratic strongholds, carried emotional weight for McCain. His campaign had been reborn in New Hampshire's primary. In Pennsylvania, desperate to win where everyone said it was impossible, McCain had invested great amounts of money and time. Next to the dot-com's news desk— circular, dimly lit, everyone with a video monitor, as if at the nerve center of a starship—a clerk sat in front of five television monitors, two with screens split into quarters, and watched the eleven feeds for news of calls.

At 8:39 p.m., Pennsylvania went to Obama.

One more breath and New Hampshire went to Obama.

Cillizza, done with his webcast gig, hurried back to his laptop, the battered purveyor of ten thousand words a week. The Fix sat in a corner at the far north of the newsroom, a twelfth-floor corner with a sweeping landscape view that included the Lincoln Memorial, the Washington Monument, and the U.S. Capitol. The view alone was reason enough to bang away at the laptop until you wore the letters off its keys. Cillizza did not hammer his laptop for the fun of it. The Cillizzas had a Fix Baby on the way, due in April. So he cashed the *Post*'s checks and kept his editors happy, as with his 9 o'clock question to Liz Spayd, the dot-com's second in command: "Is that what you want, a new lead at the top of every hour?"

"Or whenever," she said.

"Okay," said Cillizza.

"My whip," Tom Wilkinson said. "Where is it?"

He was seventy-one years old, an editor who had worked in every news department and knew everything. He sat in his little office at the back of the newsroom. This night he wore a T-shirt carrying the name of his hockey team, a gang of ancient icemen who called themselves The Geri-Hat-Tricks.

A long time before, political reporter Maralee Schwartz had told him there was only one way to keep copy moving. She gave him a bullwhip, eight feet long, braided leather with a wooden handle. Now, on big news nights, he was the deadline sheriff. He walked the room, the whip coiled across his shoulders.

He hadn't used it since February 5, the night of the Super Tuesday primaries. "What drawer did I put it in?"

There it was, in the middle drawer of a filing cabinet.

"Ready," he said.

On primary nights throughout the campaign season, Bob Kaiser closed himself in a tiny office just off the National staff's area. As a proper gentleman should and most journalists don't, the Yale man put his suit coat on a hanger, then slipped it under his topcoat on a hook at the door. He loosened his tie just so and draped his half glasses from a lanyard. At 7 p.m. on this night, he was at his computer ready to chat live on Washingtonpost.com, answering in real time hundreds of questions from website users around the world. This was the future he had first seen on a trip to Japan sixteen years earlier.

"Good evening," he began. "We've done this often, but I think tonight is going to be special, and memorable . . . The Washington Post newsroom is buzzing in a way it only does once every four years. Dozens of journalists are deployed, and I can walk around and ask questions, so don't be shy about asking. Washingtonpost .com gives you a zillion ways to follow what's going on—take advantage!"

Questions came to him from coast to coast, from the heartland of America, from Sweden, Japan, England, the West Indies, and Australia.

At 10:03, I tapped on his door and asked for an update.

"It's over," Kaiser said

"When did you decide?"

"Ohio," he said. "About twenty minutes ago."

At that point he had typed, "CBS has just called OHIO for Obama. We have seen this coming. I think it means that Obama will be our next president, but that's just me talking. The Post will make a more formal call later."

Wilkinson and his bullwhip moved through the room. The vise of time was closing. At the news desk, page designer Jon Wile created a first-edition front page carrying the headline:

EARLY RETURNS SHOW OBAMA
ON PATH TO HISTORIC VICTORY

Even before he transmitted that page to the presses in suburban Virginia—with the touch of a computer key—Wile had prepared a final-edition draft that now, just after 10 o'clock, showed a large headline:

PRESIDENT XXXXXX

He wanted better.

Then, at 11 o'clock, from a television above the news desk, CNN anchor Wolf Blitzer cried out, "CNN has projected Barack Obama as president! He will be the first African American president of the

United States!" Three minutes later, ABC made the same call, and Jon Wile's eyes never moved from the monitor in front of him. He was twenty-eight years old, buzz-cut to a Marine look. Out of Kent State University in 2002, he started as a sports agate clerk at the *Cleveland Plain Dealer*. No fun there: agate clerks shepherd those tiny-print game results, batting averages, box scores. Because his place in sports put him near a page designer, he asked how it was done; the next month, he was doing it. Two and a half years later, he came to the *Post*. In September 2008, gearing up for this night, Wile was moved to the A1 design chair. In advance of this night, he had played with designs on his laptop at home. He had the page done, with a horizontal photograph of Obama in victory. All he needed was the headline.

"We wanted to avoid a two-line, long-winded headline," he said. "I wanted it to be punchy, big, and bold, a hundred and ten point." Wile settled his fingers on the keyboard as a handful of editors and kibitzers formed a semicircle behind him and suggested headlines. Someone liked the simple "President Obama." Or the simpler "Obama!" Then someone called out, "Obama makes history," and Wile instantly said, "Yes!" And he typed it in.

OBAMA MAKES HISTORY
FIRST AFRICAN AMERICAN ELECTED AS PRESIDENT

Good. But Wile still wanted better. Now the news desk operated at a quickened pulse rate. News editor Vince Bzdek, standing behind Wile to watch the design, asked photo editor Michel DuCille, "We still horizontal with Obama?" "Yes," DuCille said. And then came Len Downie's call on the state of Washington: "Yep! We'll call Washington. That puts him over the top."

John McCain had seen defeat coming for a long while, probably longer than he could admit. Kaiser had suggested as much three months earlier in his piece on McCain, the "romantic fatalist." His concession speech became McCain's finest moment of the campaign. The shrillness was gone from the voice that had snarled in debates and in his stump speech. He was no longer a man seething with unspoken anger born of ambition denied. The man who charmed everyone eight years earlier when he defeated Bush in the presidential campaign's first primary election—that man suddenly reappeared. Gone was the man who wanted the presidency so much that he had compromised not only his principles but his personality in cooking up red meat for the conservative base. Gone and good riddance, for in that suffering man's place came the real John McCain—the McCain that Fred Hiatt had admired. This man, in conceding defeat, twice gently scolded his audience for booing at the sound of Obama's name.

"I wish Godspeed to the man who was my former opponent and will be my president," McCain said. "And I call on all Americans, as I have often in this campaign, to not despair of our present difficulties, but to believe, always, in the promise and greatness of America, because nothing is inevitable here. Americans never quit. We never surrender. We never hide from history. We make history."

Near midnight, the day's history maker appeared in Chicago's Grant Park. And in the *Post* newsroom, young Jon Wile had a new headline ready for the final edition:

OBAMA MAKES HISTORY
U.S. DECISIVELY ELECTS FIRST BLACK PRESIDENT

Photo editor DuCille, rolling behind his people in a desk chair, watching thumbnails of photographs appear on monitors, said, "First picture of him we get." No time for artistry, no time for deep thought, not when you're a quickening heartbeat from deadline. First picture in the house is the best one! Go with it!

Obama stood smiling in that great park in that great city. He stood on a stage that at its edges held two giant pieces of bulletproof glass. The walls of glass had been lowered into place by cranes that afternoon. The walls were three inches thick, ten feet high, fifteen feet long. They were transparent reminders of an opaque darkness in the land. Between those walls, the man who would be the forty-fourth president of the United States began his victory speech, saying, "If there is anyone out there who still doubts that America is a place where all things are possible, who still wonders if the dream of our founders is alive in our time, who still questions the power of our democracy, tonight is your answer."

And to those people who came with him on the most implausible of political journeys, he said the victory was not his. Instead, it proved that "more than two centuries later, a government of the people, by the people and for the people has not perished from this Earth. This is your victory."

Even as Obama's voice sang with its Lincolnian echoes from a television above the news desk, Bzdek checked an inventory of sto ries due to copy editors. "Ed, we're running way behind," he said. "Ten stories out." The news desk's boss, Ed Thiede, bounced off his chair to roust the tardy. Bzdek now looked at the big headlines on Wile's page and turned to Phil Bennett. They spoke with deadline terseness.

Bzdek asked, " 'Black' okay?" Earlier they had used "African American."

"What's style?" Bennett said.

"Interchangeable."

"That comes from the copy desk?"

"Yeah."

"Okay."

From the stage in Grant Park, Obama spoke of a voter in Atlanta, Ann Nixon Cooper, a woman 106 years old, who was born a generation past slavery and had lived through a century of darkness and light, heartache and hope. He said, "America, we have come so far. We have seen so much. But there is so much more to do. So tonight, let us ask ourselves, if our children should live to see the next century, if my daughters should be so lucky to live as long as Ann Nixon Cooper, what change will they see? What progress will we have made? This is our chance to answer that call. Ths is our moment. This is our time . . ."

At the news desk, as Obama said, "and may God bless the United States of America," photo editor Bonnie Jo Mount said she had pictures from a street celebration outside the White House and pictures from Grant Park and what pages did they want them for? Someone answered, "Thirty-three, thirty-four," and last-second advisories flew to people with a need to know: "We're only going into five pages, 1, 25, 28, 38, and 45," and "We're moving that ad inside, putting Broder at the top, and Obama's speech at the bottom, it's only forty-five inches," and "R.B., there was a big thing on U Street," which caused R. B. Brenner, the Metro editor, by then scurrying back across the big room, to shout over his shoulder, "We're there."

At his computer, Dan Balz wrote a hundred words on Obama's speech to be dropped into his analysis between its fourth and fifth paragraphs. He had said, "You don't want it to read like you'd written it all in advance. You want some sense of the moment in the piece." In the last edition, then, Balz quoted Obama saying, "The road ahead will be long. Our climb will be steep. We may not get there in one year or even one term, but America—I have never been more hopeful than I am tonight that we will get there. I promise you—we as a people will get there."

Some days, especially days like this—and most newspaper days are like this if you do the work right—I swear, over the objections of my wife and to the dismay of bill collectors, and even without Chris Cillizza's view of the monuments, I would do this work for free. I guarantee you that Jon Wile would have paid for the privilege because now, at three in the morning, at 1600 Pennsylvania Avenue, the page designer six years removed from sports agate stood on the sidewalk looking at the White House.

He carried with him a proof of his front page.

Cars honked their horns. People danced in the streets.

Out in front of Barack Obama's next home, Wile thought the moment was surreal. And people came to him and they asked what he had in his hand, and he showed them the front page he had created for *The Washington Post*.

Someone said it, and everyone agreed: "Dude! Cool!"

Just before 7 o'clock, by the dawn's early light in suburban Virginia, ten minutes from the White House, a little white car moved slowly down a leafy street. It moved in a long S pattern, from one side of the street to the other. The car was a Honda CR-V. The driver was Muhammad Amin. He was a fifty-year-old Pakistani who had come to Virginia twelve years ago. His first job in America was delivering *The Washington Post* and he now did it seven days a week. He snapped papers through his window toward houses on the left. For the right side of the street, he reached his left arm far out and performed the Koufaxian feat of pitching the *Post*, in its translucent yellow bag, over the roof of the car and into a yard.

He was late this morning because his four hundred newspapers had come late from the Springfield presses to his pickup spot near Alexandria. "Election news, always late," he said.

His wife, Nighat, sat in the backseat of the Honda, squeezed between hundreds of newspapers. Her job was to slide the papers into their yellow bags and pitch them up front into the passenger seat. Amin then delivered the papers according to the customers' orders. "People tell me where they want it, I throw it there or I stop the car and take it to the place. I hit trees, flowers sometimes. But never cats or dogs." All that throwing caused me to ask if he had played Pakistan's national game, cricket. Perhaps he had been a bowler, the game's equivalent of a baseball pitcher. No, not a bowler. "But this is maybe good practice for the bowling, yes?"

Then he had to get going, down to the next block. It was already late. I watched for another two or three minutes until the little white car moved into the shadows of trees, disappearing.

Part V

"MARCUS WAS AS GOOD AS BRADLEE AND DOWNIE"

20.

SOMETHING MUST BE DONE

The morning of September 21, 2009, Bob Woodward delivered the kind of story that long before had prompted the British press lord Alfred Charles Northcliffe to say he coveted *The Washington Post* because it reached the breakfast tables of the capital's leaders. In the more pungent Bradlee vernacular, Woodward had done a holy-shit story that rattled coffee cups in the White House, the Pentagon, and perhaps in the mountain redoubts of Afghanistan.

He was at work on a book about the Obama administration when he came into possession of a document that he thought was too important to hold. He read it on Friday, September 18. In its grim report on the war in Afghanistan, he came to see traces of the Pentagon Papers of 1971 that reported the misguided conduct of the Vietnam War. He also remembered how the Bush administration, late in 2002, had misused a hastily prepared National Intelligence Estimate that, in the body of its text, cast doubts on its own sensational summary that Iraq held weapons of mass destruction. Rather than sit on information that could frame a national debate on war, Woodward negotiated an agreement with his source to write a newspaper story immediately.

At 8:28 p.m. that Friday, Woodward e-mailed Marcus Brauchli: "Marcus: I have obtained a copy of the classified McChrystal assessment (66 pages with annexes) that has some significant new material. You may want a story. Thoughts? Guidance? I'll be up reading. Best, Bob." At 11:09 p.m., the editor replied: "Hi, just seeing this. Yes, assuming none of our folks have seen. Can we chat in the morning?"

General Stanley A. McChrystal was the commander of U.S. and NATO forces in Afghanistan. He believed the war against the Taliban was going badly. That much had been reported for weeks. Why he believed it, and what he would do about it—those details were in the general's secret report to his commander-in-chief. On Thursday, September 17, Secretary of Defense Robert M. Gates told reporters at a Pentagon briefing that the McChrystal assessment remained classified because Obama deserved the right to "absorb the assessment himself" with questions answered by top civilian and military officials. "We need to understand," Gates said, "that the decisions that the president faces . . . on Afghanistan are some of the most important he may face in his presidency, about how we go forward there." The *Post*'s news story that day reported that the Pentagon had distributed copies of the assessment to select members of the House and Senate.

A secret report? Distributed to politicians? Already in the hands of civilian and military officials? This is secret? Not in Bob Woodward's world.

"When I was in high school," he once said, "I worked part-time as a janitor in my father's law office, and I was able to rummage through everything in the office. That may have sparked an interest in finding out the secrets that people keep."

Now he had uncovered another.

The *Post* had been drifting. That summer, Katharine Weymouth had made two rookie-publisher mistakes that could haunt her for years; meanwhile, the paper lost money in such historic amounts that Don Graham told her, indirectly but firmly, that the honeymoon was over. Brauchli was eleven days past his first anniversary on the job and neck deep in a print-online merger that required blowing up the Fifteenth Street newsroom to rebuild it for the new operation. Adrift on a sea of confusion, the paper needed an anchor.

Here came Woodward. Because of the construction, Brauchli worked from a temporary office on the fourth floor. It was Saturday morning, September 19, when Woodward arrived for the familiar drill that he had done dozens of times with Bradlee and Downie. Calls would be made to the involved parties. Woodward would say, This is what we have. The White House would say, No, no, no, you can't print that, it's a national security issue. The Pentagon would say, No, no, revealing operational plans will put the mission and troops at risk. At that point in the dance, Woodward and Bradlee or Downie would debate what was a real national security issue and what was driven by simple political considerations. All the parties then would understand what the story would say.

The McChrystal dance began in Brauchli's office with Woodward, the paper's lawyer, Jim McLaughlin, and Rajiv Chandrasekaran, the *Post*'s man in Afghanistan.

The phone rang.

"Hi," a woman said, "I'm the security guard on the L Street entrance at *The Washington Post*. I've got a guy on the phone who says he's from the White House Situation Room."

The L Street entrance was an all but hidden back door to the building. The security guard sat in a little cubbyhole office separated from all living things. Someone who would call the *Post* and reach the L Street security guard office would be someone, to put this delicately, without a clue.

The guard went on: "He'll only give his name as 'Elliott.' Do you want us to put him through?"

"Sure," Brauchli said.

The young man named "Elliott" was charged with patching together a conference call with Brauchli, the secretary of defense, the national security adviser, a lawyer for foreign affairs, and the vice chairman of the Joint Chiefs of Staff.

But the connections were botched. Elliott had to make the calls again. About here, a wiseguy might have asked, *My national security rests in an apparatus that includes Elliott's nervous hands?*

What Woodword did was listen to the four officials warn that publishing the document in its entirety could endanger troops.

That was reason enough to delay publication until everyone agreed on redactions from the document. That agreement was reached at a Sunday meeting of Brauchli, Woodward, and Chandrasekaran with three Defense Department officials. Nearly all of the McChrystal document was declassified with certain details omitted, among them the outlines of future military operations in Afghanistan. Those decisions enabled Woodward to write.

Played in the lead position—the top right-hand corner of the front page—Woodward's story of September 21 began:

> The top U.S. and NATO commander in Afghanistan warns in an urgent, confidential assessment of the war that he needs more forces within the next year and bluntly states that without them, the eight-year conflict "will likely result in failure," according to a copy of the 66-page document obtained by The Washington Post.
>
> Gen. Stanley A. McChrystal says emphatically: "Failure to gain the initiative and reverse insurgent momentum in the near-term (next 12 months)—while Afghan security capacity matures—risks an outcome where defeating the insurgency is no longer possible."

In two thousand words, Woodward reported McChrystal's disenchantment with the Afghan government, his disappointment in his own command's failure to understand the nation's civilian suffering, and his concern that the Taliban insurgency, already "muscular and sophisticated," would come to control significant portions of the country. "Toward the end of his report," Woodward wrote, "McChrystal revisits his central theme: 'Failure to provide adequate resources also risks a longer conflict, greater casualties, higher overall costs, and ultimately, a critical loss of political support. Any of these risks, in turn, are likely to result in mission failure.'"

The *Post*'s publication of the McChrystal assessment did, in fact, begin a national debate on Obama's decision making on the war. To Woodward, the longtime newspaperman, the dance with the White House and Pentagon served another purpose at well. He saw the new editor at work. He saw Brauchli stand firm against Pentagon pressure, particularly in that Sunday meeting.

"Marcus was as good as Bradlee and Downie," Woodward told me, "in dealing with the White House and Pentagon on a sensitive

national security story. He was tough, informed, personally involved, and would not be pushed around. Also, he was sensitive that
we not publish anything that might endanger the lives of the troops
or forecast future operations. I would give him an A plus, and I
don't give those very often. The *Post* editorship is in strong hands
once again, and that is really encouraging to those of us who still
labor in the news vineyard."

Did I say the newspaper was adrift on a sea of confusion? To
extend the metaphor, there were times when the newspaper was
up a creek without a paddle.

Graham, the old Metro reporter, put this tight lead on his 2008
annual report to shareholders: "Well, that was something."

His friend, the ombudsman Deborah Howell, called the year "a
psychological nightmare." There were the journalistic triumphs
of six Pulitzers and wall-to-wall coverage of a historical presidential campaign. But there was also an operating loss of $192.7 mil-
lion, the newspaper division's first loss in thirty-seven years as part
of a publicly traded company.

Beginning with the first buyout five years earlier, Graham had
seen his family's newspaper disappearing. More than 100,000 subscribers had left, twenty thousand of them in Weymouth's first
full year. By the time of the fourth buyout in 2009, nearly four
hundred newsroom staffers were gone—a fifty percent reduction.
A shadow of sadness fell on everyone. After a lifetime in journalism, Howell said she was "pessimistic" about the industry's future.
"Don asked me, 'Is it all over?' I couldn't bring myself to say a
word. We just sat in silence."

In his annual report dated February 24, 2009, Graham wrote,
"Poking our heads up from the rubble, we at The Washington Post
Company would like to say: prospects look reasonably good going
forward at our largest business, but 2009 will be another very
rough year at the media companies." He accepted the 2008 losses
and knew that in the following year the *Post* would lose even
more—"substantial money," he called it. As long as the losses could
be considered an investment in a business that would be profitable

again, he was fine with it. But he dropped in a gentle warning: "*Post* management knows the losses must diminish in 2010."

It was not a make-money-or-be-gone ultimatum because Graham knew it was foolish to imagine a return to the flush days. In fact, the problems might be solved only when the paper returned to a miser's budget. "Today," Graham wrote, "it isn't obvious that even the best-run, most successful newspaper can be consistently profitable. But the *Post* will get every chance."

Still, the curt message to *Post* management—Weymouth's team—was a reminder that every big-time paper lived with the possibility of failure. Print revenues continued to fall ten times faster than online revenues rose. Some analysts proposed online only; others insisted websites would never make real money. No one knew anything, really, except that something had to be done.

His *Wall Street Journal* boss once described Marcus Brauchli as the very picture of "the swashbuckling banana-republic foreign correspondent." A good thing, too, because that was no hill that Weymouth wanted taken, it was a damn Everest. The publisher wanted him to meld the *Post* and Washingtonpost.com into a single news organization operating on all media platforms while doing world-class journalism. And, oh yes, do it with fewer people and less money each year.

Looking more like an affable lawyer than a practitioner of Nicaraguan derring-do, Brauchli was forty-seven, tall, thin, balding, and well turned out in light grays that whispered of fine tailoring. He pleasantly took offense at the "outsider" talk, pointing out that in the previous sixty-two years, two of the *Post*'s three executive editors came from outside the newsroom: Russ Wiggins from the *New York Times*, Bradlee from *Newsweek*. Only Len Downie was pure-bred *Post*. While Brauchli had never worked in Washington or covered politics, he came with advantages. An important contributor in a *Journal* project integrating that paper's print and online newsrooms, he had worked in a news organization as widely respected as his new one and he brought a sense of urgency no longer obvious in Downie.

In April 2009, he announced a newsroom reorganization. Entire sections of the newspaper disappeared. Stories were edited for a tighter newshole. The Sunday magazine became a slick city guide. Washingtonpost.com put up a new local home page. Downie's newsroom—Bradlee's before that—had operated with assistant managing editors overseeing departments such as National, Metro, Sports, Style, Business. To create a production line that would work for both print and online, Brauchli remade the organizational chart.

"He restructured the paper by separating the creation of content from the production of content." So began one editor's e-mail explaining the new schematic:

> On the creation side, he split reporters and their editors into two groups: Local and National. Working under managing editor Liz Spayd, the two groups were then organized by subject matter instead of geography. The Maryland, Virginia, and District desks, for instance, were replaced with Group Leaders in Education, Social Issues, Cops and Courts, Local Government, etc. The ratio of reporters to editors was greatly increased as the ranks of editors were thinned via buyout. The assistant managing editor role was eliminated in a cost-saving move that also flattened the structure.
>
> He took all the production people—from copy editors at the newspaper to web producers at the website—and placed them on a Universal Desk. The desk was given responsibility for taking the content created by the Local and National staffs and delivering it in newsprint, on the web, and on other platforms such as mobile phones.

One reporter told me he worried that the plan would undermine "the greatest strength of any newspaper newsroom," the reporter-editor relationship. Previously, a story was a shared responsibility; by challenging a writer's every thought, an editor invested his own ego and reputation in the story. "That's an awfully powerful engine," the reporter said. The new structure seemed to be an assembly line of editors handing stories off to other editors. "There's an alchemy to producing great journalism," he said. "It's something that works just because it does. I fear we're about to fuck mightily with that."

Two questions dominated a Brauchli staff meeting on the reorganization plan. What changes were coming? Did any of it mean new money? He could answer the first because managing that change was his job. The second, no one knew.

"We are in a really dynamic industry facing profound challenges," Brauchli said. "But I think, realistically, this organization has the best chance of not only surviving but flourishing of any news organization its size because of a mix of things from the commitment of the owners to the nature of a Washington committed to news."

Yes, something had to be done.

So Brauchli landed running.

"If I have a worry," he said, "it's that we're doing too many things all at once. Putting in a content management system, which is a big, complicated exercise. We're bringing into this newsroom— the *Post*'s—people who haven't worked here who have their own views of what happens downtown. And, of course, everyone here has their views of what happens over in Arlington. Preserving the best qualities of both cultures is a challenge. And we're going to have to actually build physical space, which is another complication, moving people around. We're doing a redesign of the paper, and some of the website."

About here, a business reporter asked the kind of cut-to-the-chase question that reporters often ask—though perhaps not that often of a brand-new executive editor arriving in mid-crisis.

"How will all this make us a better business?" the reporter asked. "We'd have to quadruple our Internet traffic to make significant advertising gains. Will all this get us more advertising, will it increase the physical paper circulation?"

Brauchli said, "It will not do those things." It was a little about money—savings would come with the merger—but more about reorganizing the newsroom for new chores, among them the creation of "news alerts." Those snappy little mini–news reports went mostly to mobile devices during users' workdays. They were important, Brauchli said, because "operating competitively is really really really important." He added, "You want people to think of *The Washington Post* as the place they first learn of things."

Yes, the new editor of *The Washington Post* had declared that hundred-word news alerts were really really really important. The idea of news alerts was to reach people when and where they wanted to be reached while raising awareness of the *Post* brand. It had nothing to do with the kind of journalism that built *The Washington Post*. But, in these times, it had everything to do with survival.

In an interview later, I asked, "With everything that's happening, what's the long-term strategy now?"

Brauchli: "At a strategy session that Katharine initiated, the *Post* settled on being 'for and about Washington,' being the indispensable guide to this city. For the audience outside Washington, we have to do the best job of explaining politics, policy, and people in this seat of power. For the Washington audience, we have to do that—plus help readers know their communities, find restaurants and theaters, follow their school board or local council, make decisions on voting. These are the central objectives of any great metropolitan newspaper. We are not in a retreat in any way from the serious journalism that defined the *Post* for decades. We have to continue to do that but also a great deal more because we now compete with many new layers of media, ranging from blogs or individual websites to mobile platforms that bring national and international competitors into our marketplace. But we continue to believe that strong, original, inspired journalism will draw an audience that will enable us to remain profitable."

DK: "How important is it to regain that profitability?"

MB: "No news organization can long thrive as an independent organization if it's financially dependent. Obviously, we're part of a larger company and we always have some financial interdependence with our parent company. But I think we cannot survive as a ward of the corporate parent. We won't be able to do the kinds of journalism that are important to us and our readers if we are not financially independent and strong. None of us wants to be a money-losing enterprise. None of us wants to be carried."

DK: "Isn't that the position right now?"

MB: "Yes. But Kaplan lost money for many years, too. If you think you are losing money in the short term because of various factors, secular or cyclical, but you think you'll ultimately be profitable, the way to see those losses—if you can afford them—is as investments in your future. If you believe, as I do, as we do, that information has value, and that great journalism has great value, then we will find a path to realizing that value. But we may have to invest in the short term to get there."

DK: "How do you plan to 'get there'?"

MB: "Nobody has the proverbial 'silver bullet.' What we have to do, at many levels, is perform. My primary concern is that we continue to be ambitious, taking on the great causes, tackling the big issues, explaining the dense but important, writing better, thinking smarter, delivering more compelling content than anybody else. If we do that, that gets you part of the way there because that keeps your audience. And if we maintain our audience, if we do the journalism, if we have good products, we will survive."

Managing editor Liz Spayd had told *Portfolio*'s Lloyd Grove that Katharine Weymouth would move forcefully and fast. "Hold on to your hats, cowboys," she said. "We're going for a ride." And late in 2009, Weymouth drew a deep breath, smiled, further considered the question about how the ride had been so far, exhaled, and said, "Unbelievable."

Through 2008, the *Post* reported losses of $3.4 million a week—and 2009 was no better. Because, again, something had to be done, the publisher earlier had approved an idea to make some money.

The idea was a really really really bad idea, and had she ever been a reporter, if only through one day's lunch with a source, she would have known she couldn't do what she planned to do. A newspaper can never take money from the subjects of its coverage.

It does not make it better to bring those people to your home for a private dinner. It makes it worse.

It does not make it better to invite other interested parties that the subject of your news coverage would want to see. It makes it worse.

It does not make it better to say that all the conversation at the dinner bought and paid for by the subject of your news coverage is off the record. It makes it worse.

But she planned to do all that and do it eleven times at private dinners bought by sponsors at the rate of $25,000 a night or at the bargain rate of $250,000 for the series. Sponsors would mix with movers and shakers. The *Post*'s marketing staff had produced an advertising flier promising sponsors that these evenings would sparkle with "news-driven and off-the-record conversation. Spirited? Yes. Confrontational? No."

Weymouth's grandmother was famous for her dinners with Washington's powerful. An invitation to Katharine Graham's table conferred on its recipient the ego glow that accompanied acceptance among the elite. But Weymouth, as yet without her grandmother's achievements, was not conferring status in return for unspoken, unreported agreement of thought. Today's Katharine was simply selling seats to representatives of special interests.

This was influence peddling. Unseemly for anyone, it is unforgivable in the better journalistic circles. Yet here was *The Washington Post*, the most righteous of righteous papers, promising to put special-interest operatives alongside decision makers. The newspaper that chased lobbyists into prison would, for a fee, facilitate a sponsor's lobbying. The newspaper that made its reputation uncovering secrets now would create them.

Had Weymouth ever worked in the *Post* newsroom, she would have known that secrets have a short shelf life in Washington. This one went viral the morning of July 2, when *Politico* posted a story online that began:

> For $25,000 to $250,000, The Washington Post is offering lobbyists and association executives off-the-record, non-confrontational access to "those powerful few"—Obama administration officials, members of Congress, and the paper's own reporters and editors. The astonishing offer is detailed in a flier circulated Wednesday to a health care lobbyist, who provided it to a reporter because the lobbyist said he feels it's a conflict for the paper to charge for access to, as the flier says, its "health care reporting and editorial

staff." The offer—which essentially turns a news organization into a facilitator for private lobbyist-official encounters—is a new sign of the lengths to which news organizations will go to find revenue at a time when most newspapers are struggling for survival. And it's a turn of the times that a lobbyist is scolding The Washington Post for its ethical practices.

Swiftly, unanimously, and often with snarkish delight, commentators decided that Weymouth had stepped in it. At the *Post*, amid a newsroom uproar, Weymouth and Brauchli said the flier had been a marketing executive's mistake, that it had gone out without their seeing it, and did not represent what they had agreed to. The next day, Weymouth canceled the dinners; two days later, she published an apology to readers.

David Carr of the *New York Times* wrote, "Theoretically, you can't buy *Washington Post* reporters, but you can rent them." Jack Shafer of *Slate*:

> To gauge just how unkosher the Weymouth salon is, consider a smaller-scale version of the same practice: A reporter throws a poker party at his home. The guest list includes legislative aides and junior lobbyists. That's OK, right? It's just a poker game among a bunch of guys who live in Washington. But the minute the reporter starts charging the lobbyists money on the promise that legislative aides will attend, he's crossed the line. He's no longer hosting a party; he's arranging a lobbying session for personal profit. His editors would tan his hide. Then they'd fire him . . . What really stinks about the now-aborted salon-for-dollars scheme is that Katharine Weymouth appears to have contemplated the sale of something that wasn't hers to sell—The Post's credibility.

Post ombudsman Andrew Alexander called the plan "an ethical lapse of monumental proportions." (Deborah Howell opted for a reporter's jargon: "A giant fuckup.") Alexander interviewed the publisher, the editor, and marketing executive Charles Pelton, who had been hired only six weeks earlier. While Weymouth and Brauchli both took responsibility and expressed embarrassment, they mostly tossed Pelton under the bus.

He was a genial, gray-haired Californian hired to be general manager of a new business, Washington Post Conference & Events. The Weymouth salons were to lead to perennial major conferences worth millions of dollars. Such conferences were common among media heavyweights such as *The New Yorker*, the *Atlantic, National Journal,* the *Economist,* and the *Wall Street Journal*—though none of those promised to use their reporters as connectors to policy makers and lobbyists.

Briefly and carefully, Pelton suggested to me that Weymouth and Brauchli had not told the entire story. "Who knew what when was not fully explained in the ombudsman's piece," he said. He asked that I not use his *Post* e-mail address because it "is being monitored." He gave me a private e-mail address and said we might talk later.

In mid-August, I asked if he was negotiating a severance settlement. "Who told you that?" he said. "Anyway, I'm not doing any interviews until *after* my situation with the *Post* is cleared up." He had promised an interview to the ombudsman first.

On September 3, I asked Weymouth if Pelton was still a *Post* employee.

Emphatically, "Yes."

"For long?" I asked.

This time, silence.

A week later, Pelton's resignation was announced. My further e-mails went unanswered and he issued a statement: "Given the current circumstances with regard to the resources needed to launch [an events business], my family and I have decided not to relocate to Washington, D.C." The ombudsman, Alexander, had spoken to Pelton only long enough to arrive at a wry conclusion: "I gathered he was calling from his yacht."

Brauchli argued that cancellation should outweigh planning. "Nothing that's happened is deeply egregious," he said. "We made a couple of missteps that we probably should have seen and not done. I regret that we allowed the idea to advance as far as it did without thinking through the way it might impugn our credibility."

I asked, "Was the money the problem? The off-the-record?"

He said, "Oh, the off-the-record thing was the only problem as far as I was concerned. We had laid out some very specific conditions on what we would consider acceptable. There had to be multiple sponsors; the news department had to choose the topics; we would moderate the discussions but not participate as opinion leaders because we don't do the opinion thing; we would ensure that anyone participating was part of a genuine dialogue and we weren't putting people in the room that were shills; and it had to be a real journalism thing, not a bunch of people sitting around celebrating their point of view.

"I also had originally indicated that we would only do it if we were able to use the material under what the British call the Chatham House rule. [The press can use the information but not name its source.] But I allowed the thing to slip into an off-the-record thing—mainly because, frankly, I didn't pay sufficient attention."

To judge by Brauchli's later admissions, he apparently paid no attention at all. In a letter to Pelton dated September 25, 2009, Brauchli said the off-the-record nature of the dinners "was never hidden from me by you or anyone else." At two slide presentations, he had heard them so described. He also had discussed it with Pelton. And, yes, Pelton had e-mailed to Brauchli marketing materials and correspondence with the newsroom that contained the phrase. "I should have said something at that point, but did not," Brauchli wrote. "And you certainly should not be faulted for my not speaking up. Please feel free to share this letter with anyone who questions whether you kept me informed about the way the dinners were being promoted."

In our conversation about the embarrassing salon controversy, Brauchli went on:

"The *Post* has a unique and important role in this town and its reputation for journalism is shining bright lights in dark corners, and we should not have been creating dark spaces for monied interests to meet with the people they would seek to influence.

"Now, I would add, we didn't, in the end, do this.

"The marketing department sent out a brochure that was egregious in its description, a caricature of what we intended. It served to starkly remind us of how this sort of thing would be seen and we called it off with all the attendant bad publicity. We didn't do it. We called it off. It didn't happen. Our ombudsman wrote a column saying this was 'an ethical lapse of monumental proportions.' Well, actually, it wasn't. We didn't do it. It was a judgment lapse. We shouldn't have proceeded down that particular avenue. But we did not do it."

In those last twelve sentences, Brauchli told me seven times that the dinners had been cancelled. Better if he could have told me one time that they had not been planned.

The portrait of Katharine Weymouth done by her friend Matt Mendelsohn on January 21, 2008, showed her striking a glamour pose with a copy of the *Post* curled in her hand. The picture never appeared in her own newspaper, but it did run in the *New York Times* on July 3, 2009, along with a story on the salon saga.

This was irony doubled. First, Mendelsohn's work showed up as illustration for a snarky *Times* piece on a Weymouth embarrassment. Second, it came when Weymouth and Mendelsohn were the central figures in a controversy of their own.

That hoohah, coming on the heels of the salon episode, was not as sensational but to some journalists it was the more troubling of the two. Weymouth had used her publisher's hammer to kill a story because she thought advertisers wouldn't like it—and the story hadn't even been written yet. It was being reported and photographed by Mendelsohn, the publisher's friend since their Georgetown dog-park days.

He had worked a year documenting the life of Lindsay Ess. Bright, pretty, ambitious, and dogged, she was a fashion merchandising graduate of Virginia Commonwealth University. In the summer of 2007, she went to a hospital with an inflamed intestine. Surgery went wrong. A bacterial infection left her in a coma for two months. When she awoke, surgeons amputated her legs and arms to stop the spread of sepsis. The heart of Mendelsohn's story was Ess's return after the amputations to teach fashion show production at her school.

On January 17, four days before their shoot, Mendelsohn and

Weymouth attended a brunch celebration of a friend's birthday. Because everyone there knew she was about to be named publisher, someone said, "Matt, aren't you writing something for the magazine?"

Years earlier, he had done a light feature for the *Post*'s Sunday magazine on his move into wedding photography after a decade in photojournalism. Now he had a go ahead on Lindsay Ess. Weymouth, with her involvement in the newspaper about to be ramped up, was excited to hear that Mendelsohn had a story working.

"What's it a story about?" she asked.

"About a young woman who desperately wanted to be in the fashion business," Mendelsohn said. "Through a quirk of fate, she ended up losing her arms and legs two months after graduating with a degree in fashion merchandising. Then she comes back to teach fashion."

Weymouth stared.

Then she said, "No! You gotta be kidding me!"

Among her poker-night, birthday-brunch friends, Katharine Weymouth was often endearingly profane. Oaths and expletives beginning with the earlier letters of the alphabet were recurring features of her repartee. It was possible if not probable that she seasoned her response to her dog-walking buddy with a lively adjective, but Mendelsohn said only, "I went home and told my wife, 'The weirdest thing happened at the brunch today. Katharine made some bad jokes that indicated she thought Lindsay was not a good story for the *Post*." He also remembered her saying advertisers wanted happier stories, not depressing ones.

That, he figured, had to be a joke. Lindsay Ess's story was not so easily labeled. Her moments of depression came less often than moments of the kind that had her at the end of a fashion show runway shouting to the models, "Sex it up, ladies! Sexier! And Shera—no more tanning." The story, he thought, was that she lived her life the way it demanded to be lived. Because Ess's mother was her twenty-four-hour caregiver, Mendelsohn's wife one day told him, "This is a story for a Mother's Day." He agreed. "It's about a mother and daughter's love."

Then came an e-mail from an editor at the *Post*'s magazine.

Its first line was, "We need to talk."

Uh-oh.

" 'We need to talk' ranks up there with 'It's a routine surgery,' " Mendelsohn said. "An editor told me Katharine had been using the story in many a business meeting at the *Post* as an example of what not to do. And I said, 'But the story isn't written yet.' The editor said, 'She's using the story idea—of a woman with no arms and no legs . . .' "

Weymouth beat that no-depressing-stories drum insistently. She did it as early as her second month on the job when she didn't like that Style picture showing a toothless old woman dying in bed, and she did it in the summer of 2009, telling friends the Sunday magazine lost $3 million a year because it chased away advertisers with long stories on sad subjects. To which I say—as a reader who admired the magazine's deeply reported, elegantly written pieces—oh, please.

Hoping to rescue his story, Mendelsohn finally wrote it—nine thousand words—but editors could not get it in the magazine. On receiving Mendelsohn's e-mail that the publisher wanted "happier stories," Ess replied, "WTF?!? How rude."

Eventually, Mendelsohn's story and pictures ran on a photographers' website, for free, and was carried by America Online, for free, instead of running in *The Washington Post*, which might have paid $6,000 for a magazine cover story and photographs. "The money never mattered," he said. "The irony is, when everybody's trying to get out of print journalism, I'm trying to get back in. I hoped Lindsay's story would be my way back."

It all was an unfortunate case of bad timing, Weymouth said. The editorial shift in the magazine came just as Mendelsohn did his story.

"What Matt had told me, I did think it represented the feature that is informative but really depressing stuff in a depressing year," she said. "But I was not involved in the magazine deciding to kill it or run it. I did use it—I probably should have kept my mouth shut—as an example of the kind of thing we publish that makes me crazy."

"Still," I said, "you are you . . ."

234 | DAVE KINDRED

"And part of the 'me' is that I'm very frank. I read his story—he sent it to me when he finished—and it's a beautiful story, and there's a very uplifting tale about difficult circumstances—to the extent that a tale like that can be uplifting. It's well done. But I do think the magazine should take a different direction. I'm sorry that he got caught in the crossfire."

At home that night, I sent Weymouth an e-mail with one more question about the Mendelsohn story: "I was told that in your using it as an example of depressing stories that you'd rather not have, you said 'the advertisers' don't like that kind of story. Connecting 'advertisers' with judgment on news stories is always a slippery slope, so, did I hear the story correctly?"

She replied, "What I intended to convey was that, although the magazine has published many beautiful, moving, and important stories, I believed that it had gotten away from its readers and that the tone had become increasingly depressing. It has also become harder to sell. The magazine is a reader initiative and while I was not looking for a glowing, upbeat candy magazine, I did think we could do a better job of serving our readers and giving them a product that they would want to pick up every Sunday. And when you get readers, advertisers generally follow."

I took that as a yes.

Great newspapers didn't work that way. They insisted that editorial decisions be made without reference to advertisers' desires or demands; their reporters and news space were not for sale. Weymouth's hopes for the salon dinners and her intervention in the Mendelsohn magazine story stood in stark contrast to a Ben Bradlee/Katharine Graham decision of a generation earlier.

Bankers in town were upset by the *Post*'s investigation of savings-and-loan practices that targeted poor blacks. For months, the young reporter Len Downie had worked on the story. "Then, one day, Bradlee came over to me," Downie said. "I hardly ever had any contact with Ben, this great figure, and he said, in his booming voice, 'What are you working on?'

"I started to explain, in my nervous way, and he cut me off. 'That's way too complicated for me,' he said. 'But that's all right. I don't need to know anything else. I just want to say that in my office there was this delegation from the savings and loans industry. They told me you were working on something they didn't like and if we publish what you're writing, they'll pull all their advertising.'

"My heart stopped. I was waiting to hear the next thing. After a long pause, he said, 'Just get it right, kid.' And left. We finished the story, published it, and they pulled all their advertising for a year. And I had to find that out. I had to ask. No Katharine Graham came to me. Nobody ever said boo to me about it. And that was a lot of money back then, maybe a million dollars."

Henry Allen could talk you some talk, such as, "All the good-looking babes that used to flock to work here have been replaced by Dan Balz—no offense to Dan, but really . . ." He was a survivor of the *Post*'s golden era who first knew Woodward and Bernstein as "a cub and a fuckup." He was there in Bradlee's rambunctious years for "the creation of the hot-shit *Washington Post*." Now, he said, "Doom has been creeping up on us the last five years. I don't know what the future is, but it's over there," and with that he waved a hand toward an outside wall, indicating Washingtonpost.com's headquarters across the Potomac.

I stopped at Allen's desk in the early fall of 2009 to ask what he thought of Brauchli's insistence that the only problem with the salon idea was that he allowed it to slide into off-the-record status.

"I think," Allen began, raising that deep, loud voice that filled most every room he entered . . .

And he stopped because he remembered where he was, which was next to Brauchli's assistant, Pam Kendrick, temporarily camped among the Style folks.

He dropped a decibel or two to say, "Call me, we'll talk."

21.

HAMMERIN' HANK

Before Henry Allen and I could talk, he punched a fellow Postie in the face.

It happened on a Friday afternoon, October 30, 2009, just outside Brauchli's temporary office, only fifteen working days before Allen's long-planned retirement.

Henry Southworth Allen was sixty-eight years old, sturdy, vigorous, and decorated with a Hemingwayesque beard. No one in the building could remember the last time an editor had conferred in exactly that manner with a reporter. But no one could remember another Henry Allen, either. "Intense. Mercurial. Bald. Bearded." So ran a self-description with a website's gallery of portraits and landscapes he had painted. "Journalist, poet, novelist. Pulitzer Prize for criticism, 2000." At no time did he describe himself as a pugilist, because he believed nothing of much importance had happened on the Friday in question. "In the old days in the sports department at the *New York Daily News*, we had so many fights that we didn't even look up."

Back then, the *Daily News* newsroom in midtown Manhattan was in "Front Page" mode with every newshound's senses under assault by smoke, clattering typewriters, and whiskey drained from bottles left to clank in metal file cabinet drawers. Today's newsrooms were clean, polite, and numbingly professional. Allen certainly was old enough to know better than to get physical in a newsroom, though maybe a Marine never gets that old. (The last time he threw a punch, it was 1963 and he was at Parris Island studying up for Vietnam.)

The to-do began when Allen, working as an editor under contract, had heard enough from one of his writers, Manuel Roig-Franzia. Early in the week, they had exchanged unpleasantries during a news meeting; the writer reached across a table for Allen's notebook and ripped a page from it. Allen growled, "Give me my fucking notebook." Twice more, aspiring for a certain level of quality, Allen had raised questions about Roig-Franzia pieces. First time, the writer responded by calling the editor a "dick." Second time, he said, "Henry, you're being a cocksucker." On hearing the enhanced version, Allen shoved Roig-Franzia and followed with the right hand. The writer backed away, this time running silent.

Style was Ben Bradlee's baby, born a year and eleven months before the wandering Henry Allen came in from the New Mexico desert to sit one night on the copy desk and never leave. At last he had landed among kindred spirits whose intelligence, wit, sophistication, and daring made Style the coolest thing in journalism across nearly two decades—with Henry Allen as cool as anyone writing for a newspaper anywhere. Gene Weingarten would call him "very possibly the best feature writer who ever lived." David Von Drehle, once Style's top editor, thought of Allen as a "dazzling and original talent," a master of "experimentation, of risk-taking, of form-busting" who "took newspaper journalism to places no one realized it could go."

June 12, 1977. Allen on lists:

I didn't frighten my mother with my first list, which I wrote when I was ten, and left on my bureau. In fact, Mom stashed it in her family archives, along with the report cards, crayon drawings, and cuttings of baby hair in glassine envelopes:

RUNAWAY GOODS
1 tight suitcase
2 pairs of dungarees and 2 undershirts and underpants
3 pairs of shoes
4 pairs of shirts

coat and jacket
money
cantine
drinking cup

I've been reading, writing, reciting, lulling myself to sleep and whiling away 3 a.m. drives across Nebraska with lists ever since: all the countries and states I've visited (twenty-five and forty-one); places I've lived (thirty-five); the New York Yankees of 1951, including the hard-to-remember Bobby Brown on third base; plus the usual collection of drugs, lovers, fistfights, used cars, important books, and so on. Hasn't everybody?

For most of Allen's years, a Style appreciation on the death of a noteworthy personality was a marvel of the genre. But when attention spans came to be measured in nano-seconds, a thoughtful piece was all but a relic. Besides, the paper's news hole had been reduced and there went any room for the unique stories done by Allen and his cohorts (including Roig-Franzia). But Erik Wemple, the *Washington City Paper*'s editor and estimable *Post* critic, said, "My take is that Allen's frustrations don't lie so much with the *Post* as they do with the industry. The stuff that has him so mad has been steam-rolling newsrooms for the past five or six years, if not more. I'd say he should consider himself lucky that the *Post*'s stewards warded off these sorts of changes for as long as they did, long enough that Allen didn't boil over 'til he was almost out the door."
February 21, 1991. Allen on an Army media briefing in Riyadh:

The Persian Gulf press briefings are making reporters look like fools, nit-pickers and egomaniacs; like dilettantes who have spent exactly none of their lives on the end of a gun or even a shovel; dinner party commandos, slouching inquisitors, collegiate spitball artists; people who have never been in a fistfight much less combat; a whining, self-righteous, upper-middle-class mob jostling for whatever tiny flakes of fame may settle on their shoulders like some sort of Pulitzer Prize dandruff.

After the fisticuffs, huzzahs for Allen came from inside the building and across the land. "The best press since Lindbergh landed in France," he said. Anyone googling Henry Allen still found Henry "Red" Allen, Jr., the noted jazz cornetist, but at the top of the page there was Henry Allen of *The Washington Post*. "Winning a Pulitzer gets you some attention," Allen said, "but I think the committee might want to consider holding a boxing smoker next year."

The City Paper's reporting of the dustup prompted dozens of user comments. My favorite came from a Jeff Houck, who wrote, "If Henry Allen clocked me in the face in a workplace setting—whether or not I deserved it—I'd designate that spot on my cheek a place on the National Journalism Historic Register. Then I'd spend every morning of my life looking in the mirror at the abrasion and laughing my ass off. We should all be lucky enough to be walloped by such talent." Someone signing in as Walter Lippmann typed, "I only wish he had slugged more of those nitwits on his way out."

When Allen wrote to his son that he next expected Chuck Norris jokes, Peter Allen replied, "Henry Allen doesn't edit an article. He just stares down the page until the words change on their own." A neighbor, Richard Weil, wrote a poem, "Battle Him of the Republic (of Takoma Park)":

Our Henry is a bard ass editor
Careful how you write the scoop
He tends to edit content and punks
Henry, he don't take no poop.

His passion at the Post is legend
Don't ever take him for a sucker
Or if you do, you just might visit
All his knuckles when you pucker.

I guess I'll end this poem 'write' now
As it may make some grown men cry
But I know many editors are smiling
And many Marines are yelling 'Semper Fi'!

Marcus Brauchli helped end the tussle outside his office door and then ordered that Allen stay home for the remaining days of his service. No doubt the editor's decision was good management, especially with Allen a short-timer. Still, kicking Allen out kept the *Post* on a losing streak beyond the financial reverses that had reached the hundreds of millions. Every six months, another report showed circulation falling in twenty thousand-reader chunks. Credibility took a hit in the salon debacle even before Weymouth meddled in the magazine's business. And now a Pulitzer winner was banned from the newsroom, and not just any Pulitzer winner but this one, for thirty-nine years a craftsman whose stuff made the hair on your neck quiver in applause. Von Drehle told Wemple, "I was sad because instead of being banned from the building, Henry should have a statue in the lobby—and, yes, it should have prickles all over it and a grumpy look on its face."

January 28, 2009. Allen's appreciation of John Updike:

On Christmas Day 1960, when I was 19 and had every intention of becoming the greatest living stylist in America, I opened a present, John Updike's "Rabbit, Run," and saw from the first few pages that as long as he lived—and he was only nine years older than I—I would not succeed. He was a dragon who would be unslayable.

Instead, he stalked me for 35 years, breathing the cool, ego-crushing fire of a style that didn't just evoke reality but also seemed to violate one of our most ancient taboos, the one against the making of graven images—a style that created eerie holograms with 100 percent correspondence to the material world.

And then, one morning in June 1995, I looked across a gallery at the Whitney Museum in New York and saw him, the dragon himself. Taking notes like me, staring at the Edward Hoppers with mild eyes and beaked nose familiar from dust jackets, he seemed immense, "taller far than a tall man," as Sappho described the god Ares. To speak to him or not to speak? I remembered that he reviewed art for Barbara Epstein at the *New York Review of Books*. We were working colleagues for a moment, Updike and I.

I approached a slender, slightly stooped man who shrank reassuringly as I neared him.

"Aren't you John Updike?" I asked.

"I seem to be," he said in a low, careful tenor, the voice of a friendly dentist reminding you to floss, but a dentist who might have something going on with the receptionist . . .

It was Henry Allen's last appreciation. He said, "Style as a place where readers can find writing, evocation, wit, and even some literary art is gone. There is NO full-time features editor on the assigning desk. I was the last one, and I was half-time . . . The big push is for arts coverage. Arts are easy to assign, and easy to edit. They are format pieces, close to standing features, which makes them easy, but they are often tediously written. Relying on arts coverage guarantees we will always come in second to the *Times*.

"Bradlee's masterpiece—Style—is over. It came out of a generation of people who wanted to be tough, hip, ironic, funny, and sophisticated—the Humphrey Bogart template . . . Over and done with."

Henry Southworth Allen, the last and best of the high-wire walkers (he'd written about the daring Wallendas) who created the soul of a great writers' newspaper, would read a Brauchli memo on the appointment of a "multi-tasking editor" whose job was "content management optimization." He would recognize in it the dispiriting bureaucratic language of the twenty-first century's merged website/print newsroom. He said, "Now the nameless process zombies have taken over."

It was, then, a good time to go to his drawing, his painting, maybe some writing. The *Post* could no longer be the paper that Bradlee, Downie, and the Grahams had created any more than today's world could be their world of a generation past.

Still, he wondered why the dustup caused such fuss.

"If this had been two guys in an insurance office, nobody would have cared," he said. "Why care about this?"

Here's why. It didn't happen in a time of degenerate newsroom hacks slugging each other over a bar tab. It was a twenty-first-century moment when even the best and brightest knew that their beloved newspaper business had gone all to hell. So in any future telling of Legendary Moments in *Post* Journalism, no one will remember the run-up of insults between Henry Allen and Manuel Roig-Franzia. They'll remember Hammerin' Hank's right cross to his antagonist's jaw as a last, shimmering, beautifully defiant act of rage against the dying of the light.

EPILOGUE

Len Downie and Bob Kaiser wrote a book about newspapers and television news organizations across America. *The News About the News* was an academic examination of journalism. In my pitch for this book, I told Downie, "What you and Bob did, that's what I want to do. But only about the *Post*—"

Downie jumped in. "Good idea."

"—and sexier," I said.

He laughed. "That won't be hard."

We talked in the summer of 2006, maybe the last time an executive editor of a major metropolitan newspaper laughed about anything. By the next summer, the joy was gone. By the summer of 2008, Downie himself was gone.

The news about the news became more miserable each day. Late in 2009, circulation figures hit their lowest level since 1940. While U.S. population had doubled, newspaper sales had fallen 25 percent. The *Post* sold 582,844 papers daily and 822,208 Sundays—a 5 percent drop in a year. Money vanished even faster; the *Post* company's newspaper division, primarily the flagship paper, lost $359 million through 2008 and the first three quarters of 2009. Small wonder that Don Graham informed the *Post*'s top managers that he expected better in 2010.

A second insult came in a survey. Sixty-three percent of Americans believed the news media often couldn't get its facts straight. That was "the lowest level in more than two decades," according to the Pew Research Center. In virtually all demographic units on all questions—political party, age, education, geography, bias, ethics, openness, fairness—the press fared poorly.

As I worked on this book, newspapers died. After 150 years in business, Denver's wonderful tabloid, the *Rocky Mountain News*, closed its doors. In Seattle, the *Post-Intelligencer* went dark. Suddenly, the *Post*, the *New York Times*, the *Chicago Tribune*, and the *Los Angeles Times* weren't feeling too good themselves.

The malaise touched even a veteran newsman proud of journalism's work in Watergate and the Pentagon Papers. Speaking at Harvard late in 2008, Anthony Lewis, twice a Pulitzer winner for the *New York Times*, cited the Bush administration's violation of a criminal statute on wiretapping; its direction of torture of detainees in violation of treaties, law, and American tradition; and its taking "this country to war on the basis of false assertions of fact." Lewis asked, "Where was the American press when those things happened?"

Shortly after John Carroll resigned the editor's job at the *Los Angeles Times* in 2006, he imagined the once-unimaginable. At a gathering of journalism leaders, he said, "If, at some point in America's newspaper-free future, the police decide that guilt or innocence of murder suspects can be determined perfectly well by beating them until somebody confesses," he said, "who will sound the alarm, as the *Philadelphia Inquirer* did in 1987? Or, if those federal scientists who tell our doctors what drugs and what dosages are best for us are secretly allowed to take salaries and stock options from drug companies, how will we know if the *Los Angeles Times* is not there to tell us, as it did in 2003? . . . More routinely, who will make the checks at City Hall? Who, in cities and towns across America, will go down to the courthouse every day, or to the police station? Who will inspect the tens of thousands of politicians who seek to govern? Who—amid American's great din of flackery and cant—will tell us in plain language what's actually going on?"

Without *The Washington Post*, who would work months to unravel the bureaucratic tangle that deepened the wounds of already wounded soldiers in Building 18 at the Walter Reed Army

Medical Center? Who would go to the Iraqi desert and put at risk his legs, his hands—his life—to bring that senseless war's horrors to the breakfast tables of the nation's leaders? Without such a newspaper serving its community of readers, who tells them everything about the evil that brings death to a college campus where youth lived an hour before?

Shortly after moving into a new office as a *Post* vice president at large, Downie began work designed to make certain those questions would always be answered. He and Michael Schudson, a Columbia University professor, did a report entitled "The Reconstruction of American Journalism," commissioned by Columbia's Graduate School of Journalism and its dean, Nicholas Lemann.

Downie and Schudson said they saw "abundant opportunity in the future of journalism." From their report: "We have seen struggling newspapers embrace digital change and start to collaborate with other papers, nonprofit news organizations, universities, bloggers, and their own readers. We have seen energetic local reporting startups. We have seen pioneering public radio news operations . . . We have seen the first foundations and philanthropists step forward to invest in the future of news, and we have seen citizens help to report the news and support new nonprofit news ventures . . . Now, we want to see more leaders emerge in journalism, government, philanthropy, higher education, and the rest of society to seize this moment of challenging changes and new beginnings to ensure the future of independent news reporting."

News organizations must do that. They also must accept a mission defined by John Carroll as more daunting than any they have ever faced. They must work to ensure "the existence, long into the future, of a large, independent, principled, questioning, deep-digging cadre of journalists." The mission is not merely to do good stories, nor is it merely to save newspapers. "It is—and this may sound grandiose—to save journalism itself."

Late in 2009, all across America, the salvation train sat at the station. Where it would go, no one knew. How it would get there, no one knew. But they all knew they'd better get on board. They knew it at 1150 Fifteenth Street in Washington, D.C., where, curiously, a violin virtuoso may have given them words to live by. When

Gene Weingarten asked Joshua Bell to play at a Metro stop, the showman briefly considered the possible harm to his Stradivarius if not his reputation. Then he said, "Sounds like fun. What the hell."

The violinist's words could be a journalist's, as good and true as Bob Woodward's reminder that reporters are expected to speak truth to power even in-house: "All good work is done in defiance of management." Put them with Katharine Graham's lecture deliv ered gently when the boys from Metro were investigating all the president's men: "Never? Don't tell me never."

Only a dreamer believes *The Washington Post* can ever again be the *Post* of the late twentieth century. Because those money-machine days will not return, the newspaper will never again pro-duce the cash necessary to put together a nine-hundred-person newsroom. Yet only a fool says the *Post*'s days as a major player are over. Woodward believes the paper could be effective with a news-room half the size of years past; during the Pentagon Papers and Watergate reporting of the early 1970s, the room's population was under 350.

The *Post* will survive. The greatest assurance of that was the continuing work of Don Graham. The company's chief executive officer had emotional attachments to the flagship newspaper that deepened his resolve to see it through its most profound crisis in seventy-six years. He had built a diversified company able to sus-tain a struggling division. *Post* executives were smart enough to stay away from the highly leveraged deals that pushed other media companies into bankruptcy; they also had shown the will and dis-cipline necessary to cut costs. The newspaper's problems were partly of its own making, allowing editors to overspend, and fail-ure first to anticipate the Internet and then to comprehend its impact. But most of the damage came when the Internet's rapid maturation coincided with the collapse of the national economy. No one could stand in that tsunami.

Once the waters recede, and the *Post*'s survival as a news organi-zation is a fact, the question will be one of franchise identity. Will there be a newspaper? A daily, or Sundays only, or three days a week—what? Washingtonpost.com will be available every minute every day everywhere. The website could be invaluable to both users and advertisers if it is engaging, informative, and entertaining while delivering the goods quickly to every imaginable wireless device. Maybe then there would be no newspaper at all.

There would be websites and journalism, yes. But still. Newspapers—a newspaper in my hands!—had been my university. Half of what I knew about anything, I learned because a newspaper story piqued my curiosity. Weingarten once explained that serendipity:

> Newspaper reading at its best involves incongruous juxtapositions and the pleasurable discoveries of the new; a headline grabs your eye; a photograph pulls you into an article, or vice versa; a tidbit shared with a partner over breakfast leads to an impromptu discussion or fight, or a swapping of sections to compare discoveries. I never read what I think I will read. I never find what I already knew I would find. I don't read the newspaper so much as it reads me. By contrast, when I read the news online, I seek out and find what I knew I wanted in advance: a specific article, a specific issue. It confirms knowledge, instead of expanding it; for me, at least, it offers up news as a consumable item instead of educating me.

However the delivery system changed, David Hoffman said, the essential elements of journalism could not, must not, change. After twenty-seven years at the *Post*, first as a White House reporter and last as the foreign editor, Hoffman took the 2009 buyout. In his farewell speech in the newsroom he told a newspaper story.

"It was September 1972, a few months after the Watergate break-in . . ."

The boys from Metro, Woodward and Carl Bernstein, were in Ben Bradlee's office briefing him on a story about Attorney General John Mitchell.

Bradlee interrupted to say, "Listen, fellas, are you certain on Mitchell? Absolutely certain?"

They nodded.

"Can you write it now?"

Then, Hoffman said, "Bradlee stood up and waved his hand— 'Well, then, let's do it.' They did. And we all know what happened.

This moment happened right here, in this room, in our time, and it has happened a hundred times since then. We did the gutsy, hard work of finding the truth."

He told another story. As people fled the violence of Darfur in 2003, the foreign correspondent Emily Wax found a group of displaced teachers. She told Hoffman: "Huddled under trees, these educated women wrote letters to international leaders begging for help. They weren't sure they would make it. They wept, wondering about the bombed-out school they left behind, their students, all their hard work. Two years later, I saw a few of them again in a refugee camp in Sudan. They were still without their homes, without their schools. But they were going to open a school in the camp soon. We all hugged. And we all wept, all realizing how much time had passed and how the war was still going on."

Hoffman had heard enough fears about journalism. "The only thing that can extinguish our light is forgetting who we are. Forgetting our legacy. Forgetting Ben's wonderful determination and Emily's remarkable courage and empathy. This is what we are about—we discover, we reveal, we explore, and we must have no fear. Please, as I leave you, I beg you—don't be deterred from this great mission. Don't let the doubts distract you from our highest calling. You are the ones who will save the *Post*. You are the ones who will save journalism. Do not forget who you are and what you must do."

The sports columnist Sally Jenkins knows who they are— they're kids on fire, and the fire is familiar. "The future of the business is its past—the Internet is the soul of journalism," she said. "It's full of rabble-rousing pamphleteers, the penny press, and samizdat. It's what journalism is supposed to be. We weren't supposed to be an industry. We weren't supposed to get so comfortable." No money? No problem. "If I have to give up the good apartment, so be it. I became a journalist because I couldn't believe I could get so lucky as to have someone give me a plane ticket to someplace interesting, so I could find out more about something that made me curious."

In today's kids, she saw yesterday's. "Give them a laptop and a digital recorder and some meal money, and God almighty they're thrilled. And they beg for more work. *The Washington Post* will be fine, even if 'controlling costs' means handsomely paid veterans like me have to go away. The future is a bunch of kids in wrinkled clothes and backpacks who don't give a shit what they're paid, who have a knee-jerk distrust of all forms of power, who are happy to live on hot coffee and bags of smoked almonds, whose eyes flame with enthusiasm for their jobs, and who love the fatigue they feel after deadline. Well, hell. Isn't that how we all used to be?"

There once was such a kid who came to the *Post* out of the navy.

Could've gone to law school, didn't want to wait around that long.

Harry Rosenfeld, the hard-ass Metro editor, gave him a two-week tryout and said, "You don't know how to do this," to which the kid said, "Thank you. But I found out something. I love it. I don't know how to do it, but I know that I love it." So he went to the bush leagues to learn how.

A year later, the *Post* hired him back.

He worked night cops, 6:30 p.m. to 2:30 a.m.

Single, on fire, he woke up early, worked day shifts, too.

Nine months in, on June 17, 1972, he was assigned a cops' story.

D.C. police had arrested five men who had broken into the Watergate Hotel.

And in court that day, when one of the five muttered that he was retired from the CIA, there began the rest of Bob Woodward's life.

By the fall of 2009, he spoke of himself as an old guy. But he kept reporting stories that ran at the top of the front page.

He also imagined the *Post* of the future. "In ten years, it may not be a printed paper, it may be online-only. Maybe *The Washington Post* print edition for old hands like myself will be a sixteen-page newsletter, daily, weekly, who knows? Maybe like the *Daily Racing Form*, there would be a real premium price on it for those who want it. But we know the information business will continue to exist; the demand for good, solid, dependable information is as great as ever. How it's delivered, who delivers it, what you pay for it—those are the questions no one has figured out."

Imagine this: In 2020 *The Washington Post* sells for five dollars a copy as a sixty-four-page, slick-paper tabloid five days a week. Woodward says you'd have to buy that newspaper if it "scoops the world every day with good, original, exclusive, dazzling information." At the same time, Washingtonpost.com is ubiquitous, essential, and irresistible. The website gives a global platform to the newspaper's work even as it creates its own news reports, hyperlocal databases, and entertainment video in high definition.

And on a marquee at the front of the newsroom, these words in lights:

"All good work is done in defiance of management."

"Never? Don't tell me never."

"Sounds like fun. What the hell."

SHIRTTAIL

Reporters and Editors

BRADLEE, BEN

"Sally's thrilled by getting me the hell out of the house," he said, meaning his wife, Sally Quinn. Eighty-eight in the fall of 2009, he came in to the *Post* every workday. He said the author Jeff Himmelman "had interviewed the hell out of me" for a biography. "I gave him my files, too. I have not led a terribly ordered existence. In one file, we found a sandwich."

BRODER, DAVID

He continued as the *Post*'s op-ed political columnist. He called himself "reasonably optimistic" about the industry's future, "based on the continuing high quality of the people coming into the newsroom and our growing understanding of the opportunities opened by the multiple channels of communication."

CILLIZZA, CHRIS

He became a White House correspondent. On February 24, 2009, his wife, Gia, gave birth to the couple's first child, Charles Henry Cillizza, aka Little Fix.

DOWNIE, LEN

He joined the faculty at Arizona State University's Walter Cronkite School of Journalism and Mass Communication. Before

Knopf published his first novel—*The Rules of the Game*, starring, of course, an investigative reporter—he had a second outlined. A lifetime of deadlines will do that to you.

GRAHAM, DON

Late in 2009, I asked him, "Is anyone ever going to make real money on the Web—the kind of money it takes to sustain a big-time newsroom?"

He said, "I can't answer that question yes or no, but that's sure as hell what we intend to do." A pause. "We've got to prove it."

HOHMANN, JAMES

He was in newspaper limbo. His second internship—he covered metropolitan transportation—was extended to the last day of 2009. "They say my future will depend on the company's financial situation at the end of the year. My fingers are crossed."

HULL, ANNE

She quit reading the Romenesko newspaper blog on the Poynter Journalism Institute website. "It's an obituary," she said. Her work continued to focus on "the dispossessed, those people in exile or shoved to the borders and reaching to get closer."

JENKINS, SALLY

Done with the presidential campaign, she returned to the subject that was really important in the nation's capital, the Redskins. On a regular basis in her sports column, she called for the impeachment of the football team's owner, Dan Snyder.

PINCUS, WALTER

"I cannot see a time when I am not working for the newspaper, though Herblock's record remains more than a decade away. For me, separation from the *Post* is almost as inconceivable as separation from Ann, my wonderful wife of forty-five years."

PRIEST, DANA

She was really puzzled when I asked what kind of work she would do if she were told she could no longer be a reporter. There was a long pause. Her delicate brow became furrowed with worry. I said, "You know, what would you be?"

Plaintively, she said, "A German shepherd?"

Late in 2009, she was deep into an intelligence project a full year in the making: "Truly a multimedia experiment. The Web presentation should be, if all works out, even more important than the newspaper articles. I hope to produce several stories, videos, chats, blogs, and interactive things I can't even name yet."

REID, TONY

He became director of the Writing Center at the Hill School in Pottstown, Pennsylvania. "The future of journalism is essentially here now. Journalism and media have moved from the page to the screen. Most of journalism will be video—more as time goes along. National papers like the *New York Times*, *USA Today*, the *Wall Street Journal*, and the *Financial Times* will live on, at least for a while. Some local papers are prospering because they have a monopoly on the news their audience wants. I can't see them going away. That's the way a lot of big-city papers, such as the *Post*, will have to go to survive—ultralocal."

SHADID, ANTHONY

In mid-September 2009, he resigned from the *Post* to join the *New York Times*. He said the *Post* had changed in ways that affected him personally and professionally. His mentor, Phil Bennett, was displaced as managing editor (and resigned to teach at Duke University). Shadid's immediate boss, foreign editor David Hoffman, took a buyout. "I adore the *Post* and Don Graham is still an inspiration to me," Shadid said. "But they're going a different direction in foreign, a lot more about policy, not going head to head on daily stories." In the summer, Shadid married Nada Bakri, a Lebanese journalist. Both will work for the *Times*.

WEINGARTEN, GENE

He took the 2009 buyout and stayed on at the *Post* under contract to do his Sunday magazine humor column and the "Tuesdays with Moron" online chat once a month. He was at work on a screenplay and a comic strip. A collection of his feature stories, titled *The Fiddler in the Subway*, was scheduled for publication in 2010 by Simon & Schuster.

WEYMOUTH, KATHARINE

She planned on giving a second life to the salons/conference idea, albeit with improvements. In the face of all that criticism the first time, she said, "You could go overboard and say, 'Oh, God, we can't do that.'" Instead, the *Post* would do an "intermediate level of briefings with a couple hundred people and possibly a big event."

WOODWARD, BOB

After his scoop on the McChrystal assessment of the war in Afghanistan, he said, "The old media is still kicking." His next book, on the Obama administration, was due for publication in the summer of 2010. His old boss, Bradlee, said, "He did, what, four books on Bush? Four! God couldn't get four books out of that guy."

A NOTE ON SOURCES

This book is based principally on my interviews of reporters and editors. A hundred and more people spoke to me on the record, telling me their stories. Occasionally, a subject asked to speak on background, meaning I could use the information but not name the source; in those cases, I did my best to use the fair and honest answers and leave the others in my notebook.

In the course of three years' work, I also searched for material in more than 125 books. The introduction's John Boyle O'Reilly definition of newspapers was found in James Jeffrey Roche's compilation of the Irishman's poems and speeches, titled *Life of John Boyle*. Chapter 1 draws heavily from several historical sources, foremost Merlo J. Pusey's magisterial biography, *Eugene Meyer*. That book also provided a line from Agnes Meyer's diary as well as the Lord Northcliffe quotation. Evalyn Walsh McLean's autobiography, *Father Struck It Rich*, is an odd little book (befitting an odd person) that recounted the years her even odder husband, Ned McLean, owned the *Post*. Katharine Graham's life with Phil Graham is told in beautiful, agonizing detail in her *Personal History*. Chalmers Roberts's history of the *Post* in its one hundredth year was invaluable. My accounts of the early days in the careers of Don Graham and Len Downie benefitted from two extraordinary character studies done by Barbara Matusow for

Washingtonian magazine. She profiled Downie in the July 1988 issue, and Graham in the August 1992 issue.

Interview subjects, 2007–2009: Michael Abramowitz, Joel Achenbach, Frank Ahrens, Andrew Alexander, Henry Allen, Muhammad Amin, Rick Atkinson, Paul Attner, Peter Baker, Dan Balz, Jim Barnhart, Mark Benjamin, Phil Bennett, Andy Beyer, Bob Blunk, Tom Boswell, Ben Bradlee, Jim Brady, Marcus Brauchli, R.B. Brenner, David Broder, Vince Bzdek, Ruben Castaneda, Rajiv Chandrasekaran, Chris Cillizza, Steve Coll, Rob Curley, Tim Curran, Roger Cushman, John Diener, Janice Downie, Len Downie, Jill Drew, Michel DuCille, Steve Fainaru, Mark Fainaru-Wada, Doug Feaver, John Feinstein, Omar Fekeiki, Marc Fisher, Emilio Garcia-Ruiz, Bart Gellman, Susan Glasser, William Goodfellow, Cynthia Gorney, Don Graham, James Grimaldi, Jill Grisco, Annie Groer, Mary Hadar, Bill Hamilton, Walt Harrington, John Harris, David Hawpe, Neil Henry, Fred Hiatt, Nelson Hernandez Jr., James Hohmann, David Hoffman, Adrian Holovaty, Deborah Howell, Anne Hull, Jim Hull, Dan Jenkins, Sally Jenkins, Bo Jones, Tammy Jones, Mary Jordan, Bob Kaiser, Bill Keller, Kitty Kelley, Ann Kornblut, Tony Kornheiser, Bill Kovach, Athelia Knight, Larry Kramer, Howard Kurtz, Lawrence Laurent, Jane Leavy, Jeff Leen, Carol Leggett, Bob Levey, Caroline Little, Mike Littwin, Bob Lyford, Bob McCartney, Annette McLeod, Rick Maese, Jason Manning, Al Manolo, David Maraniss, John Mashek, Jay Mathews, Barbara Matusow, Matt Mendelsohn, Kevin Merida, Shirley Meyer, John Morton, Jonathan Newton, Bill O'Brian, Pat O'Shea, Joshua Partlow, Gene Patterson, Steve Pearlstein, Eric Pianin, Walter Pincus, Gary Pomerantz, Mark Potts, Dana Priest, Steve Proctor, Mitch Prothero, Tony Reid, David Remnick, Paul Richard, Gene Robinson, Robert Rosenthal, Eli Saslow, Rachel Saslow, Chris Schroeder, Matt Schudel, Mike Semel, Anthony Shadid, Jack Shafer, Ian Shapira, Len Shapiro, Taylor Shapiro, Richard Simmons, David Simon, Verenda Smith, Rachel Smolkin, George Solomon, Liz Spayd, Alan Spoon, Bob Staake, Dan Steinberg, Ariel Stone, Hank Stuever, Marilyn Thompson, Suzanne Tobin, Scott Vance, Lexie Verdon, Karl Vick, David Von Drehle, John Walcott, Russ

Walker, John Walsh, Gene Weingarten, Katharine Weymouth, Michael Wilbon, Jon Wile, Tom Wilkinson, Mike Wise, Bob Woodward, Karisue Wyson, Marty Zad.

Time and again, I referred to these books:

Personal History, Katharine Graham's autobiography, Random House, 1997.

A Good Life, Ben Bradlee's autobiography, Simon & Schuster, 1995.

Eugene Meyer, by Merlo J. Pusey, Alfred A. Knopf, 1974.

The Washington Post: The First 100 Years, by Chalmers S. Roberts, Houghton Mifflin, 1977.

Behind the Front Page: A Candid Look at How the News Is Made, by David S. Broder, Simon & Schuster, 1987.

Father Struck It Rich, by Evalyn Walsh McLean, Little Brown, 1936.

The News About the News: American Journalism in Peril, by Leonard Downie Jr. and Robert G. Kaiser, Alfred A. Knopf, 2002.

The Powers That Be, by David Halberstam, Alfred A. Knopf, 1975.

The Printing Press as an Agent of Change, by Elizabeth L. Eisenstein, Cambridge University Press, 1979.

A Child of the Century, by Ben Hecht, Simon & Schuster, 1955.

A History of News, by Mitchell Stephens, Viking Penguin, 1988.

All the President's Men, by Carl Bernstein and Bob Woodward, Simon & Schuster, 1974.

The Elements of Journalism, by Bill Kovach and Tom Rosenstiel, Crown Publishing, 2001.

The Mission, by Dana Priest, W.W. Norton, 2003.

News Is a Verb: Journalism at the End of the Twentieth Century, by Pete Hamill, Ballantine Books, 1998.

The Snowball: Warren Buffett and the Business of Life, by Alice Schroeder, Bantam Books, 2008.

Test Pilot: How I Broke Testing Barriers for Millions of Students and Caused a Sonic Boom in the Business of Education, by Stanley H. Kaplan with Anne Farris, Simon & Schuster, 2001.

Arizona Kiss, by Raymond H. Ring, Victor Gollancz, 1991.

Fast Copy, by Dan Jenkins, Simon & Schuster, 1988.

Four movies reminded me of what I love about the business:

All the President's Men, directed by Alan J. Pakula (Warner Brothers, 1976).
Deadline USA, written and directed by Richard Brooks (Twentieth Century-Fox, 1952).
Foreign Correspondent, directed by Alfred Hitchcock (United Artists, 1940).
The Paper, directed by Ron Howard (Universal City Studios, 1994).

INDEX